GAY S WARRIOR

An Empowerment Workbook
for Men Who Love Men

John R. Stowe

FINDHORN
Press

First published in 1999

ISBN 1-899171-82-7

British Library Cataloguing-in-Publication Data.
A catalogue record for this book is available from the British Library.

Library of Congress Catalog Card Number: 99-64837

Layout by Pam Bochel
Cover design by John R. Stowe, Tahlia Vanabel and Mike Goettee
Illustrations by John R. Stowe

Printed on acid-free paper and bound by Data Reproductions, USA

Published by

Findhorn Press

The Park, Findhorn,   P.O. Box 13939
Forres IV36 3TY   Tallahassee
Scotland   Florida 32317-3939, USA
Tel 01309 690582   Tel 850 893 2920
Fax 01309 690036   Fax 850 893 3442
e-mail: info@findhornpress.com
http://findhornpress.com

ACKNOWLEDGMENTS

I feel deeply grateful and quite humble to realize how many people have helped to create this book. Andrew Ramer planted the seeds and gave unrelenting encouragement until they sprouted. The Lifebridge Foundation provided funding to assist with workshops, printing and distribution of the initial manuscript. Many people have offered support and encouragement throughout the process – Al Cotton, Gary Kaupman, Franklin Abbott, Mark Thompson, Larry Auld, King Thackston, Rob Nixon, Jonathan Lerner, Bill Bergeron, Carter Rhodes, Jay Beard, Bruce Parrish, Sarah Hall, Tom Sechrest, Dominique Sire, Leon Lashner, among numerous others. Miguel Molina shared the magic of his movement to help me create the illustrations; Gary Kaupman, Tahlia Vanabel and Mike Goettee gave invaluable support in bringing them to fruition. Thierry and Karin Bogliolo at Findhorn Press have given their gentle and generous support to bring this vision into the world.

For inspiration and ongoing support, I honor the hundreds of loving men who have shared their dreams, visions, teaching, healing, and hearts at Gay Spirit Visions, in workshops, through correspondence, and elsewhere. The path of Spirit is broad -- and the debt to those who have gone before is deep. I have been blessed over the years by the wisdom of many teachers. Their contributions weave through every bit of the material I've presented.

Finally, I give thanks to my partner-in-life, Monty Schuth, for his patience during every stage of this process and to him and the rest of my family for their treasured love and support.

Throughout the book, I have changed names to protect the privacy of those who have shared their stories here.

This book is dedicated to all the men – past, present, and especially future – who walk the paths of Gay Spirit.

CONTENTS

PART 1 FOUNDATION

PREFACE

Mark Thompson

Like most things born in the Twentieth Century, gay identity has not so much gracefully aged as exploded. Secretly conceived in the midst of Cold War angst, the state of being we now call gay didn't take long to burst upon the scene with kick-ass joy. Once weaned of paranoia and shame, gay identity wasted no time in liberating itself from prior notions of homosexuality, which defined sexual variance only in terms of sin and sickness.

Thirty years have passed since that signal act, enough time, one might think, for the mantle of pride and self-determination to become a comfortable fit. Yet who among those in possession of a gay identity hasn't felt its pinch and bind? It's a cloak with a better label, for sure, but — can one size really fit all? What's it made of? Is it still our shining suit, or can it be getting somewhat threadbare?

Thoughtful gay men, such as John Stowe, are asking these and similar questions. Like many others, he too seeks true inward identity in preference over outward appearance. Such investigation has meant divesting himself of all kinds of trappings. For he knows that gay identity can become as much a disguise as any other, if not continuously re-envisioned.

Gay Spirit Warrior is a workbook for the new millennium, an opportunity to conduct our own inventory, even a stripping to the bone. The invitation should not be lost.

Most gay men today seem stuck between desire and fulfillment — twin poles of want and need. What is wanted is obvious: civil rights, autonomy, and someone to love. These are needed things as well, of course, and gay identity has proved a useful tool in obtaining them. Over time, social justice is being met.

Yet beneath the wanting there lie still deeper needs — less tangible and thus harder to list. These are needs reflected by the questions asked here: Who are we gay men, truly? What is our actual potential? How can we see ourselves more fully, moving beyond past wounds and present predicaments? Why is just being gay increasingly not enough? When is it appropriate to ask for more?

John Stowe says: The time is now. One way to begin is to delve into the alternatives and answers he offers here. His book is smart, fun, useful — a much recommended investment in one's future. As fast and far as we've come, gay men have only just begun to imagine the distance ahead.

This collection of wisdom is a step in the right direction.

INTRODUCTION

Andrew Ramer

In a conventional book I would be required to write this introduction without telling you that John and I have known each other since 1990. We met at the first Gay Spirit Visions Conference in North Carolina and have been friends ever since. But this is not a conventional book and we men who love men are not conventional people either.

Conferences tend to be heady places and I felt right at home there, for I'd learned to survive my childhood by living in my head. But in the midst of talks, lectures, and workshops, there was John, reminding us to move, dance, and feel our way into our bodies. His guidance was exactly the medicine I needed, as I'd forgotten that whatever we know about Spirit comes to us through our bodies.

This book is an antidote to two thousand years of religious teachers telling us that our bodies are bad and the world is bad. That approach to life has brought us the atomic bomb, pollution, and one holocaust after another, our own included. But there is another way to live on this planet, as a human being and as a man who loves men.

John is a master at weaving together body and soul, through words, dance, memory, and dreams. Over the years he's taught me how to do that myself, and as you travel through his book, you too will learn how to be grounded in your body in a spirited and spiritual way. But we cannot transcend two thousand years of bad programming overnight and you cannot race through this book either. To go on this journey with John requires time, focus, and a willingness to remember who you really are, beneath the defensive strategies we all had to adopt in order to survive here.

Chapter by chapter, John will welcome you to a sane and satisfying new world and give you all the tools you need to thrive and prosper here. But the magic of John's work is that it isn't something he delivers to you. Rather, as you move through this book, you will be invoking and working with your own deepest visions and moving to create for yourself, your tribe, and for all of humanity a way of living on this planet that is healing and profoundly creative. There is nothing conventional about this. Rather, it is ordinary, inevitable, and utterly magnificent, all at the same time.

Part 1
FOUNDATION

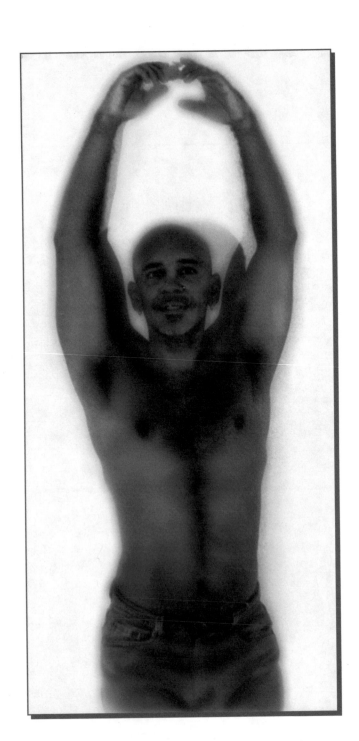

1 **Introductions**

AN INVITATION

Gay Spirit Warrior is dedicated to the tremendous healing, vitality, creativity, and passion carried by men who love men. It is a journey of self-discovery and transformation for men who believe that loving their brothers intimately and wholeheartedly is a cause for celebration. It is for men willing to move beyond conformity and stereotype, to turn wounds into strength and exile into inclusion. It is for men ready to resolve doubts, put aside self-judgment, and honor the unique gifts they were born with. If you are a Gay or Bisexual man ready to claim the full measure of health, power, and personal fulfillment that already lives within you, this journey is dedicated to you.

Why empowerment? Because you have an incredible number of gifts to enjoy and share. The capacity to love other men is just the tip of an iceberg, the most visible part of a way of being that goes far beyond attraction and sex. You have an enormous range of talents, dreams, and desires that can make your life rich — and you have the right to explore them. You have the right to enjoy satisfying relationships in whatever form you choose. You have the right to feel good about who you are, to have rewarding work, and to walk in the world with pride and respect. You have the right to discover the full range of your own passions and to express your creativity fully. You have the right to claim your power to make your life whatever you would have it be.

In truth, men-loving men cover the full range of human experience. We're born in every part of the world, in every part of every nation. We've been here always and we're here to stay. When we learn to accept ourselves and share who we are without fear, we have the potential to transform society. Quite often, we see things differently from the mainstream. The way of loving that comes naturally to us is a powerful alternative to the aggressive, competitive maleness our culture seems to worship. As a group, we share a quality of consciousness that makes us creators, explorers, and innovators. Because we tend to bridge the seeming polarities of masculine/feminine, spirit/flesh, vision/reality, we are in a position to offer deeply needed perspectives in a society plagued by imbalance. It is no accident that we fill professions related to the arts, caregiving, spiritual ministry, and teaching. When we value ourselves enough to live openly and fully, the entire world is enriched.

Many cultures have recognized these unique talents and honored our special place within their communities. Unfortunately, our own homophobic social traditions have caused our gifts to go unrecognized and, in the process, have inflicted great pain and wounding. As a result, most Gay and Bisexual men carry fears, hurts, judgments, and misconceptions about ourselves and our bodies. Most of us learned to distrust our natural desires for touch, sharing, and pleasure. We learned to shut off any parts of ourselves that didn't fit the overwhelmingly heterosexual expectations we saw around us. We came to deny anything inside us that seemed "different" or too close to our core. So doing, we often renounced our most valuable and glorious gifts. Even men who have lived out, open, and healthy Gay lives for many years can still be haunted by old, nagging doubts and fears.

It is time to move beyond the wounding once and for all. **Gay Spirit Warrior** is a personalized journey designed to help you recover the parts of yourself you once denied. On this journey, you'll discover **for yourself** what loving other men means in your life. You'll make peace with your body, embrace your desires, and explore the full extent of your gifts, dreams, and talents. You'll gain tools to vanquish false beliefs that once sabotaged your health and happiness. You'll lay the foundation for new relationships based on support and satisfaction. You'll access the wisdom to create personal vision, direction, and goals, as well as the power to fulfill them. You'll learn to change where you come from in life to a place that allows clarity, respect, and fulfillment.

If you were able to create whatever kind of life you wanted, what would it look like? In reality, you already have that power — and it is your right to use it. **Gay Spirit Warrior** is an invitation to step forth and discover the full extent of your own being. It is an invitation to stand tall, proud, and empowered. It is an invitation to take charge of your own life and be all you can.

GAY SPIRIT VISIONS

The seeds for **Gay Spirit Warrior** were planted in autumn, 1990 at **the mountain**, a conference center in southern North Carolina. Return with me there for a moment. At 4000 feet, the weather is cool and very damp. Gray, misty clouds have turned our camp into a shadowy island. Here, at the very edge of the Blue Ridge Mountains, ancient white oaks stand like twisted sentinels outside the open windows of the wood-paneled lodge where we are gathered.

Eighty men have answered the call: "Come to **the mountain**. Let us explore together what it means to be a Gay man on a spiritual path." Seated in a large, irregular "heart circle," we make a diverse assemblage. Although I know that "back there" in the rest of the world we are doctors, teachers, waiters, lawyers, gardeners, students, executives, and members of every other profession, here in the safe confines of our circle the differences fall away. Looking around, I see splotches of color and bits of personal expression that stand out amidst the jeans and sweatshirts. An older man sits across from me whose long hair and grizzled beard contrast sharply with a hot pink sweater. Beside him, a burly black-haired "bear" sports leather chaps and jacket. Other men make their statements more quietly. I see a bright red vest on one side of the room and many men who wear feathers, leather, or bits of jewelry. Almost universally, the eyes I see are bright with expectation.

We come from many places and follow many paths. Some of us are fully out, others still deeply closeted. Some have learned to feel good about ourselves, others struggle even to meet the eyes of another man. Some are blown away just to be in a room with this many Gay men. As we take our turns speaking, I hear the words we use to describe our spiritual paths — "Buddhist," "ex-priest," "Judaic," "Protestant," "radical faery," "Native American," "pretty much atheist." One by one, we share stories, dreams, hurts, fears, hopes, and joys.

A young man with three earrings and a tribal tattoo asks the Circle, "I've always felt that being Gay means something very important, but I'm not sure what it is. Can you show me?"

Two lovers sit together. One stands to say, "It's our fifteenth anniversary next month. We're here to celebrate with men who appreciate how valuable relationship can be. We still love each other and still giggle as much as we did that first night."

Another man, whose face shows the premature aging and purple blotches of illness, tells us, "I miss my friends who have died. I've learned too much these past few months to put up with people who bullshit me. I'm here to make friends who will be honest."

The man in pink stands up with a story. "I remember my friend Billy, how much we loved each other at 16, how much fun we had touching. One day he told me at school that what we were doing was wrong and started to pretend he didn't know me. It hurt then. It still does. I want to make the world a place where boys can love each other openly."

Across the Circle, another echoes the same sentiment. He leans on a carved wooden cane and speaks slowly, with effort. "When I was thirteen, I found the word 'homosexual' in the dictionary. Each day for months, whenever I was alone, I looked it up again and again. It was my secret proof that I was not the only one. I, too, want to tell the boys of today not to waste time hating themselves."

In a voice so soft we have to strain to hear it, a man of about thirty-five tells us, "This is the first time I've ever sat with other Gay men. I've always known this is who I am, but couldn't bear to face it. I was scared to tell my wife and kids where I was going this weekend, but I had to come."

Our words weave a powerful presence. I feel in them an almost palpable hunger for affirmation, for validation, for someone with whom to share this path. Almost universally, they express a feeling that being Gay involves more than what our culture has given us. Many voice dissatisfaction, not only with the restrictions of mainstream society and religion, but also with a Gay community that seems to ignore spiritual issues altogether. There is a consensus that being Gay is an important, powerful gift, something to be cherished, nurtured, and claimed in its full measure.

That gathering in 1990 was the first of many Celebrating Gay Spirit Visions Conferences at **the mountain**. It began a process of deepening connection that continues to nourish and sustain me and hundreds of other men. At that first Conference, Harry Hay, who founded the Mattachine Society in the early 1950's, spoke of the fear and persecution that governed the lives of homosexual men at that time. Andrew Ramer spoke to us of tribal identity and the long heritage of healing and wisdom carried by men who love men. Through the years, we've been blessed with the wisdom and inspiration of many other elders and teachers. We've explored a host of topics from leather sexuality and tantric massage to healing, poetry, dance, and connection with nature. We've shared tears, laughter, hugs, loving, a good deal of outrageousness, and an ongoing support most of us had only dreamed of when we started.

Looking back, I'd say the greatest of all the gifts we've shared at **the mountain** has been the satisfaction of watching each other unfold, lower defenses, and become more and more confident in our own abilities. Together, we've enjoyed a growing realization that the answers we seek lie within ourselves. Each one of us has insight, healing, humor, and wisdom to share with the rest. In sharing, we foster strength. In sharing, we've found that the path we sought doesn't lie outside us like some yellow brick road waiting to be discovered, but right here as we create it one step, one moment at a time.

GAY SPIRIT WARRIORS

In our discussions at Gay Spirit Visions, one of the terms that comes up repeatedly is "Warrior." At first, the word disturbed me every time I heard it. The images it conjured up of jack-booted soldiers and brutalizing Rambos were the very antithesis of the qualities we spoke of wanting to develop. It took me a long time to realize that these hyper-testosteroid machos, though widely admired in our "masculine" society, are actually gross distortions of true warriorship. The true Warrior is quite different — and learning to embody him is actually central to our quest for empowerment.

The true Warrior is an ideal figure who carries great power within the human psyche. Living in the realm of archetype — the shared, collective consciousness which we access through myth, dreams, and symbols — he's an inner persona accessible to everyone. In societies with greater wisdom than our own, the Warrior was known to embody the very highest principles, able to act powerfully while still maintaining balance, alignment, and total self-control.

Archetypes like the Warrior express uniquely through each person. Men who love men often manifest the Warrior in ways that are distinctly different from what we see in the rest of society — hence the term "Gay Spirit Warrior." Even allowing for differences in personal style, the Warrior usually comes through for us with a more balanced mixture of masculine and feminine energies and tends to combine action in the human realm with simultaneous awareness of other levels.

Any one of us can be a Gay Spirit Warrior. When you embrace it fully, the path of the Warrior allows you to live with power moment by moment. All it means is acting with integrity. How it looks varies. For Greg, it has meant staying sober for ten years. For Sam, it meant daring to come out to his co-workers. For Jack, it meant being true to himself while nursing his dying lover. For Charles, it has meant lobbying the national board of his church each year to consider Gay issues. Where might the Warrior help in your own life? Learning to welcome him there is one goal of our journey together.

For Gay and Bisexual men, this journey to empowerment has two stages. Initially, we must create safe space in which to heal whatever wounding we still carry. Although the steps *you* take in this part of the journey will be personal — and at times challenging — the healing you accomplish will be both deeply rewarding and vital to any further growth. Somewhere in the process, you'll find that you've already begun the second phase, which is self-actualization. This part the journey is open-ended. It entails learning to define yourself on your own terms and exploring your passion for life in every way. As Warrior, you claim the power to make your life an ongoing adventure of discovery and fulfillment.

THE JOURNEY OF HEALING

Let me share with you a vision. He's strong, the one I see, bigger than life, a shining man-god profoundly sure of himself and his purpose. He's powerful and full of vigor. In fact, he lives as the joyful embodiment of spirit in flesh. Where? Right here. I've seen him. I've caught glimpses of him hovering behind the faces in our circle at **the mountain.** I've seen him striding among the participants in a Pride parade or gyrating in celebration on a half-dark dance floor. In fact, he seems to be around whenever a group of Gay men come together in a spirit of affirmation.

He's here, fully realized, just beyond physical form, somehow a part of our being and yet more. His eyes are strikingly deep, old with wisdom, at the same time young with playful magic. He knows beyond doubt that loving other men is a gift of Creator. His form seems to shift, taking on the face of one man, then another. His beauty is vital and healthy, a graceful rapport of body and mind. He's the **Magic Boy** who glories in himself and delights in his world. He's the **Sacred Androgyne** who blends the strengths of male and female, the **Shaman/Healer** whose clear inner guidance taps the secrets of healing and life. He's the **Divine Lover** each of us seeks, the mysterious twin who transforms reality with soulful passion. He's the voice of the **Elder** imparting the lessons of a lifetime with perspective and humor. He's the spiritual **Warrior**, sure of his power, who calls on the triune strengths of intention, stillness, and action. He's the **Explorer,** the inventor god who serves his people and helps the world.

What shall we call him? A Gay spirit? A Gay angel or god? The terms seem so loaded, they don't do him justice. Whatever we call him, though, he is real. He lives in all of us, the embodiment of our hopes, dreams, and desires. His strength helps us survive when the world seems hostile. His essence permeates the impulse that makes us seek our own kind, that defies all attempts to make us "normal" or less than we are. In fact, if you want to name him, give him your own name, because he is a very real part of **you.** You see his beauty and strength reflected in other men. You hear his voice urge you to live with integrity. He's the fullness of your own potential that calls you onward, one step at a time, until finally one day you look in the mirror and see him smiling back at you fully realized.

Even if you don't take the images literally, let them remind you of the place in yourself that seeks growth and understanding — that in fact called you to pick up this book in the first place. You have the ability to embrace your whole self right now, to become as gifted, beautiful, and powerful as you choose. That's the purpose of the journey.

Why a journey? Because most of us forget who we are inside. Imagine the man-god we've described. Imagine that he's born, like some ugly duckling, into a society that hasn't a clue about his true nature. Imagine Apollo born into the center of the Spanish Inquisition or Osiris into 1960's America. Imagine what that boy-god growing up would learn from the people around him. Imagine how he'd feel about himself and his place in the world. Imagine what he'd do to himself trying to conform.

Do you know what I'm talking about? Almost every one of us carries scars inflicted by society's homophobia, anti-eroticism, and fear of difference. Whether it was the well-meaning advice of parents, the more direct pressure of adolescent peers, or the fire and brimstone of a bigoted evangelist, you probably got the message right from the start. If you were lucky, the rejection was gentle. If you weren't, it was abusive or violent.

In order to survive, many of us became chameleons who hid our true selves in an attempt to blend into the rough background of accepted male behavior. We learned to doubt our own feelings and fear our natural desires for love and intimacy. We internalized the homophobia that was directed against us until we came to feel flawed, defensive, or unworthy. Like our man-god born in the wrong time, we became shadows of our true selves.

Do you recognize the patterns? Internalized homophobia manifests in many ways. For some men, it is dramatic and debilitating. Do you suffer the loneliness of rejection by family and friends, stay in an abusive relationship, or live in fear of losing your job? Do you struggle with self-loathing, self-sabotage, or addiction? Too many men still do.

On the other hand, maybe you're one of the many men who live openly and well, for whom the wounding manifests more subtly. Have you ever felt that even though life is basically good, you're still missing something important? Have you ever sold yourself short or held back from reaching for your full potential? I know lots of men who have. I think of John, who came out in college and got a good teaching job, only to spend the next decade bored to tears trying to be as "normal" as he could. Brian went the other way, working as a "professional queer" for one cause after another, yet never letting himself explore his deeper dream of becoming a lawyer. Barry, who works out at the gym until he looks like Adonis, still feels his body's not good enough. Bill wants a relationship with another man desperately, yet is afraid to open to anything more meaningful than occasional, anonymous sex.

For you, as for the man-god in our story, growing to full power is a journey of opening and transformation. You'll approach it step by step, gently examining the sources, content, and ongoing consequences of your own wounding. Knowledge of yourself is a major tool for living well. Bringing old pain to the light allows you to release it. Ultimately, your wounds will provide a map to trace backward and inward to the very core of your being. From there, you'll work to shift perspective and undo old habits of self-compromise. As an empowered Warrior, you'll turn negative to positive, release the ties that bound you to the past, and reclaim the sacred, wonderful gifts that comprise your spiritual heritage.

DEFINE YOURSELF IN YOUR OWN TERMS

We've come a long way since the dark days Harry Hay told us about, days in which Congressional witch-hunts and McCarthy-era persecution made it dangerous for homosexual men and women even to gather, much less discuss things like "Gay identity" or changing the status quo. In the intervening half-century, we've made strides socially and politically that would have seemed mind-boggling to people living then. Who'd have dared predict that we'd be able to live so openly, that issues like Gay marriage or serving in the military would be front page news? There's more to do, of course, but we've come far and fast. Still, despite our success at claiming civil rights, making ourselves a place to live more openly, and surviving a plague in the process, I wonder if we're any closer to answering the most fundamental question — "Who are we?"

Growing up, coming out, living in the world, we've all had to deal with the voices of negativity. In learning to speak about who we are, we've always needed to respond to critics before anything else. The voices of homophobia — both the strident ones in society and the more subtle ones in our own heads — have largely dictated the course of our discussions. As a result, our definition of self is only beginning to emerge from the shadow of what we're **not**. "We are **not** sick, **not** evil, **not** sinful, **not** perverted, **not** child molesters, **not** anti-family, and in terms of basic humanity, **not** all that much different from anyone else."

Saying "NO!" to homophobia is one the healthiest steps any one of us can take, yet when our whole self-definition is based on negation, we miss something vital. We know what we're not, but we still don't have answers to the same basic questions, "Who are we?" "What does it mean to love as we do?"

Why is self-definition so important? Because **beliefs are creative**. What you believe about yourself colors every aspect of your life. It forms the structure by which you order events and interpret experiences. Beliefs tend to be self-fulfilling. As long as you're driven — consciously or not — by negative images of Gays that come from outside yourself, you are living by someone else's script. Whether you believe the lies or rebel against them, you still don't call your own shots. Only by searching deeply, cutting through the layers of "otherness" to meet yourself at your core, can you make your life truly satisfying and fulfilling.

So how would **you** respond if someone asked what it means to be a man-loving man? Would you focus on the physical, as in "free to have sex with whomever I want?" Would you focus somewhere else, as in "sensitive, artistic, colorful?" Would you say we're "just like everyone else except for what we do in bed?" Do you still have doubts about whether we're "sinful," or "sick," or "perverted?" I wonder how far down the list you'd go before words like "spiritual," "powerful," or "self-actualized" came up — or how long it would be before you thought of someone who's an exception to any category you could dream up.

We all know that being Gay or Bi means loving other men. Yet, beyond that very general definition, it's virtually impossible to come up with a set of characteristics or values that applies to all of us. In fact, we're an extremely diverse group. We represent the entire range of cultural and ethnic backgrounds. And so the answer to our question, "Who are we?" is not one answer but many. And the only valid way to find out is for each man to answer first, "Who am *I?*" and "What does loving other men mean in *my* life?"

To find your own answers, you'll have to turn within and seek the truth of your own experience. This book is intended as a map to help you navigate the deep territory of your own self. The exercises you'll explore are general enough to allow you to find your own answers. At the same time, they'll help you integrate your discoveries into a healthy, empowering understanding of yourself as a man who loves men.

THE JOURNEY TOWARD WHOLENESS

You're on this journey already. In fact, you've been on it all your life. The goal of **Gay Spirit Warrior** is to help you make the journey with greater ease and awareness. I invite you to use it as a shamanic quest to the very core of your being. Because you set your pace and determine your goals, you can adapt the process to meet your own needs. Your experiences on this path will be unique and personal. The insights and healing you find there will serve you in every part of your life.

In Part One, you'll embark on your journey — buying a journal, setting goals, learning to support yourself for the duration of the trip. You'll examine the sources, content, and consequences of negative beliefs — even if they're totally subconscious — and learn how to change them for the better. You'll make your body your ally so that you can support it — and it you — all the time.

In Part Two, you'll travel through the realm of your own inner being. This is where you'll meet the greatest challenges — and also reap the greatest rewards. One step at a time, you'll face and conquer old fears, uncover and heal old wounds, and reclaim the parts of yourself you learned to deny. There will be work involved, some of it hard, but you won't have to do it alone. You'll have the help of seven allies, from Magic Boy to Lover to Explorer, parts of yourself who will guide and strengthen you on your path. As you work with each one, you'll learn to call on all the insight, wisdom, power, and humor that live within you to create new, effective solutions to the challenges in your everyday life.

This may not be entirely new territory. Perhaps you've already explored some of the same issues in therapy, have read about archetypes, or learned by experience how to think positively. This is good. **Gay Spirit Warrior** is intended to help men at every level of self-awareness. For some, the material will be entirely new. For others, it will be a chance to explore yourself more deeply as you fine-tune and *put into practice* what you already know. The exercises are designed to help you tap the wisdom of your own body and then integrate it with mind, feelings, and spiritual awareness. In the process, you'll shift where you come from energetically to a place where you actually live what you believe. You'll be surprised at how effective this process will be.

In Part Three, you'll return from your journey with a new understanding of yourself. You'll focus on ways to be self-directed as you chart a course through life that is enjoyable and meaningful. You'll reclaim your spirituality and the ability to support yourself. You'll learn to share the gifts you were born with in ways that enrich your life as they benefit others. You'll learn to live in the world with self-affirmation and power.

The benefits of empowerment are practical and concrete. Living with power means claiming your right to love other men, still a radical concept in our present society. It means to love and support yourself just as you are, to acknowledge your right to fulfill your deepest dreams and desires. It means living with strength every day, going for the job you want, daring to stand up to anyone who would condemn you. It means claiming your right to be intimate, to love, and to express yourself honestly. It means knowing that you are worthy and that your relationships can be validating and healthy. It means freeing yourself of long-standing doubts and opening to fulfillment, satisfaction, and joy. It means creating your life as **you** would have it.

I invite you on this journey because I believe you deserve the kind of life you want. I have to confess, though, to another broader motive. I want you to share who you are with the world. Your courage to live with integrity will make it easier for others to do the same. The satisfaction you feel in expressing your gifts will touch others. You'll find, ultimately, that whatever gives you the greatest fulfillment will also make the greatest contribution for change and healing in the rest of the world.

The world needs that healing quite desperately right now. Globally, we face a state of crisis/opportunity that might well determine our future on the planet.

Ecologically, culturally, and in terms of values, old structures are breaking down and very little has appeared to replace them. Every person on the planet is being called on to reach deep inside and to contribute whatever he or she can toward healing the problems that affect us all.

Men who love men have an important role to play. Already, many of us are on the forefront of social change. Having been forced to deal with a myriad of challenges — from isolation and rejection, to homophobia, to the difficulties of the AIDS crisis — we're learning new ways of supporting ourselves. Experimenting with non-traditional families and relationships, exploring the nuances of our own sexual expression, we set examples that often filter into more mainstream awareness. Working more openly than ever before in the realms of politics, organized religion, entertainment, and social services, we are making important contributions directly and visibly.

Having sat at **the mountain** and spoken with men-loving men in many places, I believe that claiming our uniqueness and the power of our truths is not only possible, but vital. At this point, we can ill afford to lose even the smallest gift that might help the world to shift. To the degree that wounding or homophobia keeps you from sharing, the world is weaker. The urge that you feel to make your life as healthy and satisfying as you can is the same urge that encourages us collectively to step beyond limitation into power — **now, before it is too late.**

No one of us takes this journey alone. You are surrounded by a hundred thousand brothers, members of this Tribe of Men-loving Men. I'm writing because I want companions on the path, an army of lovers around me, an army of beautiful, strong men proud to love men. Are we ready to be empowered, satisfied, healthy, and *fabulous*? Are **you**? I think so. In fact, I dare you!

2 Beginnings

LET'S GET STARTED

Whenever you set out on a journey, it pays to prepare carefully. If this were a trip by car, you'd check the oil, fill the gas tank, and be sure to put air in the spare tire. You'd take a good map and pack clothing to serve you in a variety of situations. In the same manner, as you embark on your path of the Gay Spirit Warrior, a few simple preparations will make the time you spend much more profitable and enjoyable. The focus of this chapter is to help you cultivate habits and attitudes that support you on the way.

First of all, honor the fact that **your path is unique**. Even though you may have companions to travel with, no one else can take the journey for you, nor can anyone tell you exactly what you'll discover. Certainly, you face many issues in common with other men-loving men. Still your own background, needs, desires, and goals are distinctly personal. Avoid the temptation to judge yourself. Toss out expectations about where you *should* be or what issues you *should* already have handled. You'll do best to take the journey one step at a time and see where it leads.

Second, **cultivate an attitude of openness**. The exercises in each chapter will serve as a clear road map to lead you onward — *if you let them*. Be careful not to sabotage your success by nit-picking about language or inconsequential details. The tools here are effective. Take responsibility for using them and, if necessary, adapt them to fit your own circumstances.

In terms of language, let's start by defining "Gay." Throughout the book, I use it broadly to signify any man whose affectional preference is for other men. You may or may not be comfortable applying the word to yourself. Human sexuality is extremely fluid and coming up with a single term that suits everyone is nearly impossible. If you prefer to describe yourself with other terms — "queer," "bisexual," "homosexual," "open-minded," or just "sexual" — feel free to translate as you read. Don't let the terminology get in your way.

Approach each exercise as an experiment. Ask yourself, "What can I learn here? How can I apply this to **my** life?". You'll find that some of the exercises call you very strongly. These, of course, you'll want to explore fully. There may be others that you need to adapt slightly to fit your own situation. For example, if an exercise asks you to list your father's beliefs about being Gay and you, in fact, never met your father, you can still gain a lot of insight from examining the beliefs of the men who did raise you. A few of the exercises may not apply at all. In that case, just let them go and move on.

Make a commitment to stay focused. Choose a pace that works for you and **stick to it.** The best way to do this is to set a schedule. A good place to start might be to aim for completing one chapter a week. Set aside fifteen minutes a day, half an hour every other, or an hour three times a week and then adjust your schedule as you discover what works best for you. However you set it up, scheduling pays off. By investing a moderate amount of time on a regular basis, you'll not only produce satisfying changes, but also create a momentum that helps you move through any places that seem sticky or uncomfortable.

Give yourself time. Even though the exercises are sequential, your journey is basically nonlinear and internal. Much of the action goes on beneath the surface of your consciousness. It takes time to break old, negative patterns and rebuild them positively. It takes time to digest each new concept and integrate it into your awareness. Sometimes you'll feel like you're making great progress. Other times, your movement may be less obvious. Trust yourself. You're growing organically from the inside out. Keep at the process and you'll be amazed at where it takes you.

Finally, remember that **this process is experiential**. Your greatest benefits come from actually doing the exercises. Writing this, I remember myself as a boy of twelve. I was fascinated by the pictures of teenaged surfers in California and Hawaii, so I bought a book called *How to Surf*. In my bedroom, three thousand dry miles from the swells and breakers of the Pacific, I read all about how to choose the right wave, "hang ten," and recover from a really bad spill. At some point, it dawned on me that I wasn't surfing at all, I was reading. If I'd really been plopped onto a board, I'd probably have fallen off within five seconds.

If you want to surf, you need to be at the ocean, on a board, using your body. If you want to become a Gay Spirit Warrior, you've got to get your feet wet, dive in, and risk a few spills. Otherwise, you'll never feel the triumph of standing tall and proud of what you've accomplished. You'll only be reading.

MAP THE TERRITORY WITH YOUR JOURNAL

One thing you will need to pack for this trip is a notebook to use as a journal. From now on, this is where you'll record every step of your empowerment process. Your journal will become your traveling companion, a cherished, nonjudgmental friend in whom you confide the most intimate, personal details. Here you'll share fears, hurts, and challenges. You'll savor discoveries and celebrate triumphs. You'll compose letters to — and from — people in your past, your present, and even your future. You'll write letters to yourself. As you cultivate a relationship with your journal, you'll discover that you're actually cultivating the most important relationship of your whole life — your relationship with yourself.

Recording the in's and out's of your process is vital to your success. Often, new insights are short-lived and ephemeral. The mind is slippery and will do anything to cling to its old ways. One of its tricks is to explain away or trivialize even the most striking discoveries. Your journal will help you beat the mind at its own game and reinforce your new ways of looking at yourself with an accurate, black and white map of your trail.

The number one rule of journaling is *"**Keep it private!**"* Nothing squelches spontaneous self-examination like the threat of an audience. The ego is a strong protector and the minute it thinks you're writing for someone else, it will start to edit, trying for more pearls, less muck. At times you'll want to share insights or even excerpts with a sympathetic friend. That's fine, but leave yourself the option to do it at your own discretion. Don't leave your journal lying around and, for now at least, don't give it to anyone else to read. The success of your journey depends on truth. Honor the privacy of your own thoughts!

What kind of notebook should you get? I recommend a plain, spiral-bound one like you'd use for taking notes in class. Get one that is bound instead of looseleaf, to help you resist the urge to edit out parts that aren't so enjoyable or pretty. Over the years, I've bought all sorts of elegant, beautiful, and *expensive* blank journals that totally intimidated me. Most of them are still sitting empty on the shelf. Their fanciness seems to call for words too polished or calligraphy too meticulous for everyday use. I'm still waiting to be wise enough to use them. Growing is messy. You need a journal that won't feel out of place beside the breakfast dishes or jammed between the smelly socks in your gym bag. Get one that you can use right now.

Your journal

Exercise

1.   *Buy yourself a notebook to use as a journal. Find one that you like, that's easy to carry, and has plenty of room. From now on, use your journal to record every step of this journey. Enjoy yourself!*

SET YOUR COURSE

The first thing you're going to do in your new journal is to choose a destination. On any voyage, it's important to know where you want to go. Even if you change your mind and decide halfway to Chicago that you'd rather hang out for a month in Punxatawney and then head south to Miami, keeping a destination in mind gives you an important sense of direction.

You're going to choose a destination for this journey by setting goals. Even if you're not sure yet where you want to go — "I don't care, as long as it's better than here!" — creating goals helps you personalize your adventure and make appropriate choices along the way. It doesn't matter if your priorities shift later. You're not going to etch anything in stone. As you gain clarity, you'll have the opportunity to refine or rewrite any goals that don't work for you. Just take stock of where you are right now.

Goals

Exercise

2. a. *On page one of your journal, make a list called "**CHALLENGES**." Put down any problems, issues, or concerns you have that you think are related to loving other men. Be honest with yourself. Until you choose to share it, you're the only person who will ever read this list. What's bugging you? What's not working for you right now? What don't you like about yourself or about who you are?*

   Don't edit. The only thing that matters is that what you write rings true for you.

   b. *Now, make a second list entitled "**GOALS**". Make each item on this list a positive statement of something you'd like to create in your life. "I choose to make friends I can be open with." "I'd like to work where I can be openly Gay."*

   Write whatever is important to you. Be sure to include each statement in the "CHALLENGES" list, rewritten as a positive goal. For example, if one of your challenges was "feeling isolated," you could turn it into a goal that reads, "Create meaningful relationships with other people." Leave a little room at the end of the list to add other goals as you think of them later.

Congratulations! You've set your course. For the time being, don't do anything with these lists. Sometimes, as we grow day by day, looking in the mirror, we don't notice how tiny changes add up to big ones. These two lists will be a sort of "before" picture for you. When you refer back to them later, they'll give you a sense of just how much progress you've made.

SUPPORT YOURSELF ALONG THE WAY

Daring to embrace your capacity to love other men is an act of radical audacity. Setting out on this quest of empowerment is exciting. The path will lead you deep within. Things will surely come up that you don't expect — memories, long-buried fears, resentments, grief, or even pain. You'll battle fierce dragons as sharp-tongued doubts fight hard to keep you hostage. You'll rediscover a deep tenderness for yourself and gain a new appreciation of your own strength. Stories you've told yourself for ages will look different. You'll see relationships with friends and family in a new light. You'll feel tired at times and vibrantly alive at others. You'll feel like writing, drawing, dancing, singing, or calling someone you haven't seen for twenty years.

Expect to triumph on this quest. Every effort you make will reward you many times over. At the same time, honor the fact that breaking the hold of negative beliefs takes energy. It is work, soul-work of the highest degree, that at times can be quite strenuous. If you're an athlete, you know that how well you perform depends directly on how well you take care of yourself. The same principle applies here. You'll achieve your goals much more easily if you take care to support yourself physically, emotionally, and mentally.

First, there's your body. This is a *physical* process. To operate at your peak, you need adequate rest, exercise, and a healthy diet. Pay attention. Your body may make requests that are different from what you're used to — more rest, different foods, a dance break, or an invigorating, mind-clearing walk. Listen.

Emotionally, be *gentle on yourself.* At times, your journey will lead through places that feel vulnerable, fragile, or painful. Visiting these places is necessary in order to heal them. No matter how well adjusted you are as an adult, you have a boy inside who can feel hurt, scared, or angry. Support yourself by acknowledging his feelings and creating an atmosphere in which he feels safe and trusting.

Avoid the urge to beat yourself up. All of us have a voice inside that can be harshly self-critical. Sometimes, we forget that we're human and measure ourselves against standards that are impossibly demanding. Allow yourself to have feelings. Allow yourself to make mistakes. Forgive yourself for not being perfect. Pamper yourself if you need it. Even very small gestures — taking a warm bath, having dinner with friends — can support you heartily when you give them to yourself with love and generosity.

Beware of your mind. It won't always understand what you're doing. Your mind likes to keep things safe by organizing every experience into a nice, neat package. For the mind, "safe" means whatever it already knows. Even when things are unpleasant, it almost always prefers the imagined safety of the *status quo* to the scariness of change.

Your mind uses lots of tricks to defend itself. One of its best schemes is to **distract** you by creating external drama. It may suddenly urge you to do something reckless — quit your only job **right now** just when the mortgage is due, pick a fight with your lover, or scream at your mother in the middle of her bridge club because twenty years ago she once described her hairdresser as a "fag." Having to soothe the waters you've so rashly stirred up will quite effectively keep you from dealing with the real issue — your own growth.

Another of your mind's defenses is **procrastination**. Though it is appropriate to take time off when you need it, don't let go of your momentum. If you feel you're barreling along the razor edge of overwhelm, take a night off. Put your feet up and rest. Then, make a commitment to work through the rough spot. Otherwise, it's too easy to let your mind sabotage your growth. How does procrastination look? Suddenly, everything else in the world seems more important than continuing. "Oh, I'll do that exercise tomorrow. You know, it's been ten whole years since I cleaned out my sock drawer!" "Yeah, I'll look at how I hurt my first lover, but first, I promised to clean that dust from behind the fridge before Mother comes at Christmas. Goodness, it's almost August!" You could go on forever until the book is dusty and forgotten and your life is the same as it's always been.

You are much more than just your mind. On this journey, you'll learn to connect with your **whole** self — body, heart, mind, and spirit. Ultimately, you'll explore not just new ways of thinking, but an entirely new way of **being**. If you're trained, like most of us, to value logic and rationality over the messiness of actual experience, the activities you'll explore may at first seem unfamiliar or scary. Don't give in to the mind's fears. In time, it will come to enjoy these different approaches to life and even start to defend **them** as the new **status quo**.

Support yourself

Exercise

3. *In your journal, list ten things you can do when you want to support and nurture yourself. What activities feel safe, nurturing, and comforting? Fix a nice dinner? Buy a bouquet of daffodils? Take a warm shower? Snuggle with your puppy? Work out at the gym or in the garden?*

Beside each item on the list, indicate how recently you gave yourself time to do that activity? How often do you treat yourself?

YOUR SUPPORT NETWORK

Choose the people you share your journey with very carefully. Having friends who will listen to your fears or help you savor your triumphs **without judgment or criticism** is a great help. At the same time, opening vulnerable parts of yourself to someone who treats them with skepticism or negativity is risky. When a child first learns to walk, you don't send it out alone onto a busy street. When you're learning new behaviors, it's better to contain them at first and get used to the way they feel before you put yourself in a situation of having to defend them too strongly.

Your friends are like mirrors that show you different parts of yourself. Because you share something in common with each one, different friends mirror different parts. Think about it. Who reflects the happy, playful kid in you? Who would you call when you want to slip away from work for a sunny afternoon in the park? Who, on the other hand, do you call when your misery wants company, when you feel like a ten hour "woe is me, I'm a victim" bender at the bar? Who shares your idealism? Who reinforces your own doubts with stab-in-the-back comments like, "I'm glad you feel proud to be Gay, but why do you have to flaunt it?" or, "What would your mother say? This would kill her!"

Each of us has his own path. For now, be true to yourself by sharing only with people who really support you. Take some space from those who don't. Trying to argue or change their ideas at this point is an unnecessary burden. Save your energy and your breath for your own growth. Better to instruct later, by example.

One good way to create support is to find a friend or a group of men who'd like to explore this process with you. Set up weekly or biweekly meetings to discuss one or two chapters at a time. As you set out, make an agreement to listen to each other without judgment and to be available for mutual support whenever you need it.

If you're doing the journey on your own, spend some time creating a support network for yourself. Make an agreement with at least one friend who will be there if something comes up you need to discuss. If you're seeing a therapist or counselor, make them aware that you're exploring this journey. If you don't have anyone at all, make sure you know where to get professional help if you need it.

What about professional help? There will be parts of this process that bring up challenging or difficult issues. That's normal and to be expected. Most of the time, you'll be quite capable of handling whatever comes up. If at any time, though, your self-exploration puts you in touch with issues that feel too big to handle alone, ***get the help of a qualified professional immediately.*** If you need or desire it, counseling with a good, Gay-positive therapist is invaluable. There is no shame or stigma to seeking assistance. Instead, it means you value yourself highly enough to do whatever it takes to have a positive and fulfilling life. Bottom line, realize that you are a worthwhile human being and that it is quite possible for you to live happily and healthily. Whatever effort it takes is easily worth it.

Choose your therapist carefully. Find someone who makes you feel safe and comfortable. Ask questions before you make any commitments. Be sure the person is Gay-positive. Any therapist who wants to "cure" your attraction to other men or who is even the least bit uncomfortable with it may be able to help you through a time of crisis, but will probably not help much in the long run. If you feel after a reasonable amount of time that the person you're seeing isn't helping you, look elsewhere.

There are resources to help you find a good therapist. Ask around. Some of your Gay friends may be able to recommend someone. Most large cities have Gay centers, newspapers, and help lines which can also offer help. Many (though unfortunately not all) colleges and universities have Gay-sensitive counseling centers.

Your support network

Exercise

4.a. *Make a list of the friends with whom you'd be comfortable sharing the details of your growth process, who would be okay talking about, say, the feelings of your inner boy or your fears about being more open in the world. Who would you call if things got scary or challenging? If you can, call that person and ask if he or she would agree to be available if you need to talk.*

b. *Now list those you would definitely **not** share this process with, at least before you've completed it. Include friends with whom you feel unsure of yourself, defensive, or from whom you have to hide your real feelings.*

c. *If you don't have anyone listed in part a, make a note of who you could call if you happened to need professional help. This is not to say that you will need it — you probably won't. Just knowing that you have backup support, though, will let you feel more at ease through your entire exploration.*

COMMIT TO THE PATH

A remarkable alchemy occurs whenever we make a true commitment to do something. Goethe said,

> "Concerning all acts of initiative and creation, there is one elementary truth — that the moment one definitely commits oneself, then Providence moves, too."

I have a friend who states it more simply, *"For every step we take, the Angels take ten to meet us."* Suddenly, something shifts. Whether it's because of Providence or angels or some new alignment inside yourself, all at once the whole world seems to support you.

Life, like this journey, is inclusive. You are a whole being. Any shift you make in one area ripples outward to touch every other part. Your intention to explore one aspect of your consciousness engages others. Your dreams will begin to comment on your experiences with symbol and humor. Your subconscious knowing will begin to bubble upward when you least expect it, in the cracks between thoughts and activities — when you're driving, doing dishes, daydreaming, or falling asleep.

Pay attention to "coincidences." You'll be surprised at how timely and beneficial they can be. My friend William describes the night he was trying to outline what he wanted in an ideal relationship and got a knock on the door. It was his ex-lover, "Mr. Everything-But-Ideal." By the time the lover had left two nights later, William was a hundred percent clearer about what he wanted on his list. Gary found an article in a paper left on the seat of a city bus describing an interesting new university program. A few calls later, he was enrolled in that same program and embarked on a satisfying new career. Our overly rational culture delights in explaining away coincidences as meaningless mental artifacts. So doing, it negates one of the main ways Spirit acts in our lives, through a phenomenon Carl Jung called "synchronicity." Rather than rejecting synchronicities, why not embrace them as gifts and opportunities?

Dare to expect help. You are not in this alone. Once you truly commit to your exploration, you mobilize an amazing array of inner allies, guides, and helpers. Keep your mind open. Though it may seem hard to believe at first, you'll be amazed at where your support comes from. All it takes is that first step, making the commitment.

Exercises

Set forth

To take that first step, complete either one or both of the following exercises. They will help you formalize your commitment to personal growth by linking intention with action.

5.　**Commitment contract**

Use your own words to adapt the following contract so that it reflects your own goals and commitment to embark on this journey of personal exploration.

Start it out formally,

"I, (your name) _____ hereby commit to embark on a journey of self-affirmation. I choose to honor my love for other men.

I state my intention to heal the places I've been hurt, forgive the people involved, and move beyond whatever beliefs have kept me from living fully.

I acknowledge all parts of myself — the gifts, strengths, fears, and feelings that make me who I am. I commit to treat myself with gentleness, compassion, and patience.

I welcome help on this journey.

I am willing to live up to my full potential as a wondrous, fabulous human being."

Add a summary of your goals and any other intentions you have to take care of yourself.

Sign and date your commitment contract. Leave one copy in your notebook and make another to post somewhere you will see it often as a reminder.

6.　**Threshold ritual**

You stand on the verge of a life-changing journey. One way to deepen your experience of this important moment is to acknowledge it with a short, simple ritual.

Ritual is a method of honoring intention and aligning body, mind, and spirit by performing a series of specific actions. Rituals are most effective when they use words and actions with personal significance. For that reason, even though you'll use the following process as a guideline, I encourage you to personalize it by choosing words and actions meaningful to you. Be flexible. What matters most is how well your words verbalize and clarify your intention. Read through the entire process once, then return and take it step by step.

The opening ritual is simple. To begin, find a comfortable place in which you won't be disturbed. If you like, set the tone by lighting a candle, burning some incense, dimming the lights, or taking a few slow, conscious breaths.

Your first step is to create "sacred space." Just as entering a church, cathedral, or special place in nature can heighten your awareness, creating sacred space formalizes your intention to speak and act with deep meaning. There are many ways to do this. The following is one of the simplest.

a.   *Imagine a strong, clear white light that flows around you in every direction — front, back, both sides, above, and below — until you are completely surrounded by a sphere of light.*

Within the light, affirm the presence of Spirit. Use whatever terms are most comfortable for you — God, Goddess, Creator, Universal Life Force, Jesus, Mohammed, Buddha, Higher Self, All That Is, or whatever you choose.

Invite into your space all the guides, teachers, and guardians that work with you on inner planes. Whether or not you have a clear image of them yet, they will help you on your journey.

Welcome the Wholeness of your own being, all the many wondrous parts of your diverse humanity.

Remember the people who have supported you, especially those who have been teachers or positive role models for you as a man who loves men. Invite the ones who have helped and inspired us all — Walt Whitman and Edward Carpenter, Harvey Milk and Socrates, the drag queens who fought at Stonewall and the boy who took his boyfriend to the high school prom. Make your own list of heroes and invite them to accompany you on this journey.

b.   *Your sacred space is complete. Now, in the presence of all your supportive guides and companions, speak aloud your intentions for the journey. Either read the contract you wrote in the last exercise, or use your own words to state your intentions for this journey.*

State the specific goals you've made — for relationship, healing, self-awareness, and whatever else.

State the ways in which you agree to support yourself in body, heart, and mind — and your willingness to accept help and support from others. State your intention to release negative beliefs, to heal hurts, to look at life in brand new ways, and to claim the fullness of your own being.

c.   *In completion, make a tone — with a bell, a small gong, or your own voice. Sound the tone deliberately, with the intention that it carry your prayer into the world. Listen as it grows and moves forth. Listen as it echoes within you. Sit quietly a few moments and notice what you feel.*

When you're ready, leave the sacred space you created by thanking and releasing all the energies you called, either formally by going backward through the list, or generally with a single statement, "I release all the energies I've invoked into highest light."

d.   *In your notebook, jot down your impressions and insights as you begin this next step on your journey.*

3 Early Beliefs

PULL YOUR OWN STRINGS

My nephew Jake is four this year. One of his favorite activities is "helping" his Dad around the house. Whenever my brother-in-law, Tom, gets into a project, Jake runs for his tools. If Tom's in his shop, Jake sits at a small table beside him, "cuts" a piece of wood with his red plastic saw, then taps it into place with a blue rubber hammer. The whole time, he watches Tom intently, so careful to do everything just the way Daddy does that the tip of his tongue often sticks out unconsciously between his tightly pursed lips. Jake's happy when he's helping. At the same time, he's learning about his place in the world.

When we're young, we look to adults to tell us about life. "This is a tree. It is green. That is the sky. It is blue." They tell us who we are. "You're a boy. Your name is John, or Jimmy, or Monty. This is your family. You're American, or French, or Mexican. You're Jewish, or Presbyterian, or Buddhist." Just as importantly, they tell us **how** we are. "You're a good boy. You're bad when you do that. You're tall for your age. You're smart."

The world is a mirror that we search diligently for what it tells us about ourselves. Unfortunately, for boys attracted to other boys, the mirror is often skewed, warped, and not very helpful. If you were very lucky, your family **did** support you. Perhaps you had a Gay uncle, or parents who recognized early what was going on and taught you self-acceptance. Most of us weren't that lucky, and not even the most supportive family can change the messages of the culture at large.

Until this decade, the dominant culture told us hardly anything positive about being Gay. For the most part, in a sort of soul-murder by omission, it said nothing at all. Growing up at four, and ten, and fifteen, we had no role models to reflect our developing Gay selves. The inherent message was, "You are flawed. You don't belong." When we were mentioned, the context was decidedly negative — crude jokes whispered in junior high locker rooms, false "cures" offered by misguided counselors, and active condemnation mouthed by far too many religious leaders. The media gifted us with images of lisping weaklings, perverted predators, or tragic victims whose endings were **never** happy.

It has not been the same in all societies. Imagine what your attitudes about yourself would have been as part of the Navajo people a century ago. The Navajo word for men like us is **nadle**. Describing attitudes toward *nadle,* ethnographer W. W. Hill said,

> *"The success and wealth of such a family (having a nadle child) was believed to be assured. Special care was taken in the raising of such children, and they were afforded favoritism not shown to other children of the family. ...This respect verges almost on reverence in many cases. "*

He quoted several Navajo speakers as well,

> *"They know everything. They can do both the work of a man and a woman. I think when all the nadle are gone, that will be the end of the Navajo. You must respect a nadle. They are, somehow, sacred and holy."*
>   *(from Williams, The Spirit and the Flesh)*

Among the Navajo — as well as in many other peoples from around the world — the messages you would have learned would have been quite different from what we learn here. (For more information on other cultures, see the books by Walter Williams, Will Roscoe, and Randy Connor).

Generally, we accept most of our early learning without question. Because we depend on adults for survival, what they tell us is vital. Their words and attitudes form the basic core of how we think about ourselves. If the foundation includes flaws — such as the idea that we can't be Gay and achieve happiness — we usually accept them without even noticing. These early ideas are quite stubborn, often persisting in the subconscious mind even when we learn to view ourselves differently later. Instead of replacing the old ideas, new ones tend to collect around the initial core. Unless we take care to remove them, the old, flawed beliefs sink inward where they continue to influence us without our knowing.

I've done the exercises in this chapter with some of the most well-adjusted men I know — successful, active men who have been open for years about their sexuality. When asked what they think about loving other men, their responses are usually quite positive. "Makes me creative," says Bob. "Fun, exciting, who I've always been," says James. Yet, in looking deeper, every one of these men came up with older thoughts steeped in adjectives like "perverted" or "sinful". The old attitudes die hard. For most of us, they live on unconsciously as corrosive **internalized homophobia**. Unchecked, they sap our strength and undermine our efforts to create happy, satisfying lives.

You might well ask, "Why stir up old negatives? Why not let sleeping dogs lie?" The answer is that beliefs are the blueprint around which you structure reality. Because they act as a mental filter to color your perceptions and shape your responses, your beliefs tend to be self-fulfilling. This is true regardless of whether they build you up or bring you down, whether you're conscious of them or not, or whether they have any truth to them at all. Because you think they do, that's how you experience them.

How does it work? Imagine some challenging event. Let's say that you and your lover decide to end a two-year relationship. How you respond depends to a large degree on how you feel about yourself. If your self-esteem is low, or if you believe that because you love men you have no right to be happy, you'll tend to respond negatively. You might get totally depressed, crawl into a bottle, or want to slit your wrists. If you feel better about yourself, you'd take things more in stride. Maybe you'd choose to remain friends with your ex and move on peacefully. Maybe you'd use the time to explore other areas of your life like going back to school or joining a Gay hiking club. Because your experience of life depends on your overall level of self-confidence, optimism, and independence, everything you do to increase these qualities pays off hundredfold.

Just about everyone has some internal negativity. It goes with being human. You don't, however, have to let it pull the strings while you dance like some unconscious marionette. Take the initiative to hunt out the negatives. Take responsibility for your own beliefs. Take charge of your own life.

Unconscious negatives

Let's do a little digging. How do you ask the conscious mind to tell you what's in the unconscious? Trick it, of course.

1.a.   *In the best tradition of Sherlock Holmes, turn to a new page in your notebook and number the lines from 1 to 20. Then, on each line, complete the following sentence, "**Being Gay is ...**". Remember, for this and every other exercise, if the word "Gay" isn't how you describe yourself, substitute whatever term you prefer.*

Write as quickly as you can and put down whatever comes up. Your mind will try to edit every word to make your responses acceptable. You're looking for what you really believe, which won't always be positive,

Exercise

consistent, or politically correct. The best way to beat your inner censor is to write so quickly you don't have time to think.

b.   *Repeat the exercise, this time using the sentence,*

"Because I'm Gay, I can't ..."

When you finish, read the lists. Of the statements that came up, put a mark beside anything you consider negative. Resist the temptation to judge yourself. Just because you carry negative thoughts doesn't mean you're a bad person. Uncovering your hidden negatives is what allows you to change them into something better.

ROLE MODELS

As much as we learn from what we're told, we learn even more from what we see for ourselves. I never met a man I knew to be Gay until I came out at age 23. For many years, I thought I was the only one in the world who felt this way. Sound familiar? When I finally did become aware of "homosexuals," the image I held was a shadowy composite, bits and pieces I'd gleaned from bad jokes, movies, and cheap religious tracts left in the door. Even in college, I half expected "fags" to be sleazy, sad perverts in ragged raincoats who lurked around schoolyards with bags of sticky candy. My first Gay movie, *Boys in the Band,* didn't help much, especially its quote that "the only happy homosexual is a gay corpse." Is this what it meant to be attracted to other men?

When I did come out, I was shocked to meet men who were nice, interesting, and relatively "normal" — without a bag of candy in sight! I don't think my experiences were much out of the ordinary. With images like these to go by, the fact that most of us come out at all is a testament to just how deep-seated our Gay nature really is. Still, I wonder what it would have been like to have known even one person who showed that being Gay could be positive and healthy.

 Role models

2.   *Take a moment to reflect on your own life. Where did you learn what it meant to be Gay? What were the role models in your life? Did you know any Gay men personally? What did you learn from books, TV, or movies?*

What was your early image of what it means to be Gay? Was it positive? Negative? Helpful? Harmful?

Record your impressions in your journal. Pay particular attention to any negatives you learned. You'll have a chance to work with them soon.

Exercise

THE INNER CRITIC

Often, internalized negativity takes on a life and voice of its own, living inside you as a sub-personality we'll call the Inner Critic. The Inner Critic is an expert bully. Just when you're feeling really good about yourself, ready to apply for a new job or call that cute guy you met at your friend Gail's brunch last week, the Critic hits you broadside, doing his best to rain out your parade with a load of nasty, smelly doubts. *"You can't do that. Who'd hire you after you failed 8th grade algebra? That guy won't like you — you can't tell a joke worth beans. And besides, your butt's too feminine for a real man."*

The Inner Critic is dirty. Because he knows you so well, he can hit below the belt, right where you're least sure of yourself. His accusations are usually slippery — vague enough that they're hard to disprove, yet containing just enough truth to make you listen. Okay, so you *did* fail algebra. You *are* a little shy when it comes to conversation. None of this means that you're a bad person or that you're unlikable or unhireable.

The best way to deal with your Inner Critic is to realize that he's your own creation. In self-defense, you learned very early to keep a constant lookout for any slip that would give others a way to attack or reject you. Deep inside, you recorded every reprimand or correction aimed at you by parents or other authority figures. You learned to watch for the slightest limpness of wrist, the merest suggestion of a rising pinkie, or eyes that lingered too long on the hunky boy in gym class.

This vigilance is a two-edged sword. On one hand, it helped you "fit in," at least enough to survive. It probably taught you to be an astute observer of other people. Conversely, constant self-monitoring kills spontaneity, aborts playfulness, and can make you afraid to show yourself at all.

Does this ring a bell? Do you know your Inner Critic? In a moment, you'll look at how to make him a more productive ally. For now, though, let's hear what he has to say for himself.

➤ Meet the Critic

Exercise

3. a. *On a new page, draw a vertical line about a third of the way from the right margin. Then, on the larger, left-hand side of the page, write the following affirmation twenty times: "Being Gay is healthy and good." If this statement doesn't make your heart jump with excitement, revise it in your own words until it does.*

   As you write, over and over as quickly as you can, listen to what starts bubbling up in the back of your mind — comments, rejections, editorializing. "Yeah, right," you might hear, or, "That's a lie, it's evil to touch men." "Society hates us." "I wouldn't have HIV if I weren't Gay."

Whatever comes up in this background chatter, write it immediately in the right-hand column, then keep going. It may not all be negative. It may not all make sense. Don't judge or argue. Just get as much of it onto paper as you can.

When you finish, take a look at the statements on your list. Cross off anything that doesn't make sense. Compare what's left with your unconscious negatives from Exercises 1 and 2. Look for patterns. Look for statements that come up over and over, or that really grab you. These are the ones most indicative of how your Inner Critic tries to control you.

b.   *Ask yourself where each of the major negatives might have come from. Whose voice do you hear when you read it? Whose words? Is it something you were taught or did you think it up yourself? Don't be concerned if you don't get a clear response for every statement. You don't need to know where the negatives come from to release them. Record the insights you do get beside the appropriate statements and let it go at that.*

A word of caution here. It's easy to blame parents and others for the problems in your life. This is counterproductive. The point of working with early beliefs is not to blame someone else, but to discover what negatives you're still carrying in order to release them.

MAKE THE CRITIC YOUR ALLY

Your Inner Critic's motivation is basically beneficial. In fact, all his grousing is really a misguided attempt to keep you safe. Even though his vision of safety might look more like protective custody, his underlying impulse is positive. Because he's already doing his best to support you, making him your ally will be relatively easy. To do so, however, you need to be aware of one more trick he may use to trip you up — resistance to the process itself.

Without a doubt, some exercises on this journey will bring up your resistance. You may purr along smoothly for three or four sections, enjoying your new insights, feeling clear and empowered. Then all of a sudden, in the middle of an exercise, you'll hit a wall. Something will push a button, you'll get defensive, and you'll think the whole process sucks.

First off, complete the exercise. Stopping in the middle can leave you in an unresolved, painful place. If you tap into an issue that feels too big to resolve alone, take the time to call someone who can support you. In a few cases, this may even mean getting professional help. Do it. Then, make a commitment to look at the issue — and the resistance — until you resolve it.

Resistance is subtle. Your Inner Critic will come up with all sorts of very reasonable-sounding excuses to lead you off track. They'll probably go something like, *"I don't have to do this!" "This is stupid... boring... dumb... silly... pointless...!" "This book's not going anywhere, I'm throwing it away!"*

You may be right. Some exercises will touch you more than others. Some won't apply. Watch carefully, though. Strong resistance is almost always a red flag that something behind it is worth investigating. All of us hold certain "sacred cow" beliefs, ideas we "know" with such great certainty that we'd never dream of examining them. Some of them may have been true once, like the beliefs that helped you survive a difficult childhood — "If I don't share my feelings, I won't be laughed at." Some of them came from people you trusted, or with such repetition and conviction you believed them automatically — "It's bad for boys to act like girls." Often, these are the very beliefs that hold you back from living fully.

Negative beliefs can enslave you. Indeed, to discourage free-thinking is one of the major ways that moralists, religion-mongers, and authoritarian rulers try to keep other people hostage. You know what I mean? "This is a matter of FAITH!" they say. "Do not dare to question _____." Fill in the blank with whatever authority you choose — "God," "your parents," "your leaders," "the will of your country."

Break free! It takes courage to think for yourself. But what's to fear, really? You lose absolutely nothing by examining any belief you have, even basic ones like what you think about God, your place in the world, or how you love others. Beliefs that support and resonate with your own truth will hold up under any amount of scrutiny. Those that don't, you'll do better to release, revise, or replace until they support you. Doing so, you claim great power.

➤ Critic's Corner

Exercise

4. *You can turn the tables on your Inner Critic just by knowing how he operates. He may have something to say every time you take a step. Instead of fighting him, try something new.*

Set aside a few pages at the end of your notebook which you label "Critic's Corner." Then, whenever you notice that you're self-bashing, acknowledge the Critic. "Oh, hi Critic. Are you at it again? I haven't heard from you in at least five minutes! So, what do you have to say this time?"

Give him his say. In the Critic's Corner, write whatever he wants to tell you. You don't have to believe him. After the first few times, you'll notice that he's pretty repetitive. Instead of rewriting the same thing over and over, just make marks in the margin indicating that a statement came up one more time. After a few weeks, you'll be able to get through the Critic's comments very quickly, and also have a good record of what he has to say. When he's said his piece, thank him and give him a vacation until next time.

The Inner Critic is not necessarily at work every time you feel an objection to something. Sometimes, what you feel may be valid intuitive guidance telling you that a particular course of action is not the best. With a bit of practice, you'll learn to recognize the difference. Your Inner Critic tends to act like a broken record. His objections have a certain mindlessness, a feeling of defensive panic that resists change at all costs. As you get to know him, you'll become familiar with the tone he uses and be more and more able to distinguish it from real intuition. Trust yourself. You'll know.

As you become more acquainted, you'll also be able to turn the Critic's protestations to your advantage. He's usually loudest when the status quo is most threatened. The very fact that he's screaming bloody murder is a sign that you're onto something. Check it out! Let him show you where you're hiding from yourself. Let him show you where you've been hurt in the past or are selling yourself short in the present. He's there, for better or worse. You might as well choose better.

WRITE YOUR OWN SCRIPT

To reclaim your life from the Critic's negativity, use your intention to restructure beliefs that no longer serve you. The process is simple. The effects are powerful.

➤ Affirmations

5.a. *At the top of a new page of your journal, write the heading "**BELIEFS THAT SUPPORT ME**".*

*Immediately underneath, write the sentence, "**I'm willing to replace negative beliefs with new ones that support my highest health and good.**" Then, sign your name and date it. This mini-contract may seem silly, but it sends a clear, important signal to your subconscious mind that you are serious about changing.*

To create a list of supportive beliefs, rewrite each negative statement you uncovered in Exercises 1-4. Put the ones that came up most often or that seem to have the most energy at the top of your list.

You'll enjoy doing this. Make your words enthusiastic and positive. "Being Gay is dirty" now becomes "Being Gay is clean and healthy." "God hates

Gays" becomes *"God loves me just as I am."* *You are giving your subconscious mind positive replacements for the old negatives. Push yourself. Exaggerate! Even if you just think "Gay is good," go for "Gay is great!" Make the new script you're writing as strong and positive as you can.*

b. *As you finish with each negative, use a red pen or crayon to cross it off, right in your notebook, with the universal sign of negation — the circle with a diagonal line through it. This will give your mind another visual cue telling it to release the thought.*

c. *Add any positive beliefs you came up with in the earlier exercises to the list of affirmations.*

Read the list aloud to yourself. How does it make you feel? If you need to revise anything, do it now.

Be patient with yourself. Making these affirmations a working part of your consciousness takes a little time and effort. After all, the old beliefs had plenty of time to become ingrained. New ones may take time, too, though your intention will speed the process immensely.

Two factors help install the affirmations most effectively. The first is repetition. The more often you hear, say, or read them, the more your new affirmations become entrenched in your awareness. Second, remember that the part of your mind you're trying to access is much more childlike than the logical adult you show the world. The more interesting and fun you make the process, the more successful you'll be.

Be creative. Play! See how many novel and interesting ways you can use affirmations. Make them rhyme. Copy them in colors with crayons or pastels. Use glitter. Make little posters and paste them on your refrigerator, the bathroom mirror, and the edges of your computer monitor. Paste a few over the toilet. Copy them over pictures of naked men. Record them on a tape which you play as background in the car. Write them as notes which you ask a friend to hide all over the house — in the washer, your sock drawer, and the dog food bag — where they'll surprise you at odd hours. Tattoo them to your lover's butt. Whatever you do, do it often and make it fun.

Affirmations work! When I first went through this process, I uncovered all sorts of negative chatter. My Inner Critic, the ultimate pessimist, was convinced that this was the stupidest thing since scented toilet paper. Still, I went along, dutifully at first, but with more relish as I relaxed into it.

Three months later, I told one of my clients about the power of using affirmations. He was skeptical, so I sat with him while he made his first lists. To fill time, I did it again myself. I was shocked. Somehow, my inner dialog had reversed itself. Every time I wrote a negative, my mind countered with something positive. "This will take too long," I said. Inside, I heard, "Take one step at a time and it'll pass quickly." "Being Gay is hard," I wrote. "There's nothing else I'd rather be," I heard. By the time my client had finished his lists, I was blown away by mine. Try it.

Before you go any further, make a commitment to copy your affirmations once a day for the next week and then at least twice a week for two or three more. Consider it calisthenics for your mind.

RELEASE THE NEGATIVES

Negative thoughts are like cockroaches. You can curse them all you want, call their mothers bad names, and leave the lights on all night, but until you really get in there and clean house, they keep coming back.

Get rid of the negatives before they do any more harm. You've already done the hard parts — uncovering them in the first place, understanding where they came from, and replacing them with affirmations. This last step is a short ritual that will help you release them for good.

Your subconscious mind loves ritual. Even very simple actions, when done with intention, carry a strong message to your inner self. The following ritual is quite effective for releasing negative thoughts in any area of your life.

Ritual release

Exercise

6. *Copy your negatives onto small pieces of paper, one statement to a piece. As you write, say out loud, "I release this thought from my consciousness, completely."*

   When you finish, take all the papers to a fireplace or somewhere else you can burn them. One at a time, or all at once, light the papers and watch them burn. Reinforce the action with appropriate words — "I release these thoughts completely. Let their energy be reused to create positive thoughts" — or whatever words feel good.

   Burning the papers releases the energy of the thoughts symbolically. If you can't actually burn them, do something similar — tear them into tiny pieces and flush them down the toilet. I like to dig a hole in my compost pile and burn them there, so the ashes fertilize the flower garden.

Notice how you feel when you've finished. My first time, my body responded with a little spontaneous shiver, a deep sigh, and I felt much lighter. How do you feel?

Even though the ritual is complete, be vigilant about your thoughts. Old negatives will try to come back from time to time out of pure habit. Watch carefully. If you notice yourself thinking or saying something you've released, don't freak. Just remind yourself, "I've already released that thought. My new belief is ..." and repeat your affirmation. With practice, the whole process will quickly become easy and automatic.

Clean out

Exercise

7.   *Here's one last, short, non-mental exercise. Sometime this week, clean out your closet. Give away any clothes you no longer wear. Make room for new things. Arrange everything so that it feels neat.*

If your closet's already clean, find an alternate activity in the same vein. Clean the refrigerator, your file cabinet, the files in your computer, the attic, the garage, or the tool shed. Weed your garden. Vacuum the back of your car. Whatever you choose, enjoy yourself and notice how you feel afterward.

4 The Body Connection

BODY KNOWING

"When you embrace your whole, man-loving self, you open to a spiritual wholeness in which all the diverse facets of your being express vitality, creativity, and joy." That's inspiring, isn't it? It's also true, yet how many men do you know who came out looking for "spiritual wholeness?" Very few, I'll bet.

We come out because the driving desire beneath our bellies and behind our balls gives us no choice. We come out because our bodies crave the loving touch of another man, crying out to hold and be held by men. We come out because our bodies demand it. No matter how much we try to think, talk, or pray them out of it, bodies have minds of their own. When we learn to trust the wisdom of arms and thighs and cocks and hearts, they'll lead us places we never imagined.

I speak from experience. Before I came out, all I could think of was the sex part. I didn't realize that seeking the love of another man would eventually give me a way to redeem all the parts of myself I considered "different" or "weird." I thought it was just about sex. That's what I'd repressed the hardest, and what finally pushed me over the edge into the dark, exciting unknown of coming out.

Thankfully, almost right off, I met a man with enough heart to give me the care I needed in those amazing, frantic, vulnerable first months. Those were months full of releasing. It was sexual, of course. Years of pent-up desire burst forth with ecstatic vengeance. Even more, though, it was emotional. Over and over, at odd moments and without any reason, I found myself in tears. I felt so safe in my friend's strong arms that all the years of loneliness and longing seemed to well up and out. At the time, even though I was baffled and more than a little embarrassed, I had a sense that it was the right thing.

Two months after that first coming out, I made the twenty hour drive from Tallahassee to Philadelphia for Christmas with my family. I left at dusk in order to drive all night and arrive the next afternoon. Tooling along the deserted roads of Georgia and the Carolinas, I had lots of time to think. The whole night, I played my new disco tapes, as if singing along with Gloria and Donna and Patti could make my new, still-secret friends be there to warm the cold, dark highways.

I felt dazed, excited, stimulated, exhausted, and scared. I wasn't ready to tell my family what I'd been doing, but I felt so changed inside I was afraid they'd notice anyway. I thought about them a lot, and about my friend, my new life, and all the things I was finally admitting to myself about being Gay. I liked that word, "Gay," so new and much more friendly than the overly clinical "homosexual."

It was cold in the car and I was chilled before I even got through Georgia. By the time the sun came up, just south of the Virginia line, I was alternately sweating and shivering and also beginning to feel a disturbing soreness in the groin. When I reached my Mom's house in mid-afternoon, I had no choice but to go right to bed. By then, my fever was strong and my balls were swelling rapidly and throbbing with pain.

After an exam that made me more than blush, our family doctor said it was epididymitis, an infection of one of the tubes around my right testicle. It would probably get worse, he said, before the antibiotics kicked in. He was right. All in all, it was not a fun vacation. I was in bed for over a week and, even with plenty of loving care, there wasn't a lot to do. I ate my holiday meals on a tray while listening to everyone else downstairs at the table. I put up with lots of well-intentioned jokes about footballs — (wink, wink, nudge, nudge, get it? — mine *were* almost that big, and certainly *felt* kicked). Mostly, I lay there feeling isolated, read a lot, and thought and thought and thought.

I couldn't ignore the irony of it. Here I was, finally addressing the sexual concerns I'd repressed since puberty and just at the moment of finally breaking through, I developed this enormous infection right where the whole war had been fought. I felt as if my body were letting go of all the stagnant, sick energy in one hot, swollen, painful push.

This was my first glimpse of the body-mind connection. At the time, it was just a bizarre coincidence, an interesting footnote to my story of coming out. Intuitively, I knew it was showing me something important, but I hadn't a clue about what to do with it. After I recovered, the incident stuck with me, a question in the back of my mind, waiting for explanation.

It had to wait 5 more years, until I started to study massage. As I learned to help people release muscular stress and tension, I saw firsthand that physical conditions never exist in a vacuum. Our bodies are part of our wholeness. They hold the memory of every experience, belief, and emotion in our lives. They are wise in ways that mystify the mind. They deliver intuitive messages, so-called "gut feelings" or "animal knowing", replete with vital information about our surroundings. Any spiritual path that ignores the body becomes a sterile exercise in mental gymnastics. True health comes only when we integrate all levels of being — physical, mental, emotional, and spiritual.

This chapter of your journey is dedicated to your body. As you learn to embrace it — with all its needs, desires, and idiosyncrasies — you'll gain an important ally. Hang on! After the mental focus of the last chapter, this one is going to feel really different. You'll spend most of your time in direct experience, relating to your body in ways that might at first feel awkward. Let yourself relax into the process. Be patient and take as much time as you need to enjoy yourself. The tools you'll learn here are fundamental and will serve you through the rest of this journey.

Tune in

Exercise

1. *Take a few moments before you go any further to come into your body, right in this moment. Close your eyes and shift their focus into neutral, as if you were looking inside yourself. Feel your body. Notice your posture. Where do you feel yourself being supported — feet? butt? back? Notice where your skin contacts the air. Is there a breeze? What's the temperature? Where are you relaxed? Where do you notice tension? What can you do to ease those places a bit?*

   Pay attention to your breathing. Feel your chest expand and relax. Feel the breath as it passes through your nostrils and over your upper lip. Feel what happens in your abdomen as you breathe. Feel what happens in your shoulders.

   Now listen to your heartbeat. Can you hear it? Can you sense its pulse throughout your body?

   Heartbeat and breathing are your body's most basic rhythms.

   Every single cell pays attention to them; they set the tone for everything else you do. If you pay attention, these two cycles will act as a personal gyroscope that gives you support and stability at any moment. Try it. For the rest of today, be aware of these rhythms in different situations. Notice how they change from moment to moment and how they relate to what's going on around you. Your goal is to observe, not to change anything. Just be present and see what you notice.

BELIEFS

We live in a body-phobic culture. Despite the increasing acreage of skin in advertising, most of the messages we get about our bodies are bluntly negative. Commercials for "body care" products from mouthwash and deodorant to prescription drugs and hair replacement systems brainwash us continually to distrust our own bodily functions. "You're not okay as you are," they tell us. "Your body smells bad, looks bad, feels bad, and will attack you at the least provocation." We've been sold a bill of goods that has divorced us from our most intimate connection.

The media only reflect society. Ours is built on a religious and philosophical foundation that negates the physical. In one corner, the dominant religions tell us that the "sins of the flesh" are in direct opposition to spiritual salvation. In the other, science touts the supremacy of the rational mind over "unreliable" feelings and intuition.

This is not just a Gay issue. Indeed, it touches everyone. It's a sort of cultural disease that manifests as collective alienation from anything to do with "feminine" values, sensitivity, nature, and the Earth. As Gay men, we do get a major dose. Much of our wounding is body-centered. For some of us, it came as actual violence or physical violation. For most, it was less direct and more pervasive. How many of us still hear the echo of taunts like, "You throw like a girl!" or "Act like a man!"? Worse, we learned the shame of having our most natural urges condemned as wrong, sinful, or "against nature."

Your body is unique and wise. In contrast to the mind, which lives by interpretation, your body experiences life directly. Because it offers a perspective based on how things actually *are*, rather than how you think they should be, your body is an important source of guidance. To access its wisdom, you need to step beyond all the hype and meet it on its own turf. Your first step in becoming reacquainted is to examine the beliefs that have separated you from it. Until you uncover these inner defenses, they'll sabotage any effort you make to accept and love yourself as you are. Be open to this one. Think about the relish with which you examine the body of a new lover, then bring that same degree of interest into this meeting with your own.

➤ Meet your body

Exercise

2.a. *Stand in front of a full-length mirror, so you can see your whole body. If possible, get another mirror that will allow you to look over your shoulder and view your back side as well. If you only have one mirror, do the best you can.*

Have a look at this man in the mirror, as if you were meeting him for the very first time.

> *What sort of overall impression does he make on you?*
> *What's the first thing you notice about him?*
> *What do you like about his appearance? his posture?*
> *Which parts of his body are especially attractive?*
> *Is there anything you dislike? What?*
> *Do you find any parts unattractive? Which?*
> *Which parts would you change if you could?*

Often, we tend to put on a little performance when we think we're being observed — stand a little taller, suck in the belly, flex the pecs, make the eyes smile. Look inside and take inventory of where your body is tense. Let go for a minute. This isn't a job interview, just an introduction. Your goal is to observe yourself just as you are.

Jot your impressions into your journal. Be as truthful and spontaneous as you can. There are no wrong answers.

b.   *Repeat the same exercise, this time without clothes. That's right, naked. Go through the same questions and write your responses in your journal.*

Compare the two sets of impressions. Were they similar? Was one exercise more difficult than the other? How comfortable are you with your own body?

c.   *Look at yourself one more time. This time, talk to your body. Tell it you're glad to meet it, that it really is a good body, and that you appreciate all it does to support you. Tell your body you'll do your best to love and support it in return. Then, give yourself a big hug, right in the mirror.*

If you feel a little silly, that's good. Silliness is the perfect antidote to years of self-judgment. You're setting an important precedent. Your body hears and believes every word you say about it. Starting to reframe the messages you give yourself is an important step toward reclaiming your connection.

➤ Hidden beliefs

Exercise

3.   Just as you uncovered hidden negatives about loving other men, you can do the same with beliefs about your body. Your Inner Critic is alive and well, and will have a lot to say if you give him a chance.

a.   *On a new page in your journal, number successive lines 1 to 20. Write the following sentence on each line, filling the blank each time with whatever* comes to you. Write as fast as you can and try not to think about what you're writing. It's okay for the same response to come up more than once.

The sentence is, "**My body is** _____ ."

b.   Same procedure, this time number your page 1 to 10, twice.

First sentence, "**My body is not** _____."

Second sentence, "**My body is too** _____ ."

Read through your three lists. Notice any trends, surprises, or repeats.

c.   Optional. If you feel you've uncovered the biggies, skip this one and go to Part d. If you'd like to go deeper, repeat the "unconscious negatives" exercise from Chapter 3 (page 43) in relation to your body. Use the following affirmation: "**I have a good, strong, attractive body.**"

d.   Take a quick look at where the negatives come from. Recognize any voices? Any old faces come to mind? Any idea when these criticisms first became an issue?

The first time I did this exercise, I was shocked at how many judgments about my body came from very early in life. "Butt too big, belly too soft, not athletic," all firmly established by elementary school. Most came from well-meaning parents and teachers trying to help me be acceptable. I was also surprised at how many of these ideas are reinforced by the media — all those ads for muscle systems and perfect twenty-year-old bodies.

Remember, you're not here to lay blame. By noticing where beliefs came from, you show yourself that they're nothing more than ideas held in your mind. You have the power to change your mind any time you like.

e.   Change your mind now. You already know how. Reframe the negatives you uncovered into a list of BODY AFFIRMATIONS. Be as positive and enthusiastic as you can. "I love my body just as I am." "I'm attractive because I enjoy using my body." "My body is healthy, vital, and strong." Use whatever works best for you.

Since you're already working with affirmations from the last chapter, it will be easy to add the new ones to your routine. Enjoy yourself. Be creative. Play. You are making great, positive changes.

f.   Release all the negative statements with the same burning or flushing ritual you used before. Claim this ritual as part of your ongoing spiritual practice and call on it whenever new negatives show their ugly heads.

SUPPORT YOUR BODY AND IT SUPPORTS YOU

Western society is obsessed with productivity. It offers little validation for any activity that isn't directly goal-oriented. No wonder most of us learn to treat our bodies like machines built of flesh. We think that as long as we give them fuel, oxygen, and basic maintenance they'll do whatever we need. "No pain, no gain," we hear, "so push yourself hard and don't stop unless something breaks." Unfortunately, with this model something *always* breaks.

The most obvious breaks are physical. When you ignore your body's signals — and live with a health care system focused on repair rather than prevention — disease and injury are a matter of course. Beyond the physical, cutting off your intuitive body connection robs you of a powerful source of wisdom, insight, and joy. It's time for a new model.

In the next set of exercises, you'll start building a new relationship with your body. You'll focus on nurturing and listening instead of dictating. In the process, you'll find that activities which used to be merely goal-oriented begin to feel a lot more satisfying. Exercise becomes a joyful expression of strength and movement instead of merely the means to an end. Grooming takes on elements of nurture and self-expression instead of blindly parroting the latest fashion. Sex becomes a way of sharing love instead of just "getting off." Working together, you and your body are a powerful team.

How can you support your body? First, recognize that it is wonderfully unique. What it needs from you, and how it responds to the care you give it, will be very personal. You'll find great variety, not only between yourself and other people, but also for yourself from one time to another. No fixed set of rules works all the time. Listen to your body. Make it your responsibility to learn what works for you.

Lets take a look at three major areas in which you can support your own health: exercise, rest, and diet. Take the suggestions offered here as guidelines. Then, make appropriate choices based on your own experiences.

EXERCISE

In college, deep in the closet, I spent a lot of time being depressed. Sometimes, like the weekends my roommate, on whom I had a deeply-denied crush, went home to his girlfriend, I'd feel as if I'd been kicked in the stomach. When it got too bad, I'd grab a jacket and bolt. I walked fast, trying to escape. At the edge of campus, I just kept going, out into the surrounding countryside.

To my surprise, walking actually helped. It didn't make the issues go away — only coming out three years later did that — but it did give me a way to deal with the pain. First, the urgency would leave. Then, I'd find myself walking just for the sake of it, exploring new paths, checking out those woods down by the railroad or the new houses across College Avenue. By the time I straggled back to the dorm, two hours and eight or ten miles later, I was usually pretty cheerful and ready to move on.

Aerobic exercise is great therapy. Walking, swimming, biking, running, and other exercises encourage positive changes in your physiology. Exercise stimulates your circulation. Your heart pumps faster. Your breath deepens and oxygen assists the breakdown of wastes and stress-induced toxins in every cell. Your brain releases pleasure-related endorphins. Bottom line, you feel better, think more clearly, and face life's challenges with greater vigor.

Every body needs exercise. What kind of exercise depends on you. Choose something that gets you moving, that you can do regularly, and that you really enjoy. It needn't be too strenuous. Exercise where your focus is on challenging and building muscles is good, but be sure you enjoy it and don't overdo. Aerobic exercise is essential.

REST

Most men learn to value activity over quiet and reflection. Too often we fall prey to the old work ethic that places a moral taint on taking it easy. The Inner Critic likes to call us "lazy" for even a short nap and pushes us ever onward to complete one more job.

Your body needs rest in order to stay healthy. Just how much depends on a variety of factors, including how much and what kinds of activity you engage in, your level of stress, what you eat, and your overall health. Obviously, if you're working hard, you need more rest to replenish your energy. In addition to physical work, you carry a hidden energetic load. All the inner pressures of self-doubt, fear, expectations, demands to succeed, and repressed feelings take a toll. As you work to resolve all this old "stuff," you'll free up trapped energy, which then manifests as health and vitality. In the process, your energy levels may fluctuate in ways you don't expect. At times you'll need more rest than you expect. At others you'll be bouncing off the walls. Pay attention.

When you eat, you need time to digest. When you explore new concepts, deal with strong emotions, or tackle your inner "work," you need time to process. "Down time" lets you mull things over, dream about them, and let them settle into your consciousness. Resting is as important as exploring if you're serious about making lasting change.

DIET

"You are what you eat," goes the old saying. To a great extent, it is true. What you take into your body directly influences your health, vitality, moods, and clarity. Without going into great detail, let's look at two dietary factors that will influence your journey.

First, aim for **balance**. Eat regularly and as nutritiously as possible. Get fresh foods, including fruits and vegetables, and avoid additives whenever you can. Pay attention to how different foods affect your energy. Some will leave you feeling light and clear. Others may weigh you down and take a long time to digest. In general, moderation is the key.

Second, watch your intake of substances that alter your moods. Even ordinary foods, like sugar and caffeine, can have dramatic effects. Use them moderately. Others, like alcohol, tobacco, pot, or stronger drugs, affect your ability to be clear. It's very easy to use substances, from ice cream to alcohol, to mask unpleasant feelings or avoid issues you'd do better to face directly and resolve. Watch yourself.

Quite a number of Gay men have developed substance abuse problems, partly in response to living in a homophobic world. This isn't a book about recovery. It will help to the extent that it helps you deal with underlying issues. To deal with addiction, though, you'll need stronger medicine. **Get it.** Millions of men have conquered addiction and now live strong, satisfying lives.

Give your body what it needs

Exercise

4.a. *In your journal, jot down aerobic activities that appeal to you and that fit your lifestyle. Choose activities you already enjoy or would like to try. What might they be? Different men have different answers. Miguel dances to loud music in his living room. Lanny walks to the subway instead of driving. John bikes to the post office or grocery. Gerry swims at the university pool three times a week. What would you choose?*

b. *In your journal, make a note of how much rest you usually need. What amount of sleep lets you feel at your peak? Do you take naps when you need them? How often do you move through your day-to-day routine feeling tired or less than totally alert?*

c. *Take a moment to reflect on your diet. What foods support you? How could you create habits of eating regularly and well? Carry your lunch to work instead of hitting the candy machine? Co-op with a friend to cook every other night? Store a week's worth of healthy meals in the freezer? What else?*

Jot down any insights in your journal. Honestly note any foods or substances that you tend to abuse and which you'd be better to keep in moderation.

d.   *Review your responses to the first three parts of this exercise, then write out a short commitment in your journal to support yourself in all three areas for the duration of this journey. Be specific. Also be realistic. Choose goals for yourself that you're likely to stick to with ease. You'll feel much better about yourself when you uphold your commitments.*

• What kind of exercise would you like to do. Can you commit to twenty minutes two or three times a week?

• Can you commit to giving yourself as much rest as you need? How much would that be? Can you be flexible if you need more?

• What will you do to support yourself nutritionally for the duration of this process? What foods will you include in your diet that support you? What eating habits will you encourage? What foods or substances will you avoid?

When you finish your commitment, review it to make sure you're being realistic, then sign and date it. Now enjoy taking care of yourself!

Self-touch

5.   Let's take a break from mental work. Here's an exploration of relating to your body as the sentient, conscious individual that it is. Think of this as play, not work, and you'll discover an enjoyable new way to treat yourself.

a.   *Set aside some time in which you can be alone and undisturbed. Make sure you're comfortably warm. If you like, create a soothing atmosphere — light a candle or put on quiet music, preferably without words. Take the phone off the hook.*

Either clothed or nude, as you prefer, sit or lie quietly for a few moments. Focus your attention on the breath. Feel the rhythm of inhale and exhale, and notice how it calms your whole body.

Watching the breath is a simple, effective way to focus your attention. Throughout the rest of the exercise, you'll find that keeping part of your attention on the breath will make it much easier to stay present with the experiences of your body and hands.

b.   *When you feel calm, rub the palms of your hands together, gently and briskly, until they feel warm and tingly. This energizes them and makes them more sensitive.*

Use your hands to begin exploring your body. Put your awareness in your fingertips. Be attentive, as if you were touching someone new for the very first time. "Listen" with your hands.

Start with your face. Explore the sensations, the shape and smoothness of the skin, the ways your fingers enjoy moving.

Shift focus. Notice how your face feels being touched. Ask it what sort of touch it likes — soft, firm, short, prolonged, or whatever. Let your fingers and your face create a dialog with each other.

c.   *Remembering your breath, begin to expand your exploration. Take your time. What about your ears? scalp? chin? neck? Notice how the responses vary from one part of your head to another. Do some parts like being touched more than others? Do your hands prefer some more or less? There are no wrong answers. Just observe and enjoy.*

d.   *Who is this body you're getting to know? Move downward, at your own pace, to shoulders, chest, arms. Let one hand explore the opposite arm, then trade sides. Investigate your ribs, sternum, abdomen, and sides. If it's difficult to reach your back, experiment with a backbrush or towel.*

Are you breathing? Continue your exploration with the hips, cock, balls, buttocks, thighs, moving gradually all the way to your feet. Take your time. Notice which parts you're in the habit of touching, and where it may be an entirely new experience.

The energy may get sexual, or relaxing, or stimulating, or vary from place to place. Keep breathing. Often, the body interprets **any** touch in a sexual manner, because that's often the only context in which we allow it. Self-pleasuring is great, yet sexual feelings can often override anything more subtle. There's a tendency, at the first sign of arousal, to pump right to climax. For now, stay aligned with the experience. Keep your focus on the whole body, not just the genitals. Complete the exploration, letting arousal be one of the many feelings that come up — comfort, pleasure, discomfort, delight, embarrassment, or what have you.

When you've moved gently through your entire body, give yourself a big hug. Let your breath bring you back to normal awareness.

e.   *Record your impressions in your journal. Pay special attention to new sensations, insights, or areas of discomfort.*

DIALOG WITH YOUR BODY THROUGH MOVEMENT

How do you feel? You've met your body and made a commitment to support yourself. Now, you're going to take a step further. By consciously engaging your body in movement, you'll open a line to more direct communication.

Your body is wise. From your first moments here, it's been learning about the world. Is it safe here? comfortable? welcoming? warm? cold? If I do this, is the result pleasurable or does it bring pain? Your body is an excellent student. It holds the memory of each lesson. If you were scolded for touching your penis, it remembers. If you were criticized every time you stood up tall and confident, it remembers. In new situations, it does its best to keep you safe. Most of its responses are determined by earlier experiences. Your body also reads other people instinctively. It understands the language of body. It knows if someone is comfortable, ill at ease, proud, afraid, or bluffing. If you pay attention, your body will share all this knowing with you.

If you've ever tried learning a new dance, you know how hard it is to work from the outside. If you're all caught up in your mind, trying to make something look just right, you'll probably get tangled up in your feet. If you get out of your mind, the movement will come forth on its own, smooth and natural. This authentic or "soul-full" movement is what you're after here. It allows you to bring forth what is already inside you seeking expression. It forms the basis of true dialog with yourself.

Movement meditation is going to be an important tool for the rest of this journey. The following introduction will let you get accustomed to the basics — and hopefully prove quite enjoyable too.

MUSIC

Music is vital to movement meditation. The rhythm helps you shift from linear, logical thinking into your intuitive, creative mode. It encourages your body to let go of external concerns and begin to play. Since everyone has different tastes in music, adapt the following guidelines to suit your own needs:

- Choose music you like. Enjoyment is half the process.

- Choose a steady beat and moderate tempo. The beat will help you to turn your attention inward and the tempo will keep you moving. Percussion music is often especially useful.

- Use instrumental music, without distracting lyrics. No matter how positive or meaningful they are, words tend to program your thoughts in a certain direction and interfere with the spontaneity of your experience.

- Choose music that will play for 15-20 minutes without your attention.

- An alternative to using music is to listen to your breath. Like your heartbeat, your breath is part of your "built-in" music and has the advantage of being with you all the time.

►Movement meditations

Attunement

This is a good introduction to any movement exercise, a sort of "Hi! How are ya?" warm-up to help you turn inward and connect with your body.

6.a. *Use music or not, as you prefer. Be sure you have enough room to move around freely, then close your eyes and pay attention to your breath. Feel it in your body. Feel your feet on the floor. Take stock of what you're feeling. Is your body tense? Is your mind going a mile a minute?*

As you breathe, imagine a shower of white light that flows through your body from head to toe — washing, cleansing, and clearing you of external energies. Let all the "stuff" drain through your feet into the Earth.

b. *Begin to walk slowly and easily around the room, either back and forth or in a circle. Keep your attention on your body, as if you were taking an inner tour. Where do you feel stiff? Where are you loose and comfortable? Where does your breath seem to move freely and easily? Where does it feel constricted? Where do you feel connected? Disconnected? Just watch and breathe.*

c. *Return and stand in the center of the space. Request of your body, "Show me how you feel." Repeat this request, aloud or in your mind, over and over for the duration of the exercise. Repeating the request keeps your mind occupied and out of the way, so you get a more direct experience of your body.*

Begin to move. Invite your body to do whatever it wants. Maybe it wants to stretch, or moan, or hold itself tightly. Maybe it wants to jump around the room in jubilation, or wrap into a tight, defensive ball. Observe whatever it does.

Attunement isn't about how the movement looks. Stay away from mirrors or from anyone watching you for the moment. No editing. No judging. What comes up is entirely between you and your body, so give it free rein.

d. *Record your impressions in your journal before continuing. What did you learn about your body? How might you sum up the experience?*

Exercise

Body Part dance

This exercise is another way to tune in that is upbeat and fun. Use music that is catchy and makes you want to dance.

7.a. *Take a moment to feel the breath all over. When you feel centered, invite your body to start moving. Instead of falling into your usual dance routine — the one you use to impress everyone at the club — this time ask the different parts of your body to show you **their** dance.*

Start with your feet. Let them lead. Watch as they show you what they enjoy, how they feel. Watch how the rest of your body accompanies them in response. Keep breathing. What sort of mood are your feet in? Experiment with different types of motion. See if they'll show you something you've never done before.

b. *Enjoy the dance of your feet. After a few minutes, thank them for their help and move upward to your knees. Your knees may have an entirely different take on the music. Let them show you. Take as long as you like, then move upward through hips, butt, spine, chest, shoulders, elbows, hands, and head.*

c. *Play with this process. Loosen your mind and let it dance with you. Try some non-linear explorations. What colors do you notice inside the various areas of your body? Textures? Moods? If your body were the Earth, what topography might each part represent — mountains, ocean, tropical rainforest, the frozen wastes at the North Pole? What's the weather in your elbows? Take the responses lightly, because they'll make little sense to your rational mind. Put on the music and let 'er rip!*

When you've played as long as you like, take a few moments just to breathe and stretch a little. How do you feel? Tired? Out of breath? Alive, alert, enthusiastic?

You can Body Part dance whenever you like. Not only is it a great introduction to other types of movement, it's an invigorating break anytime you need to antidote too much work or mental processing.

MOVEMENT IS LIFE!

Congratulations. You've begun a new relationship with your body. In succeeding chapters, you'll learn to take the process further, as you use movement to deepen and intensify your exploration of Gay archetypes. At this point, your mind might be asking, "Why? Isn't it enough just to understand what's going on? Why all this other stuff?". I'll tell you.

Movement is a bridge between body and mind, feeling and understanding, theory and actual experience. Since the body always tells its truth, it will show you where you still have work to do and where there are discrepancies between what you *think* you believe and what actually lives in your unconscious. Further, movement helps you integrate all the changes and insights you're gaining through the rest of the process. Holding things in your mind alone won't make them happen. Integrating them into your cells and the wholeness of your being will.

Beware of resistance. "I don't like to dance," you complain. "I can't move. What if I'm in a wheelchair and can't dance?" Baloney. That's just your mind protecting you from change. All those old defenses take energy you could use more productively — for exploring, playing, dancing, living, loving. Defenses mask fear and fear shows where you can grow. You have resistance to dancing? Here are three steps to move beyond it.

First, acknowledge and honor the resistance the same way you did for the Inner Critic. In fact, use the Critic's Corner to give your fears a voice. What are you afraid of — looking silly? being ridiculed? listening to the urges of your body? having fun? Get the fears out on paper and thank the Critic for trying to protect you.

Second, make it really safe — no mirrors, no audience, and no need to push yourself too hard.

Third, dig in and fight. Don't fight yourself. Fight the internalized judgment that wants to keep you blocked from being fully alive. Every step you take toward healing yourself, even if it seems small or inconsequential, is radical. You are worth the effort. Even in your own living room, you are a powerful warrior!

By the way, one of the most beautiful and powerful dancers I ever saw was a man at a disco in Dallas. From his wheelchair, he spun and twirled, chair and all, in ecstatic abandon. His dance encouraged the same energy from everyone standing around him and the place was hoppin'! So no more excuses, huh? Get out there and shake it!

5 Initiation

COMING OUT ... THE HERO'S JOURNEY

As an adolescent, I lived most of my life in books. Probably because I felt pretty awkward in the world of kids, most of my major kicks came while I was turning pages. Though I devoured almost anything the school librarian steered my way, some stories were special. Those, I could read over and over. They were stories about boys alone in the world, exiled, forced to prove themselves in order to be accepted. I remember two in particular.

In one, *First to Ride* by Pers Crowell, the young hero faces the trials of living by himself in some prehistoric time. In the story, he finds a wild black stallion and learns to call on his own strength, courage, and determination to become the first person ever to tame a wild horse. When he finally returns to his people, he's hailed as a hero. The second story, *Call It Courage* by Armstrong Sperry, features a young Polynesian boy who braves the perils of a long sea journey with only his faithful dog as companion. When he lands on an unknown island, the boy conquers his fears to outwit a tribe of cannibals, win a wild boar tusk, and eventually return home to become a hero and legend among his people.

These stories which touched me so deeply are modern versions of an archetypal theme reflected in the myths of many cultures — the Hero's Journey. You can probably think of other examples. Joseph Campbell, a delightful expert on mythology, mentions the tale of Jason and the Golden Fleece, the trials of young Arthur before he comes to his throne, and the adventures of Luke Skywalker battling the evil Empire, among many others. All these tales present in story form the inner process by which a boy passes into manhood. Symbolically, they depict the trials, journeys, and lessons of initiation that earn the boy a place among the men of his people.

Robert Bly, Michael Meade, Malidoma Somé, and other figures in the modern men's movement talk a lot about the problems resulting from our society's lack of male initiation. Boys, they say, have an inherent need to prove themselves against standards set by male mentors and elders. Without formalized initiation, boys fail to make the step from adolescence to mature, socially responsible adulthood.

For Gay men, the story is a bit different. Initiation is less absent. Though usually we're left without the healthy adult mentorship we need, each of us is tested as we grow up by the challenges of not fitting our society's accepted models of maleness. The doubts and questions we're called on to deal with are every bit as daunting as those confronting the young heroes of the stories. In the end, if only to avoid a life of total isolation, each of us is called on to choose the path of initiation by coming out to our true selves.

Coming out is the self-chosen rite of passage we all have in common. Though we may feel confused, defiant, or unsure in the process, the steps we take to live openly make a powerful statement. "No more!" we shout to denying our true selves. "No more!" to the charade of pretending to be straight, or normal, or other than we are. In fact, coming out is an act of self-love so powerful that the term itself has been appropriated into the language of the mainstream. Nowadays, everyone from environmentalists to people who love schnauzers "comes out" into the public eye. In an amazing reversal a few years ago, I read an article in the paper entitled "Coming Out Fundamentalist," which exhorted "true believers" to stand by their beliefs. Eye-opening, to say the least, especially for someone still nursing some pretty painful church-inspired wounding.

In theory, we all know that coming out signifies choosing to be open about our sexuality. In practice, though, it means different things to different people. How do **you** define it? Was it when you finally admitted to yourself that you were "homosexual," even though you didn't do anything about it for years? Was it telling your parents? the first time you had sex with another man? moving out from your girlfriend's to live with your first lover? However you define it, most of us reach a point of no return when the choice to live with integrity, whatever the costs, becomes irrevocable.

Each of us does it differently. My friend Robert wrote letters to his whole extended family — cousins, grandparents, even his brother's ex-wife. James called his mother one night and blurted out, "Mom, I'm queer," then hung up, too terrified to hear her response. William read an essay to his tenth grade English class, earning himself a trip to the guidance office and a call to his startled parents. I came out in grad school, when I finally got up the nerve to go over to the one queer bar in town, a sleazy place we just called "The Pit." Maybe you do it with drama, maybe with ease. What's most important, however you do it, is that you dare to come out at all.

In reality, "coming out" is only one step in a slowly unfolding journey. Usually, it begins in silence, deep inside, long before you're ready even to think about going public. From the first groping realizations that you're somehow "different," you're pushed onto a path of self-examination. The steps may be so small you hardly notice them. They can come as unpleasant awakenings, like the time you found out that your mother's lipstick wasn't an acceptable toy for little boys. They can come as questions — "I'm supposed to feel something when I look at girls. Why don't I?" They can lead to insights — "'Homosexual' ... so that's what you call it. Hmmm... if there's a word, I must not be the only one. Where are the rest?"

Each step, like it or not, teaches you a little more about yourself. Forced to search inside for exactly what it is that makes you different, you learn to look beneath the surface. Though the initial motivation is probably to "fix" yourself, or at least keep your differences from showing, slowly, haltingly, you come to grips with who you are. Once you realize that this thing is not going away and that you're going to have to deal with it one way or another, the focus of the journey starts to turn outward. Somehow, you have to share it with other people.

If you're lucky, you have help. I'm eternally grateful to the therapist who heard my choked-out confession. "You can't change it," he said without batting an eye. "All you can do is get used to it and make peace with yourself." Other men weren't so lucky. When his parents found out and started screaming, seventeen year-old Gary ended up in a detention center for "troubled youth." Both Chip and Sam submitted to painfully demeaning attempts by religious counselors to "cure" their orientation. Jimmy spent years being taunted as the school fairy. Each of them made it through, but the path wasn't easy.

Coming out is a challenge however you do it. Each stage has costs. There are the risks of losing friends, family, job, popularity, church membership, or the cherished illusion of normalcy. At times, there's a risk of physical harm. All these losses, even though they're necessary steps toward personal growth, may involve pain and grief. Though it's easy to overestimate the risks in those moments of terror before you finally act, some of them are undeniable and demand consideration.

At the same time, consider the very real costs of staying closeted. Recognize the pain of living a lie and the amount of energy it takes to remember, all the time, what story you've told which person. Acknowledge the damage to your self-esteem of believing that your true being is too awful to show anyone. Be honest about the pain of replacing your lover's picture with your old girlfriend's when your folks come to visit, or the terror that makes you laugh so loud at those cruel fag jokes your so-called "friends" are fond of telling. The costs of not coming out are corrosive. They eat at your soul like acid until you find yourself depressed, bitter, and only half-alive.

Each stage of coming out is a step toward wholeness. Ultimately, the benefits are more than worth the price. There's freedom to live your life truthfully and to call your own shots. There's the incredible amount of energy you once used to conform to false standards, now available for activities that really sustain you. There's the healthy empowerment of honoring your own being, of going for your dreams, of having friends who accept and love you for who you are. Coming out is choosing life.

I suspect the rate at which we take steps to come out depends on a balance between the benefits of staying closeted and the discomfort involved. When the discomfort finally gets too great, you take the plunge, write that letter, make that call, or leave the photo of that guy with the tires on the fridge.

Beforehand, you'll always have questions. You might ask,

- **"Does it have to be graceful?"** No. You'll probably stumble, trip over your words — or your high heels — and feel like a klutz. It doesn't matter. Some day, when you feel better, it'll all make a great story!

- **"Does it have to be healthy?"** It is healthy, inherently, and at every level of your being.

- **"Does it have to hurt?"** No, but it might. A certain amount of growing pain accompanies every step.

- **"Is it ever too late?"** No. My friend George did it in his late fifties, at a "coming out party" complete with cake, candles, and party hats to boot.

- **"Is it ever too early?"** Perhaps. It's never too early to come out to yourself. There may be situations, though, in which you're better-advised to put off coming out publicly. If you're young, for example, and still dependent on parents who might freak, or if you're in an abusive situation where coming out could put you in real physical danger, wait. Gauge your situation carefully. If you need help, get it! There are more and more sources of confidential help available. Call upon them when you can, and bide your time if necessary.

➤ How far out have you come?

Exercise

1. *What does coming out mean to you? Is there one specific event? A series of steps? Is your focus primarily internal — coming out to yourself — or is it about acting with other people? Record your thoughts in your journal.*

2. *Now, take stock.*

a. *Divide a new sheet of paper into three columns. In the center column, outline the major steps, to date, in your coming out journey. Be brief and complete. Note the major points, especially actions you took. Skip details for now.*

b. *In the left-hand column, in a different color, jot down the main challenges you faced (or face now) at each step — fear of being rejected, of losing friends, of not doing it right. Don't worry if things run together or the page gets a little messy. That's how life is sometimes, anyway.*

c. *In the right-hand column, in a third color, list the main benefits you are receiving as a result of taking each step.*

3. *List the areas of your life in which you can be open about being Gay. Can you talk with your family? Your friends? Employer? Where else?*

Congratulate yourself.

4. Here are five different ways to explore your coming out journey in a less linear manner. Pick at least one and enjoy it.

a. *Write a short note giving advice to an imaginary man who is just coming out. What would you tell him? What have you learned that could make his way easier? What do you wish someone had told (or would tell) you?*

b. *Expanding on the outline you made in Exercise 1, write your coming out story. What happened? What was it like? How did you feel? How did you prepare? Did things go as expected? How did you feel afterward?*

Take as much space as you need in your notebook. The story doesn't have to be polished or ready for publication in The New York Times. You don't have to show it to your folks. Just be honest and tell what's there.

If you haven't come out yet, write an imaginary story about what it might be like. Imagine how you might do it, who you might tell first, how you think they'd react. What are your feelings about the whole thing? What holds you back? What are your concerns? Again, be honest. You're just writing here; you don't have to do anything until you're ready.

c. **M.Y.T.H.** — *Make Yourself The Hero*

Cast your coming out story in the trappings of a mythological tale. Give yourself the perfect hero's body, complete with the most heroic outfit you can imagine. Tell the tale of this hero's exploits, the dragons he must slay (fear, perfection, being the best little boy in the world, etc.). Who gets in his way — evil queens? wicked stepmothers? ugly old trolls? What allies does he meet who help him, teach him, or show him his magic gifts? What are those gifts? In the end he triumphs over all adversity. How?

Have fun with this one. Embellish it and play.

d. *Design a ritual in which you honor your own coming out. Design it for yourself alone or for as many people as you like. In your ritual, acknowledge the challenges you faced and overcame, the courage it took for you to do so, and just how far you've come in your life. Honor your commitment to continue making choices that support you.*

If this is a ritual you'd like to perform, do it.

e. *Tune in to your body. Use the "Attunement" process from the last chapter (Exercise 6.a, page 65). Perform a movement meditation using the following requests. Remember to repeat the request over and over mentally as your body responds.*

"Body, show me how I felt before I came out," or

"Show me how it feels not to come out."

When you feel you've received a clear response to the first request, change it to **"Body, show me how it feels to come out successfully."**

Your body will have definite responses to share with you. Continue the meditation until you feel complete, then release the energy and record your impressions.

COMING IN ... FAMILY OF CHOICE AND TRIBE

New Year's at our house is always festive. In honor of another year together, my partner and I invite friends and family to celebrate. As the evening progresses, the sounds of conversation and laughter get pretty lively. In pairs and clusters, our friends share jokes, stories, hugs, a dance. Most of them have known each other for years.

At one point last year, I looked around the room. In one corner, my partner's mother entertained my ex-lover and his new beau. On the front porch, one of the neighborhood moms instructed a couple of lesbians on the ins and outs of breastfeeding. Sprawled on the floor beside the couch, two designer friends plotted a new, joint business in intense whispers. At the fireplace, our playwright friend swapped theater tales with a young actor just moved to town.

At midnight, amidst cheers, champagne, and kisses, we passed dollar bills from hand to hand to ensure prosperity in the coming year. Just for a moment, waxing philosophical, I watched the green bills flow from one smiling friend to another and saw them as a symbol of something deeper, the web of love and support we've woven together. This is our new family, our "family of choice." It's not what I'd expected.

Deep in the throes of coming out, it's often hard to see beyond the moment. Risking the rejection of friends or family in order to be true to yourself, it's easy to imagine that you're taking a step into isolation. In truth, what usually happens is just the opposite.

At Gay Spirit Visions, we like to say, "Coming out is really coming in" — coming in to a circle of friends who honor and support you the way you are. Though it may involve leaving some people behind, these are people who obviously didn't support you fully anyway. In time, you'll share friendship, understanding, love, and celebration with a whole rainbow of new folks. You'll create your own family of choice.

Let me emphasize again — you are not on this journey alone. Beyond the circle of friends you know personally, you're supported by a great, extended Gay Tribe. Can you remember the first time you attended a Pride Festival or saw a picture of the hundreds of thousands of exuberant participants? Even if the amazingly unconventional diversity startled your eyes at first, remember how it felt to know that you were no longer alone. Wherever you find yourself right now on your path, relax. You have companions here you've never even met. Men-loving men accompany you in many different roles — as lovers, friends, brothers, playmates, and mentors. Even if you haven't yet come out, you belong to this Tribe. It offers you strong support. Call on it.

The Tribe of Gay Men exists, fully realized, inside each one of us. You'll explore the inner aspects of that connection in the next chapter. Your own experience of Tribe, though, depends more on the connections you make day to day, both personally with other men and within the larger community. Before we go further, take a few moments to explore these.

➤ Connections

5.   Family of choice.

a.   *List the other men-loving men in your life with whom you presently spend the most time.*

How would you characterize each of these relationships? Is it primarily sexual? casual? supportive? buddies? "girlfriends?" Recognizing that it may be a bit simplistic to sum up a whole relationship in one or two words, wherever you can, jot down the primary focus of each one beside the person's name.

b. *Put a star beside the names of the men who make you feel positive and good about yourself.*

   Put a star beside those you'd feel comfortable turning to with personal fears, problems, or spiritual concerns.

c. *Are there men on your list you don't always feel good about, or with whom you sometimes do things that don't feel quite right to you?*

d. *Are there Gay men, either on your list or not, with whom you'd like to spend more time? Who?*

e. Your family of choice is not limited to men-loving men alone. Surely, you have non-Gay friends. In fact, a healthy support system includes many, diverse relationships.

   Repeat the above exercise, substituting the word, "people" for "men-loving men". Add any names you didn't cover the first time through.

6. **Connection within the Gay community.**

   Tribal connection is a physical actuality, created each time we interact. We live in a time of rapid expansion when Gay connections are more available than at any time in recent history. How much are you taking advantage of them?

a. *List your main sources of information about Gay issues — newspapers, TV, radio, movies, magazines, Internet, etc. How accurate do you think they are? Are they supportive? Is the information first-hand? Is it actually produced by Gay people?*

b. *What is the primary focus of your interaction with other men-loving men? Are you part of any Gay organizations? Where could you meet more men with interests like your own?*

c. *Where would you turn right now if you had a problem related to being Gay? What resources in your community are you aware of? Do you have a support network you can turn to if you need it?*

Examining your connections with others is the first step toward creating a network that actually supports you. Sometimes, especially if you've felt isolated for much of your life, the desire to belong to a group, **any** group, of men-loving men overwhelms all other considerations. You tend to do whatever it takes to fit in — from wearing the right clothes to whatever else "the group" decides is right. If you have friends whose values are in line with your own, it works. If not, though, you can have problems. Think about it. Are there places in your life you feel you're compromising yourself just to fit in with a group?

The point of these exercises is not to judge others, nor to try to change anyone else. It **is** to begin making choices that honor **you.** Honoring yourself means spending less time with people who bring you down. It means making fewer compromises, finding new activities, joining a new club, or taking an evening at home instead of partying yourself to exhaustion one more night. As you grow and change, so will your friendships. Some will drift away. Others that support your new way of being will come in. Listen to your own needs. You'll create a healthy experience of Tribe that supports you each day.

COMING OUT IS A WAY OF LIFE

Coming out means choosing to live on your own terms. It is a resounding vote of confidence in your own worth. Taken to its fullest extent, coming out goes far beyond just saying, "I love men." It says, "I trust myself enough to listen to my own voice above that of society, the church, the media, my family, or anyone else. I value myself enough to reach for my full potential, to claim all the love, fulfillment and satisfaction that I deserve." Coming out, ultimately, means **living out.**

The issue of coming out never goes away. Once you make the initial commitment to yourself, each day brings new choices. Situation after situation gives you the opportunity to say "Yes!" or "No," "I'll support myself" or "I'm not really worth it." How do you choose? Do you go for the promotion you deserve or give in to fears that more visibility will bring flack? Do you get that gym membership or give in to the old, negative self-image? Do you stay in your stuffy, boring relationship or go for what you really want? Every time you yield to the temptation to sell yourself short, you take a step back into the closet and concede a point to the fagbashers who say you're no good. Every time you make the choice to live life on your own terms, you choose freedom, strength, and continuing growth.

Singly and together, we are a Tribe who pushes limits. From the moment you consciously embrace your identity by coming out, you empower yourself to take one growth step after another. A quick look around our community provides example after example of men choosing to explore new ways to be in the world. Initiation is written in our lives. Read it in the wobbly first steps of a Halloween drag butterfly. Read it in the formalized rituals of the leathermen or the words of activists fighting for political change and religious freedom. Read it in the determination of men in recovery and the ecstatic abandon of those who dance. Read it in the strength and compassion with which we've met the unasked-for challenges of AIDS. Read it in yourself, in your commitment to grow on this journey.

You were **not** put on this planet by Creator merely to pay the rent each month and eke out some gray, unfulfilling half-life. You are here with a host of gifts and talents to share. Coming out means going for **all** your dreams, daring to reach for health, happiness, satisfaction, and spiritual fulfillment. Coming out means daring to be nothing less than **fabulous**. Now, that's what I call a life's work!

➤ Living out

7.a. *List any areas in your life where you still aren't as open as you'd like to be. Are there situations in which you feel you compromise yourself, even just a little? Be honest, but not too hard on yourself here. Sometimes, being discreet is an appropriate response to a difficult situation.*

b. *For each item on the list, think about what payoffs you get by leaving things the way they are. Payoffs might include not losing your job, staying friends with someone, and so forth.*

c. *For the same list, consider what it might cost you to come out further. Some of your answers might be the same as for part b, but also consider things like how you feel about yourself.*

d. *For each item on the list, what are the potential benefits of coming out further?*

This exercise is to make you think. Don't be hasty to act right away on anything you've discovered. Pushing things at this point could easily be premature. Instead, hold in your mind the issues you've raised as you proceed through the next chapters. They'll give you a strong focus as you explore ways to act effectively and appropriately.

CONGRATULATIONS

You've just completed the first leg of your journey. What you've done so far is quite powerful. Claiming responsibility for your thoughts, relating to your body holistically, and examining your life in order to take charge of its direction are all major, positive steps.

Congratulate yourself! Feel good! Give yourself a gold star and a big hug! You've earned them.

Part 2
ARCHETYPES
AND GAY MEN

6 The Journey Within

THE REALM OF ARCHETYPE

At this point, your journey turns inward. While theories about Gay identity can get you headed in the right direction, they can't tell you much about your own experience. The only way to discover what loving other men means to you personally is to go inside and take a look for yourself. That's what you're about to do.

This part of the journey is the true heart of your empowerment process. Do your best to approach it with an open mind. Inner reality is different from what you might expect. In contrast to the material realm where things can be touched and quantified, the world within is subjective and everchanging. It is a realm defined by symbol, imagery, dreams, and mystical experience. Having grown up in our overly-rational culture, you may be tempted to dismiss what you discover here as unreal or "make-believe". In fact, the truth is quite the opposite.

The inner realm holds the keys to your spiritual empowerment. What goes on here is valid and real — indeed, it determines the quality of every experience you have. Some of the territory you're going to explore will be challenging. Some will inspire you. Some will bring you strength and satisfaction. Some will even make you laugh. I invite you to approach this territory with an attitude of serious lightness. As you become more at home here, you'll come to value it as one of the richest parts of yourself.

As an introduction, let's look at a few concepts that will help you understand where you're going. They'll give you a map of the domain and a context to make your discoveries much more useful and meaningful.

ARCHETYPE

In recent decades, archetype has been discussed at great length by psychologists and philosophers. Rather than getting bogged down with all the details, let's agree on a working definition that is short, loose, and practical. Archetypes are aspects of collective consciousness, the pool of awareness shared by all humanity. Each one carries the traits associated with some element of human experience, creating a sort of universal character that we recognize instinctively. To clarify the concept, let's look at an example.

We're all familiar with the general archetype called "Mother." You could describe it easily, drawing on countless images from art, literature, and your own experience. The archetypal Mother encompasses a host of individual traits. Some are strongly positive, like the patience, nurturing, and protective devotion that characterize the "ideal" mother. You could also list negative mother traits — neglectfulness, overprotective smothering, and cruel self-centeredness. All these traits, whether positive, negative, or neutral, are part of the overall archetype.

At the level of pure consciousness, archetypes animate psychological dynamics and provide the underlying patterns of all our interactions. Each of us relates to particular archetypes uniquely. No single person can embody **all** the traits of any one. Look at the many styles with which the universal Mother can express. One woman might be nurturing and practical, the very image of a hippie Earth Mother. Another might be a career mom, attentive to her children but preoccupied by other affairs. A third could be a sort of "Mommie Dearest" whose kids are the target of her own bitter frustration. Each of these individuals embodies archetypal Mother in her own way.

Archetypes have been known to peoples in all times and cultures. In some, they are, or were, held as gods. In others, they people the myths and stories that carry the wisdom of society from one generation to the next. Because tales about archetypal figures represent a sort of distillation of human experience, they provide useful guidance on our personal paths through life. Some encourage us. Others warn of pitfalls. We recognize ourselves in the over-reaching ambition of Icarus and the self-infatuation of Narcissus. We see other aspects in the drunken face of Bacchus, the sunny visage of Apollo, or the sly trickster Coyote.

Our own society makes cultural idols of public figures who resonate with archetypal parts of ourselves. Men who love men seem to be particularly in touch with certain ones. What is it that made a generation of Gay men swoon over Judy Garland and Bette Davis? What makes their successors so enamored of Madonna or RuPaul? On other levels, is it just stereotype that we're more attuned to the realm of symbol and spirit than other men? It certainly seems that an inordinate number of us work in areas that depend on creative inspiration. We're masters of glamour and illusion. We thrive on theater and drama, be it a play by Tennessee Williams, the lip-synched glory of Wigstock, or the black-tinged ecstasy of a leather scene. Archetypal figures help us to figure out who we are.

One of the more compelling reasons for us to understand how archetypes work is that positive images of Gay men are almost entirely missing from our cultural heritage. Archetypal energies **always** come through, whether we're conscious of them or not. If we lack models that show us how to express them beneficially, they come forth warped and distorted into their more negative personas.

Look at the archetype of "Man Who Loves Men." This figure could manifest through any one of us as the visionary man-god we imagined in Chapter One. Remember how loving, open, and self-fulfilled he felt, while you give him the body, appearance, and individual traits that suit you. Then look at what happens to this same archetype when it is denied or repressed. The energy still comes through, but its form grows ugly and hurtful. We don't have to look far for examples. Picture the nasty, self-hating queen whose bitter humor shreds anyone else in sight. Picture the "happily married heterosexual" who spends his evenings seeking furtive, anonymous male sex in rest areas, all the while hypocritically denouncing "those queers wrecking the family." Perhaps all three images are exaggerated, but I bet most of them are familiar.

Archetypes are an important part of your own being. You're about to explore seven that are especially pertinent for men-loving men — the Magic Boy, Androgyne, Lover, Elder, Shaman/Healer, Warrior, and Explorer. The list isn't meant to be inclusive. Certainly, other archetypes are of interest. These specific ones, though, hold insights central to your spiritual quest. Our goal is very practical. By examining the ways — both positive and negative — that each archetype expresses in your life, you'll learn to access wisdom and strength that are already part of your being. Bringing them to consciousness makes them available to you in new ways and empowers you to make clear, concrete choices about priorities, relationships, and life in general.

Cultural heroes

Exercise

1. *Think about the cultural figures that have touched you most strongly. Who in the popular culture have you embraced as your own? Was it Mickey Mouse? Madonna? Freddie Mercury? Cher? Was it Will Robinson? the Beav'? Sylvester Stallone in Rocky? Even though your tastes may have changed, list the characters or "idols" who have spoken to you the most strongly over the years.*

SHADOW

As you explore the various archetypes, you'll find some aspects that are familiar and easy to access. When you meet the Magic Boy, for example, you may find that you already enjoy being playful and spontaneous. Later on, you might appreciate the fact that what you call "common sense" is actually the voice of your inner Elder. These are parts of the archetypes that you've already integrated successfully into your consciousness. All of us, however, have other aspects that are harder to recognize. These parts, though they still manifest in our thoughts and behavior, tend to stay below the level of awareness. We can give them the general name of **Shadow**.

Shadow represents all the parts of self we haven't yet learned to claim. Though there are similarities from one person to the next, Shadow content is different for each of us. One man may be so afraid of his own anger that he represses it totally, putting on such a sweet face that he almost fools even himself. Another may hide his feelings of vulnerability behind a mask of harsh gruffness. These hidden emotions are part of Shadow.

We relegate parts of ourselves to Shadow for a variety of reasons. Fear is a prime cause — fear of pain, of rejection, or of hurting ourselves and others. Other reasons could be shame, wounding, or just not knowing what to do with something. Shadow elements can be major parts of our personalities as well as smaller, less demanding ones.

For many of us, being Gay itself was once a major part of the Shadow. Personally, I remember blocking thoughts of attraction to other boys with all my might. Doing my best to ignore it, I never even gave the longing a name. I just called it "that." "Oh, *that* again," I'd think when it got through the defenses. Then I'd try to forget that "that" even existed. A regular soldier, I did my best to marshal my thoughts into the order I thought they should be. How about you?

When we consign parts of ourselves to darkness, we go to great lengths to keep them there. Psychologically, one of the most universal strategies is to **demonize** the unwanted part. In an effort to push it away, we make that part of ourselves seem so awful that we can't even imagine looking at it, much less bringing it forth. Before I came out, I believed all the ridiculous, untrue lies about homosexuality. I was sure it involved a host of horrors from child molestation to unimaginable cruelty. At one time, I even believed it was part of the Devil — lecherous, slavering, and totally beyond control. The fact that I'd heard such filthy lies at all is an issue we'll deal with later. What's important here is that judgments like these teach us to distrust even the healthiest parts of ourselves.

Another way we avoid looking at something we don't like in ourselves is to see that same trait in everyone around us. This behavior is called **projection**. Usually, projection operates unconsciously. Often, we wonder quite sincerely why a certain type of person keeps coming into our lives. "I've never said an angry word in my life. Why am I surrounded by these people who are always yelling? What's the matter with them?" Finding faults in other people is a great way to avoid looking at our own.

Trying to escape our own Inner Critic by projecting him outward almost always backfires. Resisting any energy tends to feed it. And so, the man who lives in terror of what people are saying about him makes himself into the world's greatest gossip as he wags his tongue about everyone else. The boy worried about his own effeminacy becomes ruthlessly quick to condemn the slightest limp wrist or swaying hip in another. "Sure I jump rope and carry my books like a girl, but I don't lisp like Jimmy!" Desperation breeds some pretty shallow thinking.

Beyond individual interactions, projection also affects us as a group. One way it happens is through public homophobia. Often the very people who condemn homosexuality with the greatest vigor are actually fighting it in themselves. Witness the tragically effective homophobia of J. Edgar Hoover and Roy Cohn in the early fifties. Witness the vocal condemnation of homosexuals by religious organizations whose ranks are notoriously full of closeted queers. For the most part, men secure in their own sexuality put little energy into worrying about that of others.

We're also affected by something I'll call "group projection." Humans have a great proclivity to demonize anyone we perceive as "other." For example, look at the wartime fever that makes otherwise rational people believe the most simplistic condemnations of their enemies. Does Saddam Hussein really eat babies for breakfast? How could people in Bosnia who lived side by side in peace for decades suddenly fall into a frenzy of killing each other? Look at the religious bigotry that swept Europe during the Crusades, or the mindset that made European colonists believe the native peoples they displaced were nothing more than soulless savages.

Group projection touches Gay people directly. The lies I believed as a boy are part of a widespread assault on the truth of who we are. Because for so long we were unable to show ourselves openly, it was easy for "proper" society to demonize us. No matter that we are sons, uncles, fathers, and brothers to everyone else, to a large extent we've carried the projected Shadow of a sex-phobic, puritanical society. Our only hope of changing the situation lies in breaking out of the invisibility that made projection possible and learning to stand open and firm in the truth of who we are.

Before leaving Shadow, let's mention a more positive aspect. Although the term usually conjures up images of darkness, in reality Shadow elements can also be healthy and enlightening. Often, we keep ourselves blind to our gifts as well as our faults, and refuse to believe that we could ever shine like the people we see around us. Discovering your own hidden gifts, talents, and bright places is a major goal of this journey. For a small taste of what's to come, look at the good traits you enjoy in the people around you. Are you someone who considers himself painfully inadequate at conversation, yet who's surrounded by friends who seem witty, interesting, and loquacious? Are you always in the company of artists? Or healers? Or great dancers? At the level of energy, like attracts like. There's a very good chance that the people you're most attracted to are showing you parts of yourself.

TURN WITHIN

Exploring your inner reality is simple and easy. The tools you'll use in the coming chapters are primarily nonlinear. If this is the first time you've explored activities like guided visualization and conscious movement, you may need a little time to get used to them. You might wonder if you're doing what you're supposed to or if what you're getting has any value. Don't worry. The exercises work. All you have to do is follow the directions and pay attention. They'll take you where you need to go.

What you're after here is **direct** experience through feelings, images, dreams, and memories. Phenomena like these are highly subjective. Though deeply meaningful to your heart, body, and soul, they often don't sit too well with the part of your mind that wants to analyze and compartmentalize every experience. For now, remember that you are more than your mind. Take **everything** you experience with a grain of salt. Resist the temptation to make it all literal or to act on anything right away. You're uncovering images and feelings in order to transform them. That takes time. Trust the process and before too long, all the pieces will make sense on their own terms.

Find your own pace through the exercises. As you guide yourself through them, you'll learn how to focus inward on sensations and images while still being able to follow directions and record your observations. One way to help yourself is to read through an exercise completely before you go deeper. Then, when you have a general idea where you're going, return to the beginning and follow it through one step at a time. Even if you close your eyes in order to look inward, you'll be able to maintain your focus as you open them briefly to read the next steps or write something in your journal. With a little practice, you'll become adept at balancing your awareness between both realms.

Some people visualize very easily. Some get very little at first, or what they do get doesn't make much sense. If this is the case for you, relax. Anything you experience is valid. Just observe whatever sensations, feelings, words, or bits of imagery do come. Be easy on yourself. With a little practice, you'll get much clearer. Even if it seems that nothing at all is coming, following the directions will still engage parts of yourself you're not aware of. You'll make inner connections that will come back as insights and new awareness later, often when you least expect.

If you've never done guided visualization before, you may be surprised that many of the images are already familiar to you. To the mind, this may seem a reason to disbelieve the whole process — "There, you see, I told you you were making it all up!" Not so fast, mind. Archetypes exist at the level of energy, beyond individual awareness. The only way for you to relate to them personally is to translate them into images that make sense to you. In much the same way as you can make a magnetic field visible by sprinkling it with iron filings, your mind interprets the essence of an archetype by clothing it in concepts and images that are already familiar. Rather than rejecting what you come up with because you've seen it before, realize that this is the only way your mind can work here.

Meeting your Inner Council is a good first step. The Inner Council is like an internal board of directors that helps and guides you through life. Each member of the Council is your own expression of a particular archetype. Don't be surprised if what you discover inside already feels familiar. Really, everything you see is an aspect of your own being. This exercise is your first introduction. Over the next few weeks, you'll come to know each member of your Council much more intimately.

➤ Meet your Inner Council

Exercise

2.a. **Create sacred space.**

This exercise will take about 10 to 15 minutes. Set aside time to explore it when you won't be disturbed.

Create safe, sacred space by visualizing a sphere of white light all the way around you. If you like, begin with a short prayer or statement of intention that all which transpires in this place be positive and healing. Honor your connection with all Life by imagining roots from your center that go deep into the Earth. Reaffirm your connection with Creator or Spirit and invite your inner guides to be with you. Adapt the words and images to suit your own beliefs.

b. **Council space**

Sit quietly with your eyes closed. In your mind, ask to see the space in which your Inner Council meets. This meeting place could be anywhere that feels comfortable and safe — a circle of trees or stones somewhere outdoors, a rustic lodge in which each member sits around a fire, or a board room with oak chairs around a large, heavy table. Look inside and keep asking the question until you see what your own images are.

c.   **Meet the Council**

Imagine standing in your Council space. Call the members of your Inner Council by name — Magic Boy, Androgyne, Lover, Shaman/Healer, Elder, Warrior, Explorer. Pause after each name as you watch the figure you've called enter the space. What impressions come to you as you call each name? What other impressions come to you?

Call one more figure. This is the "Self Who Knows," the one who urges you forward, who lives inside and sees your whole path. The Self Who Knows, who may have many names, is strong, powerful, and loving. He's also the one who leads you on this journey. How does he feel to you? What images come to mind?

There may be other members of your Inner Council that we haven't named. Ask them to come in and know that you will meet them all in time, on your own.

Your Inner Council supports you all the time. When they are all present, imagine reaching out and joining hands with them in a great circle of strength and support. Notice how it feels to be part of that circle.

d.   **Enlist their help**

Speak to your Inner Council. In a few sentences, thank them for being with you, and then review your intentions for the journey. Talk about what you're seeking and request their help and guidance. Let them show you their willingness to be part of it.

Before you dismiss them, ask your Council for a token of their support. A token is a symbol or image of something tangible that will remind you of your inner connection. Notice which member of the Council steps forward to hand it to you. Look down and see very clearly what the token is.

e.   **Return**

Thank your Inner Council again for being with you. Then, feel the circle grow smaller, until it can fit easily within your body. Feel it there inside you, supportive and secure.

Watch your breath and let it lead you gently back to normal awareness. Remember your roots, and let all the energy you raised in the visualization flow from your body and back into the Earth.

In your notebook, jot down any impressions. Describe your Council space. Describe the Council. What did it feel like to connect with them?

What was your token? Is it something you can obtain physically? If you can, do so. If not, make a small drawing of the token. In a moment, you'll place this on your Gay Spirit Altar.

YOUR GAY SPIRIT ALTAR

It's time to make yourself an altar. An altar is a symbolic representation of your journey, a touchstone to remind you of your intentions, your commitment to yourself, and the extensive support you have inside. Because the word may have some old connotations, let me clarify what we're doing. The altar is not something you're worshipping, nor praying to, nor is it meant to take the place of any other spiritual tradition. The altar is merely a place that acts as an outward symbol of what you're doing inside. What you make of it is up to you.

Your altar will reflect your progress on this journey. Each time you make a significant step, you'll add something new to remind you of what you've discovered or accomplished. The altar will hold together all the colorful, dissonant, harmonious, separate pieces of your journey. How you place them will become important. From time to time, you may feel the desire to rearrange. Other times, you might be happy just to sit by it and reflect on your process. With care and attention, your Gay Spirit Altar will become an enjoyable and effective means to honor your own being.

➤ Create your Gay Spirit Altar

Exercise

3. *Set aside a small space somewhere in your home for your Gay Spirit Altar. It could be part of a bookshelf or mantle, the back of an end table, a wide windowsill, or wherever else you like. Choose a spot where you can leave the altar set up for the duration of your journey. Make it private enough that you won't have to explain it to anyone or feel the need to edit what you put on it.*

   Your altar is sacred, a place where you honor yourself, your capacity to love other men, and your own spiritual path. Its design is entirely up to you. Make it feel special. Perhaps you can cover it with a beautiful piece of fabric or leather. Maybe you can use a colorful candle or a cherished stone to signify its importance. Choose the items you use carefully so that each one supports your overall intention.

When you've completed your initial setup, sit with your altar for a few moments. Quietly review your goals and intentions. Remember the guides and allies who make up your Inner Council. Place the token you received from them on the altar. If you can't use the token itself, choose something small to represent it.

THE TRIBE OF MEN WHO LOVE MEN

Just as archetype infuses individual personality and behavior, it also informs our identity as a group. The Tribe of Men Who Love Men exists at two levels — both physically and within the realm of archetype. Let's explore how these two levels interconnect.

The Tribe is a diverse, far-flung, and colorful assemblage related to every other people on the planet. Sometimes we're welcomed, honored, and respected. Other times we're scorned, put out, or forced to hide. Still, we are here. Our diversity as well as our connections with every other tribe give us an inborn gift of weaving among peoples.

This is not a Tribe we are born into in the usual sense. Very few of us have Gay parents. This is a Tribe we waken to, as we follow the call of our own cells. Somewhere in those cells lives a spark of knowing — is it DNA, or soul, or what we facetiously call "GAYDAR?" — that makes us seek others of our own kind. The call may be faint at first, but it grows stronger like the tide until it fills us and propels us through the dance of self-recognition and coming out.

How does the Tribe look? At first glance, not much different from other men. We have the same features and wear the same clothes as everyone else. Internally, though, we're a pageant of color. In the realm of dream and fantasy, we costume ourselves to please our souls. Here, we wear leather, or sequins, or both. Here, we sport feathered loincloths or shine in naked, sunbaked, glory. Mostly, we save the richness of our inner lives for Tribal gatherings. Yet, even when we don't show them off, the colors live inside where they nurture and feed us every day.

At this level, you've belonged to the Tribe from the day you were born. The spark of recognition that brought you to realize your own attraction to other men connects you to the very same spark in the rest of us. Though we form many, diverse clans — which don't always agree or even get along with each other — ultimately, we're all in this together. The Tribe is an inner network that connects us with each other.

Practically, this means you're never really alone. As you face the challenges and questions on your path, you resonate energetically with every other man in a similar place. We support each other and share healing, wisdom, and guidance. The insights you reach help others. In turn, the realizations that come to others in the Tribe help you. Although you still have to walk your own path and come up with your own answers, the fact of resonance makes it easier.

The idea of Tribe is an important one. Conceptually, it's pretty straightforward. As an archetype, the Tribe exists. As individuals, though, some of us defy easy classification. "What about those of us who are Bi," you might ask, "or who have Gay feelings we don't act on, or live celibate, or just don't know what we feel?" We are all part of this Tribe. If you have questions, use the Tribe as working concept. When you're in a space of loving other men, you resonate with the energy of the Tribe. When your focus is elsewhere, you resonate elsewhere. You still share support and connection.

Meet the Tribe

Exercise

4. This is a movement meditation that will help you get in touch with your own Tribal connection. Set aside 10 to 20 minutes in which you won't be disturbed. Use instrumental music with a steady beat and be sure you have room to move around easily.

Remember the rules for movement meditation. Don't think about it too much. Keep your mind busy by repeating the question over and over. If you have trouble moving at first, your mind is probably trying to figure out what to do. Do your best to keep it occupied with the question and start any movement at all — then see how it develops. In a short while, this will become very easy and fun.

This is a little longer than some of the other exercises. Read it once all the way through, then take it easily step by step.

a. *To begin, start the music and stand quietly. Close your eyes and create sacred space as you've learned — surround yourself with white light, acknowledge your connections with Earth and Spirit. This time, call on your Inner Council and feel them standing around you in a strong, protective circle. Imagine that all your movement takes place in the center of this circle. Acknowledge the support and appreciation of your Council with a small bow or other gesture that feels good.*

b. *Tune in to your body. Close your eyes. Focus on the in and out of your breath. How do you feel inside — connected? scattered? all in your head? Breathe consciously for a little while until you feel ready to begin the movement.*

Now, ask your body to move gently, however it likes. What parts feel loose and easy? Where do you feel tight? Take a couple minutes to shake out, stretch, and move until you feel in line and ready to go deeper.

c. *First, ask your body to remind you how it feels not to be connected. Repeat over and over in your mind, "Show me how it feels to be alone and isolated." Watch what your body does in response. What feelings come up? Does this feel natural? Comfortable? Familiar? Exaggerate — bring the movement into your face, hands, back, feet — all over. Continue for a few minutes, just to see where it takes you.*

d. *Moving gently, ask to see a sacred, outdoor space. Watch what images come up. Perhaps you imagine a beach, a field, a circle of trees, or a mountaintop. Wherever your mind takes you, imagine that your movements are taking you there. Take your time. Let details come — the softness of a breeze on your skin, the warmth of Earth beneath your feet. Enjoy this space, for here is where you meet the rest of your Tribe.*

e. *Now, make a new request — "Show me my connection with the Tribe of Men who Love Men." Repeat the question as your body moves gently. See yourself in a great circle of loving men. Feel how alive the energy is here, how loving, nurturing, supportive, and strong.*

   Continue to move and make your motions a little bigger. What images come to your "inner eye?" Look around you at the faces within the Tribe. You'll recognize some of them. Others will be new. Some will be young, some old and wrinkled, others in-between.

   *Notice what the members of the Tribe are wearing. There may be many different costumes. If you can, imagine what **you're** wearing, here in the glory of your own wholeness.*

f. *Imagine that you and the others hold hands in a great large circle. Feel how much loving strength flows from one hand to the next around the circle. Feel it touch you, fill you, and nurture the places in you that have felt alone or abandoned.*

   This is your Tribe. You belong here. You've been in this place before and can return any time you like. The energy of Tribal connection nurtures you all the time. Knowing this, ask your body, "Show me how it feels to know that I'm always supported by the Tribe." Give your whole self to the movement. Move here for as long as you like.

g. *Thank the Tribe for showing you the connections, and release the images for now. Focus on your breath and let your movement come gently to rest.*

Let all the energy you raised flow down through your feet, your roots, into the Earth, where it brings strength and health.

When you feel grounded and clear, jot down your impressions in your notebook. How was your connection? What did you learn? How did the members of the Tribe look and feel to you? How did it feel to hold hands, to be part of the Tribal circle?

5. *Place something on your altar to represent your connection with the Tribe. Is there something circular, perhaps a ring, that speaks to you? A picture? Something else? Since the Tribe is a powerful source of inner support, remind yourself of it often.*

7 The Magic Boy

HE'S IN THERE!

What was your favorite thing about being a boy? Was it going to the park on Sunday afternoons with your Grampa? Was it having an ice cream sundae with chocolate and nuts that was almost too big to finish? Was it snuggling with your puppy? Stepping off the bus on the last day of school? Fishing at the stream? Before you go any further, get your journal and list five things you loved to do when you were little.

Did you do it? No cheating. If you got all adult on me and said, "That's foolish, I'll just keep reading," stop now. Do not pass Go. Do not read past the end of this sentence until you write down those five things .... There. How's that? Did it feel good just to remember?

Let's try another. This time, write down five things you loved to eat when you were young. Peanut butter and banana sandwich? Chocolate bar? Marshmallows on cocoa? Liver and spinach? (Just kidding!) Read over what you put down. Mmmmmm! Ready to smile a little in spite of that serious adult?

A Magic Boy lives inside you **now**. No matter how old you are, or serious, or professional, or wounded, he's still there. No matter how far away he might seem, you can be in touch with him. In fact, you need to be. The only way to live a full and satisfying adult life is to create a healthy relationship with your inner child.

"Magic Boy?" protests the adult. "Magic's not real." But it is, I tell you. You were born a tiny wonder, full of enthusiasm, excitement, and boundless energy. This is a new world! So much to explore and learn! "See, this is my foot! This is a flower! This is green! This is my penis! Boys have them! Here's a kitty! There's an airplane!"

This Boy is magic in the way he lives in the moment, in the way he sees something new in everything around him. He's magic in the way he's survived inside you through so many years and changes. Magic Boy is alive and well. The next part of your journey is dedicated to him.

Because what you learn as a boy determines a lot about who you are as an adult, this chapter is fundamental to the whole rest of your journey. It will be interesting and healing. In places, it may also be challenging. The boy inside you may not feel too magic just yet. If he doesn't, take heart — you can restore it to him. You'll emerge from this adventure lighter, healthier, and with a stronger sense of self.

We'll take it one easy step at a time. Before you start, let the boy inside you know that you're coming. Right now, put your hand over the center of your chest. Say out loud to the boy who's listening inside you,

"Here I come, (name) _____. I'm here for you. I'm going to make you part of my life all the time. We're going to have fun!"

He'll hear you, be sure of it. If you felt silly, that's good. Ever watch a parent or hang out with a very young boy? You **have** to be playful and silly. Sometimes it's the only way to get through.

Get to know the boy within

Exercises

1. In order for your inner boy to recover his magic, you have to meet him as he is in the present. This visualization will take about 15 minutes and give you a chance to get reacquainted. Your first step is to create a safe place to meet him. A young boy isn't supposed to be all by himself in the world. He does best when there's a caring adult around to watch out for him. That's you.

   a. *Sit comfortably and relaxed. Close your eyes. Surround yourself with light and take the other steps you've used to create sacred space.*

   When you feel centered, visualize yourself surrounded by the Tribe of Men who Love Men. The men in this circle are your allies. Take a moment to see them again — all the Elders, Warriors, Healers, and other brothers in the Tribe. Feel their strength as they stand around you in a large, protective ring. Ask the men of the Tribe to keep this place sacred and safe. From now on, no one can enter without your invitation.

   Now, invite the members of your Inner Council to stand with you inside the ring of the Tribe. Feel their presence as they make a smaller circle around you. Feel especially the strengths of your own Warrior, Elder, Healer, and the

Self Who Knows, there among the rest. Your Inner Council is the second ring of protection that keeps your inner boy safe and secure.

Imagine standing in the center of both circles. You are the third protector. From now on, the boy in you has a guardian, companion, friend, playmate, and comforter all the time. You're there for him. You — or he — can call on these three layers of protection whenever you need them.

b.   *Imagine kneeling in the center of the circle, at kid height. Invite the boy inside you, by name, to be with you. Talk to him. Tell him you've come to help him. Promise him you're not here to criticize or hurt him in any way. Tell him that you're going to do your very best to be his friend.*

What does he do? Is he eager and quick to come? Is he shy? Afraid? Angry? If so, take your time and continue inviting him in. Tell him that here with you, inside these two loving circles, is the safest place he could ever be. He'll come when he's ready.

c.   *Look at this boy. Who do you see? How old is he? What's he wearing? What do you see in his eyes? What sort of feeling do you get when you look at him?*

Ask him how he feels. Listen to what he says. Ask him what he likes to do. What's important to him? Does he have questions for you? Is anything bothering him? Is there anything he'd like to do right now? Let him tell or show you whatever he wants.

d.   *When he's finished, thank him for coming. Promise that he can stay here inside these nice, safe circles. Tell him you're here for him whenever he needs. Then, if he'd like, give him a big, warm hug. Actually reach out with your arms and give yourself one, too.*

e.   *When you're ready, let your breath lead you back to normal awareness. Feel the energy you've raised flow from your body into the Earth. Open your eyes. Have a drink of water if you need one. Then, record your impressions in your journal. They'll be important later.*

2.   Use at least one of the following exercises to help you get to know this boy a little better.

a.   *Find a picture of yourself as a boy. Place it on your altar where it will remind you of him often.*

b.   *Write a letter **from your little boy** to your present self. Pick the age that seems to call you. Let him tell you about his life. What games does he like? What foods? Who are his friends? His **best** friend? Who or what does he* *not* like? Who are the special adults in his life? What are his secrets? What is he proud of? Where is he unsure of himself? Let him tell you all about himself.

c.   Write a letter **from your present self** to the boy you were. What would you like to tell him about himself? What advice would you offer to help him? What things in your life as an adult would interest him? What could you tell him about his place in the world? Write a letter he'll understand and enjoy.

INTO THE SHADOW: THE INNER BRAT

When you have a healthy relationship with the Magic Boy, his gifts enhance your life each day. You enjoy spontaneity, playfulness, and deep, rejuvenating sparkle. Too often, though, the Magic Boy is blocked, repressed, or overworked. In these cases, his joyful innocence tends to distort into more troublesome characters. Instead of healthy boyishness, we see the spoiled, petulant, or totally shut down persona my friend Leon likes to call the "Inner Brat."

The Inner Brat is a product of imbalance or wounding. Despite our culture's half-baked nostalgia about how idyllic childhood should be, we all know him. Every single one of us is a survivor. In general, childhood has as many ups and downs, joys and sorrows, as any other part of life. It always involves a measure of pain. Boys who show early the signs of being "different" are especially liable to be teased, taunted, ganged up on, or shamed. We aren't alone, though — all kids receive some wounding. It's part of life.

Thankfully, for most of us, the traumas weren't too serious and were balanced out by the positive aspects of a secure childhood. For some of us, though, things were harder, scars deeper, and childhood's idyll more like a nightmare. Bottom line, though, whatever your early life was like, **you survived**. You made it. You were stronger than anything that got dished out. It's important to acknowledge that the boy within you is strong and resilient.

To make it through childhood, all of us develop certain coping mechanisms to render the hard parts more bearable. Often, these survival strategies come through as the different faces of the Inner Brat. Several of them are especially common among Gay men. See if you recognize any of the following in yourself or the men around you.

First, there are the **overcompensators**, men who generally exaggerate, quite vocally, all the worst traits of childhood. "Me, me, me," is their mantra and grabbing attention is their specialty. Sometimes you see them in public, like when they make a hissy at a restaurant and torment the waiter by sending every other dish back to the kitchen. You may have met them among your friends, the ones who sulk and won't speak to you for days because of some imagined slight you never intended.

Another face of the Brat is the **little boy who won't grow up**. At thirty or forty or even fifty, this one reeks of affected boyishness. Like Peter Pan, he'll do almost anything to avoid being responsible for his own life. He begs each man he meets to be "Daddy" and screams or faints dead away at the first gray hair in his mirror. Paradoxically, the "eternal boy" doesn't get to enjoy very many of Magic Boy's gifts. Because he's forced out into the world on his own, without the guidance and protection that would be provided by a responsible adult persona, this inner boy usually ends up stressed, exhausted, and discouraged.

At the other extreme are the **Bah-humbugers**. These men spend their lives being gray, serious, and in total denial of anything childish. "Play?" they sniff disdainfully, "Not for me. Too much work to do!" Bah-humbugers live by schedule, work too much, and wouldn't dream of having a feeling. They were grown up by the age of seven and would never admit that life feels dull and pointless.

Another face of the Brat is the **professional victim**. This one makes a career of blaming everyone else. "Smile? Can't do that. My parents hurt me as a child." "Stand up for myself? Heavens, no! Don't you know that society is homophobic?" The victim uses the fact of negativity around him as a way to avoid his own responsibility. His self-pity totally negates his own power to make positive change.

Let's not lay blame here. Everybody develops defensive personas — what we're calling the Inner Brat — to help us get through rough moments. Over-compensators, eternal boys, bah-humbugers, and professional victims are the major faces we choose. They're pretty obvious once you start looking for them. If you look at the individuals around you, though, you'll also notice a broad range of personal styles. We are an incredibly inventive Tribe — and most of us learn very early to hide our true selves behind a variety of masks. Though they're all aspects of a wounded inner boy, many of these masks don't really look very bratty. Let's do a quick tour. See if any ring a bell for you.

- **Chameleon**. Try to look and act "normal," just like everyone else. Pretend to like rough sports, even though you'd rather play nurse. Keep a low profile. Maybe no one will notice you.

- **Best little boy in the world.** Never upset your parents. Study hard. Never do anything you're not already good at. Grow up to be a superhero or workaholic.

- **Pollyanna.** Live somewhere else, like books. Stay in Fantasyland so nothing ugly or painful can reach you. Never, ever, admit to feeling anything that's not sweet and rosy.

- **The Rebel.** Be in everybody's face. Hide who you really are. Keep them all on the defensive. Yell a lot. Slam doors. Sulk. Do not conform to anything.

- **Macho.** Be so butch you make John Wayne look like a sissy. Chew tobacco. Burp and fart loudly. Captain every sports team. Tease the "pansies" every chance you get.

- **Numb one.** Whatever it was, pretend it never happened. Be okay, whatever goes on. Go numb. Bury any pain so deep you don't remember it's there. Later, do a lot of drugs.

- **Superfriend.** Be nice to everyone. Never pick a fight. Carry packs of gum and give one stick to each person in your class daily. If friends argue, take both sides.

- **School fag.** Play it up. Swish. Do your girlfriends' makeup. Clutch your books to your chest. Throw like a girl. Never let on that you can feel the teasing.

- **Clown.** Take nothing seriously. Have a joke for every occasion. Mimic the teacher behind her back. Keep 'em in stitches, so they'll like to have you around.

How do you feel? Did you see through the masks? However different they might look on the surface, all of them are created by boys who are wounded, ignored, or just not allowed to come out.

At one time or another, we've all used masks. They are probably a normal part of growing up and finding our own personality styles. Boyhood masks can become a problem, though, when they persist into adulthood. If we still depend on them when the situations that prompted them are long gone, they tend to isolate us. What once enabled us to survive now becomes a defensive wall that keeps life at a distance. Then, your inner boy becomes the Brat who holds you hostage.

When the Inner Brat yells, clowns, or sulks his way into your life, give the boy inside you some attention. He needs you as an ally. The tantrums, exaggerations, or denials that look so bratty are really the only way he knows to ask for your help. Instead of beating yourself up when you recognize him, do your best to approach him with understanding. Listen to what he needs from you and then give it to him. If he feels neglected, create an activity that feeds him. If he feels wounded, spend some time addressing the wounds. Don't get stuck. Do what you can and then move on.

Exercise

Coping strategies

3.a. *In your journal, take a few minutes to review your own survival strategies. What were they? Do they resemble the ones on our list? Can you think of others? Do you remember how it felt to use them? Was it a conscious choice? What were the benefits?*

b. *Put a star beside any of the behaviors you still use from time to time. In what situations? Are they still effective? What benefits do you get from using these strategies now?*

For each of the starred items, ask yourself, "Is there a way I might do this better?" Be careful here — the goal is to become aware, not to judge or push yourself to change. Just by observing gently, you'll automatically move toward greater balance.

c. *You and your boy have done some good work. It's time for a treat. Pick at least one of the things on the lists you made at the beginning of the chapter of your boy's favorite activities and foods. Treat yourself to that item. If nothing on the lists really works any more, ask the boy what he'd like now. Then do it and enjoy!*

HEAL THE WOUNDS

In his heart, the boy inside you longs for the magic he was born with. When he acts like a brat, it's because he still feels hurt or neglected. No matter who was responsible the first time around, the only one who can help him now is **you**. If he still hurts, **you** need to soothe and nurture him. If he still feels abandoned, **you** need to start paying him more attention. To really help him — and free yourself at the same time — you need to address head-on the pain he carries. Only by reclaiming him from the old wounds can you give your boy back his magic.

You *can* do it. You've got all the tools you need. You've got the support of your Inner Council and you're going to make sure you have support in the world if you need it. There may be emotional pain, but it will be short-lived and much less intense than the first time around when you actually lived it. Sometimes, pain is part of healing. It's like the pain of lancing a boil — healing only occurs once the blocked infection is released.

Why dig up old hurts? Because they're still in there. Until you heal them, old wounds don't go away. Even if you cover them up outside, the pain is still constant inside where your little boy lives. Even if you've repressed it totally, it still comes through unconsciously, to affect your interactions and relationships in ways you may not even notice. Don't leave your little boy in there alone. You can help him right now by using your adult strength to go back and stand up for him. Most of the time it will be easy.

This process is safe and very healing. Go gently. Your experiences will depend on what your childhood was like and the degree to which you've already dealt with the issues involved. You may breeze right through. You may discover feelings you hadn't expected. Whatever you experience, you will create a stronger relationship with your inner boy.

If you're at all nervous about what you'll find, set up a support network. Call a friend who will agree to be there for you. Tell your friend when you plan to do the exercises and agree to check in again afterward with anything you'd like to discuss. Then relax. The strength and survival mechanisms that got you through the first time will assure that what comes up now is no more than you're ready to deal with.

If you have any serious doubts of your ability to deal with childhood issues, **get help**. Issues around major trauma or abuse need to be handled carefully. If you know of or suspect such issues in your past that you haven't dealt with, it is time to do so — with **professional help.** There's no stigma at all in asking for help when you need it. If you think you need external support, don't continue until you've lined it up.

Ready to get your hands dirty? Let's dig!

 ## Reclaim the wounds

4. This following movement meditation will help you get in touch with the places that are ready for healing. To prepare yourself, set aside some quiet time. Get your music ready and have your journal nearby.

a. *In the same way you did when you first met your inner boy, create your sacred space. Call on the Tribe and your Inner Council. Visualize yourself at the very center of the two concentric circles of protection. Feel the strength and support that surround you.*

Turn on your music and stand quietly, watching your breath. Invite your inner boy to come into the circle and into your whole body. Make the request, over and over, "Show me my inner boy." As you continue to repeat the request silently, let your body begin to move gently.

b. *When you feel that your inner boy is all the way present, change the question. Repeat, over and over, "Where can I help this boy? Where does his hurt live in my body?" Don't think about your response, just let your hands move to some part of your body of their own accord.*

Exercise

When you discover what part wants attention, let it lead the rest of your body in movement. "Show me what's in there. Show me what's in there." Watch what it does. Watch how the rest of your body follows. Watch the feelings that come up. Ask, "What is the hurt here? What is it about?" Observe whatever sensations and images come through.

As your body moves, see if you can identify the situation that caused the pain. Who was involved? What happened? What did your boy experience at the time? Move until you feel clear about the situation, then bring the movement gently to a close.

What you're after here are your inner boy's perceptions of the situation. Even if you know with your adult mind that there were extenuating circumstances or that no harm was intended, the important thing about the situation is how your little boy experienced it. Go with that. You may get a lot of details or you may get none at all. It doesn't matter. As long as you're letting your body move authentically, you're bringing up the situation energetically. That's all that matters.

If the situation is painful, remember that you don't have to go all the way in. You can watch it unfold from the outside, as if it were on TV. Even if you experience tears, pain, or anger, it's almost always healthier to complete the movement than to stop partway through. Keep breathing, give yourself hugs when you need them, and trust your body.

c.   *To record your impressions, turn to a clean page on the right-hand side of your journal. Write the words "TOP SECRET" in big letters. Then, on the back of that page, get the boy to help you write down what you discovered. Assure him you won't tell anyone what's in there until he gives you permission. For the experience he showed you, write the answers to the following questions:*

> *Where was the hurt?*
> *Who or what was involved?*
> *How did he feel about himself?*
> *What else does he want to say about it?*

d.   *When you're finished, give your boy a big hug, arms around yourself, and feel all the energy you've raised flow through your feet into the Earth.*

At this point, your inner boy has done his part. He's just completed some powerful Warrior work! Congratulate him. Imagine holding him on your knee. Tell him you're proud of how brave he's been and that he doesn't have to work any more. You'll take care of everything from now on.

What would this boy like to do now? Would he like to take a nap? Draw with crayons? Have a treat? Play outside? Imagine him in the circle, happily involved with whatever he wants, as you leave.

You can repeat this exercise to uncover as many buried hurts as you like. Record them in the TOP SECRET pages of your journal. If you uncover something that has strong feelings attached to it, you'll probably want to do two things. First, if you feel the need, check in with the person who agreed to be your support system. Then complete Exercises 5 and 6 as soon as possible. If you don't have time right away, make a commitment to do them as soon as you can, certainly within the next day or so. Otherwise, everything you've brought up will just sit there sour and smelly until you deal with it.

The next exercises are extremely valuable. Though they can be used together quite effectively, one or the other may be more appropriate in a given situation. Venting and forgiveness are especially important if the boy was hurt by another person. The support visualization helps in any situation, especially if the boy felt bad, guilty, or ashamed of something he did.

Continue your healing by choosing whichever situation in your "TOP SECRET" pages feels most pressing. Work with this same situation through all three parts of the next exercises. Once you learn them, these processes are powerful tools that will serve you well from now on. Use them singly or together whenever you'd like to heal and release something from the past. Be sure to use them to focus on each of the situations you uncovered using Exercise 4.

Venting and forgiveness

5.a. Venting

Identify the Villain(s) in the situation you've chosen to heal. A Villain is someone who hurt your little boy. It could have been someone really hateful. It could also have been someone who really loved the boy and hurt him unintentionally. What matters is the boy's perception. This person is the Villain because the boy thinks so.

*On a piece of paper, **not in your notebook**, write a letter from your little boy to the Villain. Tell him (or her) what your boy thinks of what he did. Rage at him, scream about the hurt, call him a slimy pigfaced jerk. Whatever wants to come out, let it.*

Your adult may try to stay reasonable here, see both sides of the issue, make excuses, not feel the pain. If so, start with a disclaimer — "Dear So *and So, my little boy wants to tell you how he feels. It may not be the whole picture, but for now we're going to focus on this part..."*

Write for your boy. Even if you have to prime the pump a little, soon you'll forget yourself and plunge right in. Don't hold back. Don't pull punches. Exaggerate. In the middle of a good vent, you might even break a pen, rip through the paper, or find yourself in tears. Great! Keep going. Your heart may get pumping really hard and you may have to punch a pillow or stamp your feet before you continue. That's fine. Just vent your feelings until you've said all that's in there.

Do not send this letter, in any case, ever. Got that? **! DO NOT SEND THIS LETTER !** It may lead you to insights or make you want to confront the person right now. Don't do it! Even if action is really called for, you are in no condition right now to decide. Wait. When you've worked through the rest of the process, you'll be clearer on what actions, if any, are truly appropriate and effective. In the meantime, we're going to work on something called Forgiveness.

Uh oh, I can hear it now. Forgiveness is such a loaded term! "No way!" you sputter, indignant. Before you leap to conclusions, let's look at what forgiveness really means.

Actually, let's look at what it doesn't mean. First, we're not condoning what went on. We're not saying that anyone had the right to hurt you or that you were wrong to feel what you felt. That's not forgiveness. Forgiveness also isn't that sticky-sweet, sanctimonious self-righteousness that has you condescending from your heavenly cloud of moral superiority to say, in just the right, sugary tone, "Oh, I know you did wrong. I know you wrecked half my life, stole my boyfriend, and ruined my best lipstick, but ... (dramatic glance toward Heaven) ... I forgive you anyway." Give me a break!

Forgiveness isn't really about the other person at all. It's about **you**. A better word might be "untying." Be truthful. How does it feel to carry in your body all the pain, anger, and puniness of being a victim? Pretty yucky, really. The feelings are healthy. It's better to feel them than to repress them or pretend they don't exist. Once you acknowledge them, though, the time comes to let them go, to untie them from your present self. After all, it's **your** body. Those emotions don't do a thing to the other person. They're in **you**. Holding them past their time just drains **your** energy, **your** health, **your** being. Let's look at how to let it all go.

b.   **Forgiveness**

Step One: *Imagine giving the Villain(s) a chance to respond. Write a letter, addressed to yourself, in which you imagine the other perspective. Let* *yourself write what the Villain(s) might have to say. Remember, this is about you, not them. Don't actually involve the other person(s). Take this chance to tell yourself what you perceive about their side of things.*

Step Two: *Do a little soul searching. Tell the truth. What do you gain by holding on to this issue? Do you enjoy the role of "you done me wrong?" Do you feel superior by knowing "I'm right, you're wrong," or "I'm better than you because I'd never do anything like you did?" Honestly, what payoffs can you see?*

Be easy on yourself. You're not blaming yourself for the original situation. You're claiming responsibility for your own state right now. Holding on to old emotions affects no one but yourself.

Step Three: *Just as you did with your negatives, release all the letters, including those you did in the venting exercise, by burning them, tearing them up, or flushing them. As you do, turn the whole situation over to Spirit, Higher Power, Creator. "**I am willing to release this energy, to have it resolved and healed. I take 100% responsibility for my own being in the present moment.**" Turn it over, let it go, give it up, and be done with it!*

Repeat this process for any of the situations in your TOP SECRET section in which you can find Villains. Take the time you need. Some may go very quickly. Others will take more time. In the end, every one is worth the effort. Then, go back and visit the situation one more time, this time giving your inner boy the support he needs.

Return to support your boy

Exercise

6.a. *Close your eyes and go into the Inner Council circle. In the safety of this place, imagine that you are going back to the scene of the original trauma. This time, the boy is not alone. You're there with him as a secret ally, friend, and protector. You are invisible, holding his hand, and whispering in his ear.*

b. *As the scene unfolds, you don't have to go into the feelings again, just watch. As you observe the scene together, tell the boy what he needs to hear in order to feel better about himself. You'll know what to say. Acknowledge for him that yes, the situation was hard, it hurt, or whatever he felt. Whisper to him that this time he doesn't need to feel the pain. Tell him that whatever happened, he's not a bad person. There's nothing to be ashamed of. You know that he did his very best, that the situation was* *wrong, not him. If he made mistakes, remind him that mistakes are part of living. Instead of dwelling on them, ask him to see what he might have learned for the next time.*

This doesn't have to take too long. When you've finished, make sure your boy doesn't have any more questions about himself and that he's told you everything he's ready to say about the situation. He will probably feel much better for having shared with you.

c.   *Invite your boy to come home. If he'd like, he can leave the situation forever and come live with you. Does he want to do that? From now on, even if he wants to look at the old situation again, you'll go together. He'll never be there alone again.*

d.   *Use this process for as many situations as you like. Each one will help the boy inside you feel better. Jot down any impressions in your journal when you've finished. How was it? How do you feel? How does he feel?*

e.   *When you're finished, ask your boy if what's in the journal still needs to be top secret. Are the secrets as bad as they were? Is it okay to share any of them with the right people?*

Listen to what he says. If he says, "No, don't tell anyone," respect him and don't. In fact, staple those pages closed until he changes his mind. If he says you can share, maybe to help someone else with a similar problem, do so if the situation arises. Never share what's in this part of the journal until he's given his permission. You're teaching him that you're worthy of his trust.

If there are parts you choose to keep secret, remember them as you complete the rest of your Warrior journey. In time, you'll have the capacity to deal with anything in your life, and things that once needed to be secret will probably lose their old energy. Give yourself the time you need.

Congratulations! You've done the hard part. That may have been some of the deepest work you'll do in this entire process. Now is a good time for some treats and celebration. Dance. Play. Rest. Ask your little boy what he'd enjoy and treat the two of you. The next section is fun. It's Magic Boy time.

CHANGE THE FILTERS

The Magic Boy has been in there all the time, playing hide and seek with your mind. Your mind usually lost — can't you see the Boy giggling in triumph? Often, it looked right at the Magic Boy and couldn't see him. How so? It has to do with how the mind works.

Your mind processes information very much like a computer, storing clusters of memories deep in its hidden files. If you ask it to bring something back to consciousness, it searches the files and gives you an answer. "The color of Aunt May's car was blue. The square root of 625 is 25. The name of that cute guy in gym class is Robert." The answers you get depend on the questions you ask.

Your mind retrieves memories based on the search clause you give it. When you ask for something, it sorts through all the zillions of tiny memory bits in the subconscious and brings back any that relate. For the answers to reach conscious awareness, though, they have to be in a form you can understand. This means that your mind can only tell you things that fit into the framework already set up by your beliefs.

Your beliefs act as a filter through which you view reality. In other words, if you believe you have a Magic Boy inside you, you'll see him; if not, you won't. Either way, your mind will supply you with all kinds of evidence to support its case. If you change your beliefs, you'll get different evidence. Let's look at an example.

Up until a few years ago, I thought I'd had a fairly unhappy childhood. I remembered all the times I stood alone on the playground, last one to be picked for the tag football team. I remembered all the times my father sat me in "time out" on the back steps, even though I forget (conveniently) what I'd done to deserve it. I remembered the greasy heaviness in my gut when I thought about being "different," not as good as the other boys, a sissy and misfit. I remembered hating myself most of the time. If anyone asked what my childhood was like, I replied without hesitation, "Miserable."

Funny thing was, when I looked at pictures of myself, I saw a kid who seemed to be having a good time. In one picture, I see a boy holding his new pet duck, just named Fritz. He's grinning. In another, he's in a cardboard store, happily "selling" cans of Campbell's soup and Chicken of the Sea donated by his mother. In another, he and his sister are dressed in witch masks and pointed black hats, clutching paper sacks full of candy. In fact, none of the pictures looked very sad. Granted, crying children don't usually end up in front of a parent's camera. The point is, though, that I'd blanked out most of the fun stuff.

I began an experiment. To see if I could change my mental filter, I asked my mind, "Retrieve all memories of when I was happy." What came up amazed me. I remembered the fun we had looking for duck eggs when Fritz (hastily renamed Fritz-Ann) began laying in the creek and all over the yard. I remembered the time I dug up clay in the woods and shaped it into ashtrays that Mom baked in the oven. I remembered when Dad took me fishing on the ocean before dawn just to see a really bright comet. I remembered the year that Bob, our milkman, came to the house on Christmas Eve with a fake beard and booming laugh. I remember the wide-eyed wonder we kids had that Santa would really come right to our house. In short, I recovered a whole set of memories I'd blocked because of the old filter. The fact that I'd found pleasant memories didn't negate the times that were difficult. It did, however, start to put them into a more rounded perspective. Want to try it?

Games

Exercise

7.   In your journal, make the following lists.

a.   What are five more things you liked to do as a boy that are not on your first lists?

b.   List five pleasant memories.

c.   What were your favorite stories as a boy?

d.   Who were your heroes?

e.   Name five people who were nice to you as a boy.

f.   Name five things you were very proud of as a boy.

8.   List five creative activities you loved as a boy. What were they? How about finger-painting or drawing with crayons? How about dancing, writing a play to put on for your friends, or building a tower of blocks?

When you complete your list, choose one activity and do it now. The only rule is that you enjoy yourself.

9.   Pick at least one of the following exercises. Make it fun.

a.   Write a story of your perfect childhood. Make it anything you like — Swiss Family Robinson, Kids in Space, Billy in Oz, whatever. Let your Magic Boy direct the process and be sure to include lots of details and characters he loves.

b.   Write what it would have been like if the adults in your life had done all the right things. Describe how your life would have been, how you'd have felt, what you'd have become. Don't get hung up on how things really were — it's all a story now anyway. If you want, you can make this the official version.

c.   Do a movement meditation on your own, a dance with happy music to celebrate the fun and good times of your childhood. Give time to the Magic Boy and to yourself so that both of you can celebrate this new connection.

MAGIC BOY EVERY DAY

You and your Magic Boy need each other. He depends on you for nurturing, good treatment, opportunities for adventure, and appropriate boundaries in the world. You depend on him to help you lighten up, be playful, spontaneous, and creative. He'll teach you the healing power of doing things your adult might never dream of, like skipping down the street when no one's looking or tossing a stone in the lake down at the park. He's there, depending on you. You're here, depending on him. It's up to you to maintain the connection.

Making the Magic Boy part of your daily routines is easy and fun. When you're driving around, imagine he's beside you in the car. Take a side trip for ice cream or just to see the flowers in the botanical garden. At work, pretend he's there. Seeing your job through his eyes will add a whole new energy. Give yourself treats. Take time for yourself. Practice being with him a lot, because this new way of relating may take a little getting used to. Eventually, you won't be able to imagine living any other way.

Commitment

Exercise

10. *In your journal, write a note to your Magic Boy. Promise him you'll do one thing for him, big or small, each day for the next week. It can be something from any of the lists you made or something else that seems fun. It might not take more than a few minutes or it could take half a day. That's up to you. Date your note and sign it for both of you.*

    At the end of the week, make a new promise to do something for your Magic Boy as often as it feels good. Do you dare commit to once a week? Could you take a whole afternoon? A whole day? It's your decision. From now on the two of you are a team. Enjoy yourselves!

11. *Place an object on your altar to represent your new, supportive relationship with your Magic Boy.*

8 The Sacred Androgyne

THE NATURE OF GENDER

We live in a bureaucrat's heaven. Look at any official form — from your driver's license to your income tax return — and notice how often you're asked to shoehorn every morsel of individuality and idiosyncrasy into a series of rigidly defined boxes — race, sex, marital status, occupation, and so forth. The forms reflect the way our society views the world. We're accustomed to reducing the complexities of personal identity to a simple list of externally defined, mutually exclusive categories. From the standpoint of the bureaucrats, it works well. For an individual who chooses to express the full range of his own being, it doesn't work at all.

Of all the categories, the one we're perhaps most conditioned to take for granted is gender. We get it from day one. Boys wear blue. Girls wear pink. Boys are strong. Girls are sensitive. Men don't show emotions. Women take care of children. Anyone who doesn't fit the gender expectations corresponding to his or her biological sex is immediately suspect. Guess who doesn't fit. Because the two-gender system assumes by definition that everyone is heterosexual, it automatically excludes Gay people.

Gender roles are limiting. By setting boundaries on appropriate behavior, discouraging men, for example, from showing feelings or women from standing up for themselves, traditional gender roles keep people from expressing the full range of their talents and sensibilities. Not only do individuals suffer, but society as a whole is poorer.

Gay men have a propensity for turning gender roles upside down. We seem to explore the extremes. Some of us opt for leatherclad butchness that shuns any touch of feminine trappings. Others go to the opposite extreme of immersing in ultrafeminine drag. Some men blend both extremes into a genderfuck melange that shocks, entertains, and transforms all at once. Most of us play somewhere in the middle, pushing limits in one area, living comfortably within them in others.

Ultimately, we come into our true power when we claim the freedom to move beyond gender roles entirely. When we are able to express every part of ourselves with enthusiasm, regardless of gender-related expectations, we tap the power of the Sacred Androgyne.

Androgyne means "male and female together". As an archetype, the Sacred Androgyne embodies masculine and feminine traits in more or less equal measure. Why "Sacred?" Fully realized androgyny includes both genders and then transcends the plane of duality altogether. The alchemy of combining two strong polarities yields a power that is different and greater than either by itself. Imagine a battery. Neither the positive ("male") nor negative ("female") pole alone can produce a current. Current only flows when both poles are activated. If you strengthen the poles or exaggerate their differences, the flow is stronger. When you learn to embody within yourself the strongest traits of both masculine and feminine genders, you reach a state of deep, spiritual empowerment.

Exploring the concept of gender identity for the first time can be eye opening. I remember my own introduction. Not surprisingly, it happened on Halloween, the first time I dared to do drag. For months beforehand, I suffered terror and excitement second only to that of my original coming out. Each step of the preparations pushed my limits. I purchased yards and yards of flowing burgundy knit for a "gown," then sat in front of the sewing machine without a clue. I layered my face with pounds of foundation, blush, and sky blue eyeshadow, then peeled it off to try again and again, totally convinced I looked like Bozo. I spent an afternoon downtown in a wig shop with five "real" girls, trying on hair. By September, anticipation had me frantic. I waltzed around the house five times a day in my new, too-high heels, and practiced "lips" in the rearview mirror on the drive from work.

The night of the party, I was wired. Half an hour before showtime, I broke a nail — those nasty fake ones never work! — which meant I couldn't dress myself alone. Instead of calmly and practically getting help, I flew around the house in a storming rage. Enter the Diva! Even in the midst of it, I was astonished. Up to that exact moment, I'd thought of myself as pretty masculine. Now, all of a sudden, here I was, possessed by the Bitch. She didn't need warming up either, but just burst onto the scene like a fully formed personality. Now, years later, I might say she was showing me her negative, Shadow side because I'd repressed her for so long. At the time, I just knew that she was pissed!

Thus began my introduction to the Inner Female. Once I got her calmed down and to the party, she was ready to be coy. We pranced. We sashayed. We flirted shamelessly. Inside, I kept up a running mantra on how to look feminine, "Shoulders low, head down, look up, eyes fluttery soft, hips loose ...." It was definitely a new way to look at the world.

The next morning, in addition to a whopping hangover and very sore feet, my body felt oddly at a loss. For a few hours, I actually had to tell it how to act "normal" — that is, masculine. "Stand tall, shoulders broad, hips still, wrist firm, voice low ..." I had to laugh. All along, I'd thought of trying to look feminine as an act. I learned, instead, that masculine behavior is just as contrived. It blew my whole idea of gender correctness out of the water.

While a single night of drag at a party hardly does justice to the complexities of feminine behavior and sensibility, it was a powerful introduction to the concept of gender. Actually, gender behavior encompasses the entire range of human expression, including both positive and negative traits, inner qualities and external appearances. Most of us have fairly clear ideas about what constitutes appropriate behavior for each gender, many of them so automatic we don't even notice. The following Gender Map will help you delineate yours.

➤ Gender map

Exercise

1.a. *Start with a clean page in your notebook and turn it sideways. In the upper left corner, write "Very Masculine." In the upper right corner, write "Very Feminine." Draw a horizontal line between these two headings. Then, on the left, under "Very Masculine," jot down all the things you can think of that describe masculinity. Don't think about it too much — just write.*

   Make a corresponding list of traits you consider feminine on the right. Think of as many as you can.

b. *Using a different colored pen, place the following activities and behaviors on the map according to where they fall on the scale. If something is very masculine, put it all the way to the left. Very feminine items go all the way to the right, neutral to the center, and so forth. For example, if you think that "cooking" is sort of neutral, sort of feminine, place it 2/3 of the way toward the right.*

   Continue until you've placed all the items in the list. It's okay to write over what you put down in the first part if necessary.

Childcare	Teaching	Gardening
Sewing	Writing	Auto mechanics
Sports	Sexual passivity	Military service
Cooking	Dancing	Religious service
Carpentry	Fashion design	Medical practice
Hairdressing	Housekeeping	Sexual assertiveness
Caretaking	Leadership	Artistic creativity

c. *Put an asterisk or star beside each trait or activity that applies to you. Is there a pattern?*

Draw a line on the map that encloses all the traits you starred. This diagram represents your place in your own gender scheme.

How was that? Was it easy to place all the activities? Was it easy to place yourself within the map you created? Does this fit with your previous ideas about your own gender roles?

EXPLORE THE POLARITIES

Gender identity is a loaded issue, and not only for Gay people. Indeed, many of the waves rocking our cultural debate right now touch on efforts by people of all persuasions to enlarge traditional roles. Witness the upsurge of women in formerly male professions and demanding the freedoms long given to men. Witness the number of men choosing a more active role in parenting. Witness the attempts by Gay people to create non-traditional families, to raise our own children, and to have our relationships recognized by society. Witness also the degree to which conservatives feel threatened by these changes.

Gay people, especially the queens, take a lot of the flack. What seems to push the most buttons is the perception that we're too feminine. We hear it in the taunts thrown our way — "Sissy," "Queen," "Nancy," — and in our own campy humor — "Girlfriend," "Sister," "Mary." Even among men who love men, there are those who consider effeminacy to be the defining factor of Gay identity. Even while enjoying sex with other men, these machos consider themselves "not-Gay" as long as they play it butch. That effeminate men are perceived as such a threat reflects shamefully on the low regard with which our society views women. In societies that value women highly, the situation is different.

Actually, gender identity has very little to do with biological sex. According to anthropologists, gender roles and even the basic concepts of gender vary widely from society to society. To those of us with a strongly Westernized world view, this is a hard concept to grasp. The idea of two opposite genders seems etched in stone. Yet other cultures, and even our own in the past, have had more fluid views.

Traditional Native American peoples, for example, recognized that Spirit speaks to each person differently. Gender roles were often determined by individual choice. Some men felt called to cross-dress or to take on roles outside of those generally considered masculine. We use the non-Native terms, "Berdache," or "Two-Spirit" to describe these men, although doing so tends to obscure the great range of variety in both tribal customs and individual attitudes.

The berdache were respected as integral, important members of their societies. Two Zuni *lhamana* (man-women) were described by Matilda Cox Stevenson, as

> *"the finest potters and weavers in the tribe. One was the most intelligent person in the pueblo, especially versed in their ancient lore. He was conspicuous at ceremonials...."*
>
> (see Grahn, *Another Mother Tongue*)

Another *lhamana*, named We'wha, was particularly valued and respected. At one point, she represented the tribe on a 6 month visit to Washington, D.C. where she met politicians including President Grover Cleveland.

Among the Lakota, *winkte* were considered sacred and holy. According to Alfred Bowers,

> *"Berdaches comprised the most active ceremonial class in the village. Their roles in ceremonies were many and exceeded those of the most distinguished tribal ceremonial leaders. There was an atmosphere of mystery about them."*
>
> (see Williams, *The Spirit and the Flesh*)

Berdaches were respected in other roles as well — as dreamers, visionaries, craftspeople, mediators, jokesters, negotiators, and as people particularly connected with Spirit. It was considered fortunate to have a berdache in the family and good luck to have one along on war parties.

Peoples honoring the role of berdache generally value the contributions of women equally with those of men. Two-Spirit people are believed to embody the best of both. Will Roscoe among others, speaks of two-spirit men and women as representing third and fourth genders and describes modern day berdaches as maybe a bit bigger than life,

> *"The berdaches I know today all have extra large egos — lots of awareness of the self .... They are what you call big queens .... They very much feel like two personalities crammed into one little body ... there's an expansiveness, a stretching outward ... I look for that intensity as the key quality of a person who is working through the berdache archetype."*
>
> (see Will Roscoe in Thompson, *Gay Soul*)

The berdache are among many examples of gender-variant men from around the world. India has the *hijiras*. The ancient Romans had the *galli*. Polynesians recognize the *mahu*. The point of studying these men is not to imitate them directly. Their roles have very specific meaning within the context of their own cultures. We can, though, learn from their examples.

Societally, men who love men have already been pushed outside the mainstream gender system. While this exile has been a source of wounding, it also presents an incredible opportunity. We are free to experiment. We can move beyond the limiting butch/femme stereotypes we were given. We can create social identities, relationships, and families that resonate with our own inclinations. We can create a place for ourselves based on who we are, rather than who we're supposed to be.

Ultimately, our goal is to move beyond the limits of societally imposed gender identity altogether. To get there, though, it's necessary to know how gender works for you now. By examining the Inner Male and the Inner Female in your own life, you'll strengthen each polarity. The energy you raise can launch you beyond the dichotomy entirely as you create your own version of the Sacred Androgyne.

The next two exercises invite you to go deeper into gender identity. With costumes, movement, and playacting, you'll consult your body about its take on the matter. Try to stay out of your mind. What comes up may not all be positive, politically correct, or what you expect. Some of it may seem negative. You're after the **whole** experience, so let it all come through. Exaggerate, even. You may be surprised at what you find.

It's funny how charged these exercises can be. Some men are totally comfortable with one aspect and yet terrified of the other. I've seen men who had the courage to walk down the street in a dress tremble in fear at the thought of going near a leather bar. I've seen others butch enough to intimidate half of America blanch in terror at the thought of putting on a skirt. Watch yourself. See where your limits are. Then, empower yourself to step beyond them.

The Inner Male

2.a. Beliefs about men

Let's check in with the subconscious. In your notebook, title a new page, "Inner Male." Beneath that, number the lines from 1 to 20. Write the following sentence twenty times, as quickly as you can, filling in the blank for each one. "Men are ...."

When you've finished, mark each trait on your list as positive (+), negative (-), or neutral (0). The list won't be comprehensive, but it will reflect some of your own attitudes about maleness.

Make a second list. This time, complete the following statement ten times, or more if you're on to something — "Men can't ...."

Finally, ten times, "Because I'm male, I can't ...."

What comes up? Are there any parts that are similar to the gender map you made before?

b. **Role models**

Archetypes always have both positive and negative expressions. Often, we know them personified as the characters in fairy tales, myths, and stories. Figures who represent the Inner Male could run the gamut from the Good Father (Michael Landon in Little House on the Prairie), to Mad Max, Darth Vadar, and Rumplestiltskin. When you think of **"male,"** which characters come to mind?

Who were the men most important when you were growing up? Make a list of the ones who made the greatest impression, whether it was good or not.

When you go back through the list, see if you can sum up what each man showed you. Perhaps your grandfather was "loving and funny." Your gym teacher in junior high might have been "hunky but sadistic." Do you notice any similarities with what you wrote in part a.?

c. **Movement meditation**

Your Magic Boy will love this one. It's time for costumes. From what you have in the house, create an outfit that makes you feel **very masculine.** What has the most charge? Carpenter's overalls? Leather chaps? Business suit? Flannel shirt and jeans? Exaggerate the aspects that make you feel most masculine. Don't worry about how it looks. What's important is how it feels. Make it **butch.**

• *Do a movement meditation with music. Follow the steps you've learned that take you into your sacred Inner Council space. Once you're there, inside the Council, invite your Inner Male to come in. How does he look? How does he feel? Observe him for a short while and get a sense of what he's like.*

• *When you're ready, ask him to dance in your body. Ask your body, over and over, "Show me my Inner Male." Watch how your Inner Male moves, how he walks, sits, where the breath flows in your body. Notice which parts of your body feel loose and which you hold more tightly.*

• *When you feel really connected with him, ask your Inner Male to show you two things. First, repeat to your body, "Show me where my Inner Male is strongest and most positive." Your body will show you movements. It will give you impressions. It will send you feelings. Observe whatever images, situations, faces come up.*

• *When you've answered the first question, ask, "Where is my Inner Male blocked?" Watch the movement to see where he comes through weakly, where he's blocked, or possibly where he overcompensates and comes through too roughly. Don't judge, just watch.*

• *When you feel complete, gently bring yourself back to normal awareness. Ground the energy into the Earth.*

As you record your impressions in your journal, remember to be gentle with yourself. This is not about right or wrong. You're simply gathering information that will help you make informed choices later. Acknowledging your Inner Male's strengths and challenges is an important piece of self-knowledge.

How was it? Did parts of the exercise challenge you? Were you surprised? Did you uncover wounding? Did you connect with strengths in yourself you hadn't appreciated before? Challenges you hadn't recognized? As you work with him, you'll embody your Inner Male more clearly and healthily.

The Inner Female

Exercise

3. Just as the Inner Male manifests in varied ways, the Inner Female also has her own places in your life. Let's shift focus and take a look at her. If you're doing this exercise immediately after the last one, change gears by taking a short break, walking around, or shaking your body off all over.

a. Beliefs about women

    *Use a new page in your workbook for the Inner Female. List her characteristics, as you did for the Inner Male, by completing the sentence, "**Women are ....**" twenty times, quickly. Try not to censor yourself. Just write what comes, even if it doesn't make sense or isn't too acceptable socially.*

    When you've finished, label each statement as positive (+), negative (-), or neutral (0).

    *Go a step further. Ten times, complete "**Women can't ....**"*

    *Now really push it, ten more times, with "**If I were a woman, I could ....**"*

    What do you notice? Was this easier or harder than working with the Inner Male? Describe the general tone of your beliefs about women? Compare your answers here with your gender map.

b.   **Role models**

In stories and myths, we've got characters like June Cleaver, Mayberry's Aunt Bea, Cruella DeVil, and the Wicked Witch of the West. Who were the female characters you remember the most from growing up?

Looking at the women in your own life, list the ones who influenced you the most.

These are the women who taught you what it means to be female. What did they teach you? Beside the names, put a word or two that sums up the relationship. Mrs. Schoop at Sunday School = serious, mean. Aunt Bonnie = crazy, fun.

How do these examples match up with your answers in the first section?

c.   **Movement meditation**

Get yourself into a skirt. It could be a real skirt, if you have one, a piece of material, a beach towel, or even the drapes (do you dare, Miss Scarlett?!). Again, your costume doesn't have to win any fashion awards, but be sure you feel **very feminine**. Don't cheat and wrap up like a jock in a towel at the locker room. Make sure what you're wearing moves and feels like a skirt.

• *Use the same music you used for the Inner Male. Go into your sacred Inner Council space. Take some time to reconnect and feel comfortable here. Then, invite your Inner Female to come in.*

Observe her. Do you have a clear sense of her? How does she look? How does she carry herself? Does she resemble anyone you know?

• *Invite her to dance in your body. Ask your body, over and over, "Show me my Inner Female," then get out of the way and watch what comes.*

If you're uncomfortable here, you may have the urge to avoid your real feelings with a burst of exaggerated, silly sashaying. Go for it! Then, let your Magic Boy take over and see what lives beneath that layer. See how this woman really feels. How does she move? How does she sit? How does she hold her body? What parts are loose? Where is there tension? How does she feel about herself?

• *Once you're aligned with this energy, ask your body to show where your Inner Female expresses strongly and positively. Repeat the question as you watch your body move. What do you sense? Do you know her very well? Where is she strong? What situations does she help you with?*

• *Finally, ask one more question — "Where do I have a hard time with my Inner Female?" Repeat the question and watch. What are her challenges? Where in your life do you suppress her? Where does she show her more negative aspects?*

• *When you feel complete, ground the energy, watch your breath, and return gently to normal awareness.*

Jot down your impressions in your journal. What did you notice about your Inner Female? What are her strengths and weaknesses? Were you comfortable with her? Do you hold resentments about women? Was the exercise difficult? How could you acknowledge your Inner Female more fully?

This isn't all about "problems". How many times in these two exercises did you find that you express gender-related energies healthily? How? Are you good at taking care of other people? Are you a skilled carpenter or mechanic? Do you stand on your own? Are you good at supporting others who need it? Can you receive as well as give?

Think back. Were there activities you were good at as a boy that didn't get acknowledged? Were you great at making doll clothes, for example, but always ashamed of your talent because it was "only for girls"? Were you the best at football but afraid to go out for it because someone might see you looking around too much in the showers? I know a boy quite well who was the very best in his whole elementary school at double Dutch jumprope, better even than all the girls. Even though he could get well past "fifteensies," he was ashamed of his skill. He got his chance to shine eighteen years later, at the big radical faerie gathering in New Mexico. There, on the gravel parking lot, with two ropes twirling, the boy jumped longer than anyone else. The others cheered. They clapped. They made the boy feel proud. Finally.

You can, too. Ask your Magic Boy how good it feels to get a gold star, a sticker on the fridge, or an A+ on your report card. Take some time to honor yourself. Find a way to celebrate all the things you've done really well. Get creative. Make yourself a medal or a hand lettered *Certificate of Honor.* Have an appreciation dinner for yourself. Draw a halo on the bathroom mirror. Toss confetti over your head. Acknowledge the courage it takes to be true to yourself, even if you do step on the toes of all those self-appointed gender police.

GENDER SHADOW

When a "girl" puts on makeup, it's never too long before that old beard starts sticking right through. In the same way, whenever we talk about gender, pieces of the Shadow lurk just beneath the surface. Often, there's a good deal of distrust, anger, fear, or even hatred for one gender or the other. It comes through in a number of different ways.

Sometimes, you can hear it in the **humor**. While irony, satire, and the ability to laugh at ourselves are some of our most valuable gifts — to the point of helping define what we consider "Gay consciousness" — sometimes the jokes have an undercurrent of real venom. That's Shadow. Watch what comes out in your "jokes." If there's spite, you'll feel it. The words will seem to have more energy than the situation calls for, or be propelled by an unspoken desire to hurt either someone else or yourself. On the surface, the jokes may look innocuous, but the way they feel will tip you off that something needs investigation.

Another piece of gender Shadow is **rigid attachment** to one role or another. Any role you choose, from ultrabutch leather motorcycle cowboy to genderbending limpwristed faerie is fine as long as it comes from within your own self. Shadow is at work, though, when you're so attached to one role that it limits your expression of others. The tip-off here is the degree to which you feel threatened by experimenting. Does acting assertive terrify you? Are you disgusted with the mere idea of putting on a skirt, even just to play? Look deeply at what the resistance is telling you.

Criticism is a third ploy of gender Shadow. Every year after the big Pride parade, the editorial pages are filled with the same obligatory letters from self-styled moral guardians decrying the extremes to which Gay people have sunk. It used to come from the mainstream press, as they sensationalized the drag queens or gasped in outrage at the leather dykes. Too often, though, now it comes from within our own community. "Too far out," we hear. "**They** won't approve. We're not like **that**!" The most likely driving force behind this type of criticism is fear, fueled by hidden, internalized homophobia. Remember what we said about projection? Be careful. Judgements of others have a way of coming to roost closer to home than we expect.

Be gentle with yourself here. Shadow behavior is almost always defensive. Look beneath the surface and you'll probably find fear, hurt, and wounding. If you discover these in yourself, do your best to get to the core. Is the venom in the jokes a way to keep women, or men, or anyone at all from getting too close? Is there fear of being hurt, judged, rejected, or touched again the wrong way? Is there fear of losing your identity or of giving in to something bigger than yourself?

You have the tools to heal these wounds. Look a little deeper. Can you trace the wounding to a specific incident? Did the jocks at school tease you for throwing like a girl? Did your parents jump all over you for any hint of "non-manly" behavior? If so, use the tools you learned in Chapter 7 — venting, forgiveness, returning and reframing — to support and heal your inner boy.

What if the negatives don't seem to come from your personal wounding? What if you get in touch with more general beliefs about one sex or the other? "Men are stupid, hurtful, self centered, ..." "Women are dirty, dishonest, manipulative, ..." Don't judge yourself too harshly. You're not in this alone. Societally, a mountain of misunderstanding and hostility exists between men and women. Like everyone else, we tend to pick it up by osmosis from family, peers, and the media. Wherever they come from, these attitudes are poisonous. They hurt **you** by making you judge or disown parts of yourself. They hurt **us** as a society by fragmenting and distancing us from each other. Again, you have the tools to heal these negative beliefs. Return to the exercises on releasing, reframing, and creating affirmations you learned in Chapter 3. Every step you take to change negative beliefs is major healing for all of us.

Shadow thrives in darkness. Like parasites, Shadow behaviors and attitudes are most dangerous when they're hidden. Often, just bringing them to awareness is enough to break their hold. In many societies, Gay men, berdaches, and others were important intermediaries between men and women. To reclaim that role, we need to heal gender issues in ourselves. Then, perhaps, we can contribute to healing society as well.

➤ Shadow

Exercise

4.a. *Who really pushes your buttons? Look at the following list:* **men, women, drag queens, leathermen, sissies, machos.** *Who do you have the hardest time accepting? Toward whom do you feel the strongest resistance? Is there someone else not on the list?*

Using the single group you picked above, complete the following sentence: **"The problem with (that group) is ...."** *List as many things as you can that you think are wrong with this group of people.*

b. *Why do you think so? What harm do you think comes when these people act the way they do?*

c. *Think about why this might be an issue for you? Are these people doing something to you directly? Is there some issue from your past that might be involved? Is this something you learned from someone else?*

d.   *Gently, look into yourself. Of the traits you listed in part a., are there any that you've fought in yourself. Any that you might feel just a little envy about? Don't belabor this point, just look.*

e.   *Do you find any wounding in yourself around these issues? How about negative attitudes? For anything that you discover, use the exercises from earlier chapters to release, reframe, and heal. Take responsibility for your own beliefs and inner health!*

THE SACRED ANDROGYNE

Our society gives us very few models of exactly what healthy androgyny looks like. Our minds are so used to classifying every trait as either male or female that they have a hard time seeing in any other way. We tend to judge gender-inclusive behaviors as "less than" one of the polar absolutes. By society's standards, a sensitive man is too often seen as "weak." A strong woman is too often called a "bitch." Androgyny is different. It implies energetic wholeness. Maybe it's easier to visualize if we look at gender in terms of its underlying dynamics.

In the realm of energy, there are two basic polarities. Physicists recognize the opposition of "negative" and "positive" charges. In Chinese medicine and other healing systems, all of nature — including human behavior — is described in terms of opposite polarities. One polarity is the energy called **Yin**. Yin energy is passive, receptive, spacious, and associated with the moon, darkness, destruction, and stored potential. **Yang** energy, its complement, is active, assertive, outgoing and associated with the sun, light, creation, and movement. Since all things embody the basic energies of yin and yang, we can come up with endless examples of how they interconnect. In order to be active, we must have rest. In order to give, we must also receive. In order to bring forth life, we must learn to accept death. Indeed, the foundation of all health is to maintain a balanced expression of both energies.

Yin and yang also give us a good model for understanding gender expression. Looking at your lists, how many of the traits you called masculine tend to be yang in nature? Yang behaviors involve using force, taking action, pushing forward, and building. What about feminine traits? How many of them match the yin qualities of listening, receiving, and taking in?

Simplistically, we might view men and women as the human embodiment of these two energies. Women are often viewed as passive yin, men as active yang. In truth, however, every person expresses both modalities. And because each of us balances them uniquely, regardless of biological sex, gender identity manifests through a full spectrum of possibilities.

The Sacred Androgyne embraces the whole range of human potential. It takes you beyond the limitation of staying in one mode or the other and offers a chance to express the fullness of your own being. Imagine standing in the center of your gender map. With a breath, expand to the left until you contain everything you consider masculine. Expand to the right and hold within you all the feminine. Now, with both extremes inside you, step off the map. You're on your own now, free to draw from the whole realm.

As you learn to express your androgyny, you'll discover new depth and power in your daily activities. For example, imagine the power of a teacher who balances the (yin) qualities of caring and nurture with the (yang) strength to lead his students through intellectual challenge. Think about the healing of a doctor who combines empathy for his patients with the determination to face life and death situations. Think about the business executive whose decisions balance courageous leadership with the compassion to consider their effects on his employees.

In practical terms, what androgyny looks like for you will be unique and different. Move beyond thinking in terms of specific activities and start to consider the new qualities that can enter your life. Are you a painter? Try expanding your palette beyond black and white to mauve, puce, scarlet, and aubergine. Are you a cook? Move beyond mere salt and pepper to the delights of oregano, fennel, cumin, and garam masala. Woodworker? Build an oak table by hand, then put a delicate vase of roses on top. Touch Earth and Sky, light and dark, the man and woman inside you. Give and receive pleasure with all your being.

The Sacred Androgyne is a gateway to Spirit. It offers a fullness of being that is rare among humans. Before you claim it, the idea of androgyny can be scary, especially if the people around you are resistant. Yet you were born for this. The Sacred Androgyne lives in you and if you'll allow, it will give you the courage to set your own standards. It will empower you to live richly and to open to satisfying wholeness. You've got it within you. Why be anything less?

Living androgyny

5. *Transformation is the result of many small steps in the right direction. Make a list of ten things you could do to honor your own androgyny. How could you expand into areas of either "masculinity" or "femininity" you haven't explored before? How could you balance the two modes in the activities you already enjoy?*

6. *Place something on your altar that represents your Sacred Androgyne.*

7.   *Dance it! With the Inner Council as your witness, explore ways to invite the Sacred Androgyne into your own body. Experiment. Play.*

a.   *Try at least one of the following explorations:*

  • *Play with the movements of yin and yang. Yin movement is flowing and lyrical. Imagine swaying like a willow, or flowing like water, being moved by the breath or a passing breeze.*

  Yang movement is outgoing and active. Imagine the strength of an oak or the dance of a fire. Move your energy toward a specific goal.

  • *Play with props that reinforce the two modes. Get scarves for yin and a stick for yang.*

  Ask your body how it would combine them, how yin blends with yang, and yang with yin

  • *Add costumes if you like. Put on your butch drag and be as femme as you can. Vice versa, put on your skirts and dance "like a man." See where the juxtaposition leads.*

  • *Combine your favorite pieces of both costumes. Wear blue jeans and flannel with silk and satin. Wear a leather jock and high heeled pumps. In "androdrag," play with both types of movement — go from yin to yang and back again.*

b.   *In costume or out of it, ask your body to show you how it embodies the Sacred Androgyne. Ask the archetype to come through you in balance. See where it takes you, where it manifests already, where it might need help.*

  Notice if one way of moving is more comfortable and familiar than the other. When you're walking or moving through your regular activities, ask the archetype to come through. Notice where you shift. Notice what feels different, even if nothing looks changed.

As you become more fluid in shifting from one gender role to another, the Sacred Androgyne will become an increasingly natural part of your life. In time, you'll transcend the duality altogether, to express the fullness of your being with grace and ease.

9 The Lover

LOVING OTHER MEN

"Love makes the world go round," isn't that what the song says? Our love, it seems, could turn the world on its head. Can you imagine a world of men free to love each other whenever and however hearts and bodies desired? Who would fight the wars? Who would waste their time worrying about the sex lives of other people? The fact that men can love each other deeply, physically, and wholeheartedly is still a radical concept for most of society. It's also no big deal.

I don't have to tell you this, do I? The capacity to love another man is the most natural thing in the world. You were born with it. Deep inside, you already know the sharp ache of desire, the rugged comfort of male arms around you, the soft teasing of eyes, lips, and tongues. You already know the delightful scratch of stubble, the healing that comes with sweaty, intense caresses, and the whole range of ways that men's bodies share joy. Even if you've never touched another man, you know in each cell of your body that this attraction cannot be thwarted by the struggles of mind, nor by quack cures, nor by screeching moralists. The love of men for men is a gift of Creator. The only sin lies in denying it.

Sharing love with another man is a way to share wholeness. The part that draws the most attention — and the most flack from outside — is the sexual part. Erotic attraction is a valuable and integral part of who we are. It weaves through everything we do and certainly deserves extensive, frequent exploring. Even so, it's only the tip of the iceberg. Sex without connection is empty. There's more to our coming together than just physical release. We come together to enjoy the caring touch of another man not only on flesh, but also on the feeling places inside. We come together to give and receive love as well as pleasure. We come together, finally, because not only our bodies, but also our souls demand it.

When it works, it's unbelievable. Bodies merge. Hearts expand. Souls shine. And our cells, who brought us here in the first place, sing in triumph, "This is why we were born!" When we know that we can truly love each other, every day of our lives is transformed. We're free to let go of old defenses and treat each other with respect. We're open to look beyond appearances and see the wholeness inside every man. We're empowered to stand tall in living refutation of the myths that say men are born only to compete and aggress. No wonder the old order sees us as such a threat.

Unfortunately, we rarely approach each other with this much clarity. Our ability to love suffers under the burden of centuries of condemnation. We tend to bring to our relationships a host of needs, fears, questions, and wounds. Through it all, though, the attraction still lives, irrefutably part of the soul.

That same soul is the part of you that knows the path to healing. If you would follow it, your first step is to look at the beliefs you carry about relating to other men. Even though your conscious thoughts may be positive and healthy, given the environment in which we all live, it's likely that underlying negatives still sabotage your satisfaction and fulfillment. If so, why not root them out and heal them right now?

Beliefs

Exercise

1.   Take a look at what's inside your mind. Since you've already used this same technique a couple of times, you'll probably be able to move through this exercise pretty easily. Remember to write as quickly as you can and to avoid editing.

a.   Ten times, complete the sentence, **"Sex between men is ..."**

Ten more times, use **"Love between men is ... "**

Then, **"Relationships between men are ... "**

What came up? Did any of your statements surprise you? Do you see any patterns? How many of your subconscious beliefs support your having loving, satisfying, sexual relationships? Where do you sabotage yourself?

b.   Now, get rid of the negatives. Use the releasing ritual you explored earlier (on page 50) to burn or flush every negative statement you uncovered in part a.

c.   Reframe the negatives into positive affirmations. Tell your mind exactly what you'd like to create. For example, if one of your statements was *something like, "Sex is dirty," rewrite it as positively as you can — "Sex between men is healthy and clean." Leave no doubt in your mind.*

Repeat your new affirmations until they become automatic. Be creative. Enjoy yourself.

MR. RIGHT

Who are you seeking, there at the grocery when your eyes scan the other men in line? Who is it you hope to meet when you watch the guys at the gym, or on the street, or at the club? Who's in those magazines beside your bed, or in your thoughts when you sigh all alone at night? Who did you think you'd found in all those men you fell in love with, for a week or a night, who just didn't turn out to be "the one?"

Mr. Right is in there, teasing. For most of us, he's like a phantom. You catch a glimpse of him in a smile across the way. You see his form in the curve of a pectoral or the firmness of a thigh. He's elusive, though, always disappearing around the next corner. Just when you think you have him, the image fades and you realize this man in your arms is not the one you'd imagined. Over his shoulder, you catch another glimpse. Mr. Right's slipping out the door. Quick! Run and catch him!

What does "Mr. Right" mean to you? Is he a fantasy daddy who pays your way and solves all your problems forever? Is he a twenty year-old studmuffin named Adonis? Is he an equal partner, a wizard to help create fireworks and magic, or a dark knight on a black horse who kidnaps you into secret realms of forbidden pleasure? Is he all of the above? Mr. Right wears many masks. Even if you're already enjoying a positive, healthy relationship, he can still be there, flitting around the edges. Before you run after him one more time, take an imaginary journey to discover just who this imaginary man really is. Then, maybe you'll catch him more easily.

Design a lover

Exercise

2. Imagine that you're walking along a beach, all alone and bummed out because of it. Suddenly, you stub your toe on something. "What the ...?" you think, "Hmmm ... looks like an antique lamp ... might be worth something ... tarnished ... maybe if I rub it a little ... Whaa ...?" You guessed it, out pops a genie. And not just any genie, either, but a great big hunk of a genie wearing nothing but a loincloth. "Your wish, Master, is my command."

You're a bit taken aback. Gather your senses. What was on your mind? Oh yeah, bummed out, alone. Hmmm, the genie looks hot, maybe he could ... but when you suggest it, he says that sex with genies isn't allowed. Okay, then, tell him you want a man, a lover, in fact, your ideal Mr. Right.

"That's easy," the genie replies. In a blur, he transforms. The loincloth becomes a three-piece Armani suit. Opening his leather briefcase, he hands you a piece of paper. "Fill out this MR. RIGHT REQUEST FORM," he says, "then we'll see what I can do."

a. *In your journal, create the MR. RIGHT REQUEST FORM. Title a new page, then draw the rough outline of a man. Don't worry about how well you can draw — just the outline will do. The genie can fill in the details.*

   Get four pens or pencils in different colors. Your body's going to tell you what to fill in. All you'll do is write down what it tells you. Relax and enjoy the process. Do your best not to edit or think too much about your responses.

b. *First, place one hand on your head. Ask your mind, "Mind, what is most important in my ideal man?" You'll get images, words, or short descriptions. Jot down whatever your mind tells you onto the diagram. For example, if it says that Mr. Right needs a degree in mechanical engineering, put that down by the head. If he needs to be over 6 ft. tall, indicate that. Continue until you've got all the mind's input.*

c. *Now, move your hand beside your eyes. Ask, "Eyes, show me Mr. Right." Your eyes will show you what's important about his appearance. In a second color, add these to your diagram. Write whatever comes until you feel complete. It's okay to write over some of what you put down in the first part.*

d. *Third, consult your sex centers. Put your hand right on your crotch and ask, "What's most important in my ideal man?" Record these responses in the third color.*

e. *Finally, put one hand over your heart and ask, "Heart, show me Mr. Right." What comes up? Jot it down in the fourth color.*

f. *When you finish, look over the diagram. How did you do? Was it easy to come up with a single list? Were there surprises? Contradictions? Did you get everything that's important? When you feel like you've described your Mr. Right as completely as you can, hand your form to the genie.*

"Hmmm," he says, whipping out his reading glasses. "Uh huh ... yes ... I think we can take care of this." Then, he disappears in a puff of lavender smoke. You fidget in the sand, waiting. Maybe you run your fingers through your hair, just to look good for whoever he brings.

Finally, the genie reappears. Beside him, in midair, shimmers a thin curtain. "Open it," he urges. Your hand trembles as you push aside the curtain. Your eyes stare ... right into a full length mirror. When you turn back, the genie has disappeared.

GET WHAT YOU WANT

The genie told you the truth. You'll never find your ideal man outside of yourself. He's too good to be true. In fact, he could be the very obstacle standing between you and the love you really desire. Mr. Right is an illusion, a chimera made of all the needs, wounds, fantasies, and unrealized desires you carry inside. He's a role you created. It's as if your subconscious mind sits in his canvas chair like the cigar-smoking director of Central Casting and measures each man you meet against his master list. If the match is close enough, the audition's over. The new man's got the part. In fact, it starts projecting all over him, like a film onto a 3-D screen. Before you know it, you fall in love with the projection, not the man.

In this materialistic society, it's easy to be swayed by appearances, to view other men as objects rather than as individuals. When you see a body or a face that resembles your image of Mr. Right, try to remember that the person inside may or may not have anything at all in common with your projection. Maybe this man is handsome, understanding, funny, rich, and packed into his jeans. He's also got feelings, fears, desires, strengths, and a Mr. Right fantasy of his own. This is a human being right? Maybe he's your long-lost soulmate. Maybe he's a jerk. Until you see past the character you've assigned him, you'll never know.

Problems arise when you're so attached to your fantasy ideal that you forget the person underneath. Even though you might bend over backwards — maybe literally — to avoid the reality, sooner or later you're in for a rude awakening. It might come first as a feeling of isolation. It might come when you suddenly realize you've been compromising for so long you don't have any of your own principles or identity left. See if you recognize any of the following patterns:

- Fred, a handsome college student, complains about how lonely he felt when he first started going to Gay bars. "I was so attracted to older men with mustaches, that's all I ever looked for. After a while, I realized I never became friends with any of them. All we ever did was have sex. None of them ever asked what I wanted or even how I was. I guess I never thought to ask them, either."

- Bill describes his first-night pattern. "All of a sudden, there he is, looking like a god. He's so hot, I'm so horny, he's so right, I'm so ready, sometimes we get it on before we're even home. Sometimes I get so swept away, I lose control of my senses and forget about being safe. How could I ask someone so perfect to use a condom?"

- Jim says of a new lover. "We'd seen each other every night for a week. When he said he needed a night off to meet friends from work, I smiled, "Sure, it's okay." Then I pouted by myself all night."

- Jack remembers, "The third time I saw him, my new Mr. Right told a really foul joke about dykes. Instead of calling him on it, I pretended he never said it. I didn't want to tell him about my best friends, Susan and Jill."

Projecting your own hopes and expectations onto someone else is natural. We all do it. While you're projecting onto him, your partner's most likely doing the same thing toward you. As long as you're aware of what's going on, there's no problem. Just remember, though, that there's more to this man than you're able to see right off. Get to know each other bit by bit. Where your fantasies agree, act them out playfully, healthily, and to your mutual satisfaction. Where they don't, treat each other with respect. Take your time and see where things go.

➤ Get clear

Exercise

3.a. What attracts you?

When you meet a man, what is it that attracts you first? Are you turned on by body? By a pleasant smile? His eyes? Do you choose youth over age or do you go for experience? Do you look for a sunny disposition or a sense of dark mystery? Are you attracted to a boy/man who needs parenting? or someone who might help you get your own shit together? Is he independent? available?

Imagine you're walking into a room full of men. List what attracts you to some more than others. Be truthful and explore your own choices.

b. What works?

Name five people you've had good relationships with — friends, lovers, co-workers, roommates, or whoever. Beside each name, write what you especially like(d) about being with that person.

• *Jack — funny, light, good sex.*

• *Ginger — can talk about anything, spontaneous, likes to eat out with me.*

When you finish, circle anything that came up more than once. Look for patterns. Do a lot of your friends share the same positive traits — playful, spontaneous, funny, enthusiastic, etc.?

c.   **What doesn't work?**

List five people with whom you've had unpleasant relationships. After each name, write the things you found especially bothersome.

* *Bill — know it all, flirted with everyone else.*

* *George — always stoned, always late, farted at dinner.*

Circle anything that comes up more than once. Are you surrounded by gossips, critics, complainers? Don't judge, just notice.

d.   **Take stock**

Check to see how well you're really supporting yourself. Compare what you find attractive with what actually makes a good relationship. Honestly, do you move toward men who could really give you what you want? Or do you sabotage yourself by always falling for men with a certain appearance, but who are aloof, uninterested, heterosexual, or already married? Again, don't judge, just notice.

It's easy to run after a fabulous body or bulging wallet. Whether or not their proud owner can do a thing to make you happy is another matter. Even for "casual" sex, physical appearance is pretty much irrelevant to the type of experience you'll have. Beauty is as beauty does. A hot bod combined with a stuck up, abusive, or domineering personality equals a lousy time. Someone who's communicative, open, and sharing, even if his body doesn't meet your highest expectations, can make you feel really good. An old queen friend of mine likes to declare, "A good ass counts for about a week. After that, you gotta have something to talk about."

Let's not overintellectualize. Attraction happens. Either it's there or it's not. Thinking won't change it. Pay attention, though. Next time you're sure you've met Mr. Right, check with your intuition. How do you feel underneath the surface? Sure he's cute and hot and flashing twenties like they're ones, but appearances can lie. Look deeper. In the quiet moments by yourself, after a date or a talk on the phone, ask yourself, "How do I really feel here, about myself, this man, my experience?" Then, listen. Maybe it feels really good. Hooray! Maybe, though, you've been so intent on having a good time that you've been ignoring some inner signals. Does anything feel false here? Does this man seem too good to be true, or does he remind you of your past three lovers who all drank too much and wouldn't listen to you ever? Take it easy. Take your time. If this one's right, he'll still be right tomorrow!

HONOR YOUR RELATIONSHIPS

When I was about ten, my father sat me down, all serious, for the big talk. "In this world, Son," he said, "the thing to remember is this. Opposites attract." Even though he never elaborated, I got the subtext — "Act like a man and you'll attract the women you're supposed to." His plan probably backfired. It wasn't women I wanted to attract even then.

My dad's words stuck with me. Though I'm sure they expressed his truth, to me they never seemed right. It took me a long time to understand why. The world is a mirror. Who you bring into your life always reflects who you are. It works energetically. Beliefs hold energy, and so do memories, emotions, talents, dreams, and fears. Whether conscious or not, whether positive, negative, or neutral, all these energies tend to attract other people with similar, reinforcing patterns. At this level, the real operating principle is *"Like attracts like."*

Call it the Law of Attraction. In spiritual terms, it means each person you meet can teach you something about yourself. It means that every relationship, from the briefest exchange of smiles to a partnership of many years, gives you a chance to learn and grow. What you learn depends on the nature of the relationship, where you are on your path, and how open you are to observing.

Sometimes, the sharing feels wonderful. You find out what works. "Dancing with someone else who likes to dance is great!" You discover new talents. "Hey, I really like being around artists. They take me seriously when I draw." You come to appreciate yourself in new ways. "Wow, they actually laughed at my jokes. I must not be such a drip after all!"

Sometimes, what you learn isn't very pleasant. You might find out the hard way what doesn't work. "Next time, I won't tell him my whole life story in the first ten minutes." You might learn boundaries. "No, you can't stay with me for a week. We just met." You might learn what brings out your own Shadow. "I hate when people talk about me. I want to tell dirt about them in return."

If you get used to viewing the world as a sort of mirror, you can learn a great deal about yourself. Pay attention to who you find attractive. If you're always surrounded by great musicians, look inside and acknowledge your own creativity in that realm. If you're attracted to men who are really strong, look inside and recognize your own strength. If you're always attracted to a certain type of beauty, look inside and honor your own. Like attracts like. These qualities wouldn't catch your attention in other people if they weren't also part of you.

Pay attention, as well, to patterns that seem to come up over and over. How many times have you attracted someone with the same annoying habits? Do you find yourself time after time in the role of provider? jealous "husband"? spurned lover? dutiful "wife"? Even though you might write it off as a fluke the first time, when the same pattern comes around repeatedly, at some point you have to look inside and start asking some hard questions. "What's going on here?" "Why is this happening again?" "What do I believe about myself that supports this pattern?" "Do I think that this is all I deserve?" "What can I change in myself to make it work better?"

Relationship takes a million forms and each one has its own value. From the tenderest kiss to the hottest orgy, the most casual friendship to a lifelong commitment, every single connection can be viewed as a sacred exchange. Each one has its own length, scope, and purpose. Each one involves sharing — of information, perspective, pleasure, learning, and more. Each one also has its own time frame, reflects who you are at a given point in your life, and inevitably evolves and changes as you do.

The next exercise outlines a process for honoring and clarifying all these relationships. It's important because every person with whom you've shared has helped to make you who you are today. Each partner has gifted you in some way. Each one has shared energy with you, especially if your interaction was sexual. Each one has been a companion on your path, responsible in some way for bringing you to this point on your spiritual journey. By honoring your companions, you in fact honor yourself and your path.

Honor your relationships

Exercise

4.   Ritual of Acknowledgment

Personalize the following ritual until it feels good to you. You will need a candle and a small bell, chime, or something else (which could be your voice) to make a pleasant sound. Though we'll approach it as if your relationships have been with men, you could apply the exercise just as well to include women.

Part 1 - Clear the slate

a.   Unfinished business

Think about the men with whom you've shared relationships. With how many of these men do you still carry unfinished business? Is there a piece of unresolved anger, sadness, resentment, or disappointment that he never really saw who you were?

Make a list of these men. Their names will come to mind when you ask, "Which men do I need to complete with?" Write the names that come easily. Don't worry if the list isn't complete. You can always repeat the process whenever you feel the need.

Set up a ritual space. Light a candle on your altar or somewhere else that feels appropriate. Close your eyes and surround yourself with light, then call on your guides and whoever else helps create your sacred space. Call your Inner Council. Imagine that they sit around you. Then, call on the Tribe of Gay Men.

b.   Communicate

Within these two circles, speak aloud to each man on your list as if he were present. Indeed, he's there, somewhere within the Tribal circle. Address him by name, and speak the truth of whatever you need to tell him.

> **"Jeff, I'm still pissed you broke that plate my mother gave me. God, you were a jerk."**
> **"William, I hated your stupid jokes about my glasses. You made me feel like shit."**
> **"Georgie, I wish I'd said good-bye before you left."**

As you complete what you have to say to each one, make a tone with the bell or your voice. Imagine that the sound carries your words to that man, wherever he is.

*Then say, **"I release you all into the light,"** and clap your hands once, loudly.*

c.   Release the unrequiteds

Think of all the men you wanted who never returned the favor. Remember your crush on the football team captain, or the weeks you lusted after the new guy at work who turned out to be the married father of two. Remember the "straight" boy at the pool who teased and teased, then pretended he'd never even noticed you. Remember the bartender who just wasn't interested. Remember how you felt each time.

Each bit of unfinished business or unrequited attraction acts like an energetic cord to hold you connected to that person. All those cords weave a web of static that keeps you from relating clearly with anyone else in the present.

Inside your Council space, call each one to mind, and then release him with words and a clap of your hands.

> **"I release you, Jimmy. You missed your chance."**
> **"I'm letting you go, Sam. I'd have loved you and I'm sorry you never felt the same. Be blessed."**
> **"I release you, Gil. I'm saving my love for someone who will return it. I deserve that."**

Clap your hands a few more times and visualize all the cords dissolving and disappearing. Stand up, feel clear, and shake off all over.

If you have time, move directly to Part 2. If you have to stop for a while, place your hands on the Earth and release all the energy you've raised. Reinvoke your sacred space before you continue.

Part 2 — Honor your Partners

d.   Acknowledgment

Call to mind all the men with whom you've shared positive relationships. This might or might not mean including some of the ones you released in Part 1. I realize that for some of us, a complete list would be impossibly long — all those one-nighters! Start with your significant relationships, then deal with the rest as a group. This ritual is designed to celebrate and honor each one.

In the presence of Council and Tribe, address each man out loud. Call him by name, and thank him for whatever he shared with you.

> **"I remember you, Jack. Thanks for all your stories."**
> **"I'm thinking of you, Thomas. Thanks for loving me when I didn't think I was worth it.**
> **"Thank you, David, for taking me to see the butterflies, and for that great sex on the beach."**

As you complete what you have to say to each man, make a tone that carries your prayer to him, wherever he is.

Each of these men is part of your lineage. Each has helped weave your connection within the Tribe. Each has related to different aspects of your being. Honoring them, you honor yourself.

Reach around and give yourself, and all your men, a big hug of gratitude. Then, release them, release the circle, and touch your hands to the Earth until you feel centered.

5. **Honor your attractions**

a. *Who are the men in your life you find most attractive? Jot down their names and what you find attractive. There's Bill, who always knows how to make you laugh, and Sam, the mechanic with the most gorgeous body in the world. Don't forget Frank at the pool, whose hugs are big enough to protect the whole world, and Roger at the clinic, who reminds you of your grandfather and who always has time to listen. As you appreciate the good in the men you know, you appreciate at the same time the good in yourself.*

b. *Celebrate the full range of male beauty. Make a collage of photos and magazine pictures reflecting the types of men you find attractive. Make it sexy! Make it hot! Expand your horizons. Your ability to appreciate male beauty is a great gift. As you honor it, you'll find that you notice the beauty in more and more of the men around you.*

YOUR SACRED COMPANION

Look at the relationships you just honored. If you could combine them into a single, composite image, you'd see an outline of the archetypal Lover who lives inside you. At the same time, because each man you relate to reflects parts of your own being, this composite also approximates an image of what it means for you to be whole.

Take it further. Imagine returning to that mirror the genie gave you. Stand in front of Mr. Right. See him there in all his strength, beauty, and irresistible charm. Now look more deeply into his eyes. See the doubts, fears, and idiosyncrasies that make him a human being instead of just a fantasy. Imagine what it would be like to love and accept this man for all that he is, to put aside the illusions of perfection and engage with him as one real person to another. This is the beginning of true relationship.

Now, go even deeper. Hold this man with love and acceptance. Look through his eyes all the way to the core of his being. There, if you look carefully, deep inside him you'll see a reflection of your essential self — complete and perfect just the way you are. As you see it, let the mirror dissolve so that your Lover stands before you in the flesh. Take a step toward each other, then another and another until your hands meet. Continue walking. Feel yourself and your ideal Lover touch, merge, and become one.

This is how it feels to be whole. Feel the strength of claiming inside yourself everything you've sought outside. Feel the power that radiates through your entire being. Imagine living in the world with this amount of integrity. When you meet another man from this place, you don't need him to give you back parts of yourself.

You're free to see him clearly as he is. You're free to approach each other as equals and to relate from a place of mutual strength.

The Lover as reflection of one's own wholeness is a powerful archetype for men who love men. In his embodiment as the "Double" or "Twin," he appears in some of the world's most ancient myths (see Mark Thompson's *Gay Body* and Will Roscoe's *Queer Spirits* for in-depth discussions). Based on the principle that like attracts like, this Lover comes into your life not to **complete** you where you feel lacking, but to **complement** you in expressing the strength of your totality.

The idea that your Lover reflects your own Self brings us to a new kind of relating based on equality and mutual respect, something Gay visionary Harry Hay calls "subject-subject consciousness." Subject-subject consciousness is one of our Tribe's greatest gifts. It dares us to stop being motivated by appearances alone, to take off the masks we're used to wearing and show each other who we are inside. It challenges us to admit our fears and desires and to allow our partners to have their own. It demands that we let go of the illusory Mr. Right and begin to value each man for who he really is. Though the concept may seem foreign at first, when you embrace relationships in this way, you open the door to intimacy that is truly healthy and rewarding.

What we're talking about is *quality* of relationship. There's a deepening that occurs when you move beyond surface appearances. Suddenly, your exchanges with others become real as never before. There's a profound sense of *presence* that allows your sharing — sexual and otherwise — to be more satisfying. In a very real way, you take your place within a Tribe of Lovers. Each man you spend time with becomes a sacred companion on your spiritual journey through life.

This is not to say that you have to negotiate a long term relationship with every man you meet or have sex with. If you approach your time together consciously, you can share deeply in the course of an hour with someone you'll never see again. It doesn't mean an end to fantasy, either. Quite the contrary. By communicating honestly, you can match your needs and desires with those of your partner. Instead of playing separate videos in your separate heads, you can create an experience that excites and fulfills you both.

So what does subject-subject relationship look like? It takes thousands of forms, limited only by the imagination of the men involved. It can be short or long, sexual, platonic, monogamous, open, caring, casual, formally committed, or taken one day at a time. It can be the sharing of elder to youth or the caring of young man for his older partner. It can be the support of a friend or the joint celebration of a happy event. You might share dinner, a walk along the beach, an evening at home, or a trip around the world. Camp, play, dance, cry, laugh, or stare into each other's eyes for hours. When you open to the full range of relating, you explore new territory each day.

What about sex? It's vital, don't you agree? And the forms it can take are endless. Each of us needs intimacy. Sexual desire is almost always what propels us out of the closet into the arms of our brothers. Sexual intimacy weaves a strong Tribal network, one hot, erotic touch at a time — and relating to each other as sacred brothers only enhances the depth and satisfaction of the sharing. Whatever kind of sexual interaction turns you on, it is only improved by clear communication and mutual respect. Good, healthy, enjoyable sexual intimacy is your birthright. Claim it and enjoy it!

Even now, in the face of the AIDS plague, don't retreat from intimacy. In fact, the challenges of maintaining healthy intimacy while being assaulted by loss, grief, and fear — not to mention drug regimens, uncertainty about HIV status, and conflicting opinions about what actually constitutes "safe sex" — mean that we need subject-subject consciousness more than ever. Entering relationships with a sense of respect for yourself and for your partners allows you to maximize intimacy. It means making and honoring decisions with each other about how to meet sexual needs in ways that are mutually satisfying as well as safe. Ignoring the facts of the disease and engaging in unsafe sex is suicidal, really just another way to sell out to low self-esteem and homophobia. Don't do it. You don't know what's safe? Find out. You don't think it's fun? Get creative. You are worth it.

"Okay," you say, "all that sounds great. The chapter's almost over, though, and I'm still alone. Are we gonna fix that?" Well, yes. And, no. There's no magic bullet that will get you laid and married happily ever after. Sorry, but it just doesn't exist. Don't give up, though, there is hope. The Law of Attraction is very practical. Think about it for a minute. How would you attract a man who reflects your own wholeness? Would you mope around all depressed, just waiting for some gorgeous knight to gallop into your life and fix everything? If so, ask yourself why someone as cool as your ideal Lover would be attracted to someone who's sad and moping all the time, anyway.

In fact, the answer is simple. To attract the man you want, be the man you want to attract. Maybe that knight will show up. In the meantime, though, don't wait around. Learn to have a good relationship with yourself. Live as fully as you can now. Accept yourself the same way you'd like him to accept you. Make yourself as interesting, positive, and understanding as you'd like him to be. Develop your talents. Explore your passions. Find activities that make you feel good about yourself. That way you'll attract other men who are dynamic, interesting, and passionate about life. And when your knight does show up, you'll have something in common.

Start where you are. You're surrounded by people. They aren't all potential lovers, of course. Even so, each one has something to share with you. Practice the qualities of relating that you'd like to enjoy with your lover. Be present. Learn to listen. Cultivate relationships with people that make you feel really good. Let go of the ones that don't. That's a good start.

Finally, remember that Spirit works in strange ways and in Its own time. Your knight will probably show up when you least expect him. He'll appear when your mind is elsewhere, when you're taking out the garbage, getting your car inspected, or dancing your fool head off. He'll get here, you can be sure of it. Until he does, though, get ready by loving yourself.

➤ The Lover

Exercise

6. **Choices**

    Every day, you make choices about how to relate to other men. No one else can tell you what choices are appropriate for you. Reflect on your own choices and where they come from.

a. *List the top several relationships in your life right now. They might be sexual or not. Then, keep them in mind as you answer the following questions.*

    How well do these relationships really satisfy you?
    How do you feel after you've been with a partner? Good? Satisfied? Bored? Lonely?
    Do you feel present while you're relating to your partners?
    Does your mind wander to fantasies or wishing you were with someone else?
    Do you feel connected? Isolated?
    Does your sharing feel joyful?
    Do you ever feel you're selling yourself short? When?
    Are your needs being met?
    Are you seeking just sexual release? Something more?
    In light of what you're experiencing at present, what type(s) of relationship are you seeking?

    Acknowledge and celebrate wherever your relationship needs are being met. Good job!

b. *Where your relationships don't meet your needs, brainstorm some steps that might help.*

    No friends? *Why not join a group? Get a pen-pal. Help someone who's sick or stuck at home. Be a friend to yourself.*

No touch? *Get a massage. Give one. Get in with a group of people who like to share hugs.*

Not enough social life? *Invite people over. Set up a group to eat out or go to the movies once a month.*

No one to share your interests? *Take a class. Start one yourself.*

Take responsibility for creating your own life!

7. Put something on your altar to honor all your relationships. *It will remind you that your ideal Lover lives inside you already.*

8. Movement meditation

   In the sacred space of your Inner Council, invite your body to show you your archetypal Lover. Use the techniques you've already learned to welcome this man into your body. Dance with him. Feel your wholeness. Celebrate your relationship with yourself. It will be interesting, rewarding, and probably different from what you expect.

   Call him whenever you feel at a loss, lonely, or down on yourself. His presence will help you make big internal steps toward loving yourself, and as you get used to the feeling, it will help you attract men you want to be with in the world. Enjoy!

10

The Elder

BEAUTY AND THE TROLLS

Imagine a society different from our own in which older Gay men are treated with honor. Imagine a Council of Gay Elders who sit together in order to share wisdom and advice with the entire Tribe. Imagine going to this Council — being sent by your parents, even — the moment you first recognized your attraction to other men. Imagine sharing your concerns with a silver-haired mentor, a man like yourself who loves other men and who listens to you with respect. Imagine how you'd feel about yourself if you could call on this man's guidance, insight, humor, and perspective whenever you need it.

The Elder is a powerful figure in the human psyche. Indeed, at the level of archetype, he lives within you now. In his most positive expression, he embodies considerable stature and authority. Through his roles as teacher, guardian, and initiator, he shares the wisdom and patience of a lifetime's experience. He teaches you to embrace life and to cherish maturity as a gift. In this chapter, you'll learn how to bring the Elder into your present life as ally and friend.

If you're lucky, you already know other men-loving men who embody the healthy traits of the Elder. Sadly, though, mentors like these are often hard to find. Many of us don't even know where to look. Images of empowered elders are rare in our society as a whole and rarer still in our youth-oriented Gay culture. I suspect that many of us are much more familiar with the negative, Shadow aspects of the archetype. When I recall my own first impressions of older Gay men, there's not a positive image in the whole lot.

I came out in my mid-twenties into a flesh-filled extravaganza of bars, baths, and discos. Early on, I noticed a strange phenomenon. The Gay scene appeared to be inhabited by two very distinct species. First were the Beauties. Fresh, young, exuberant, and frantically horny, the Beauties made the scene. We fed on the beat, demanded constant attention, and arrogantly viewed ourselves as the pinnacle of Gay evolution. We'd invented Gay liberation, hadn't we? Of course we had, and just as an excuse to celebrate the wonder of our own being!

Around the edges, leaning against the walls or perched at the bar, lurked the others. Outlandish creatures with dyed hair and slack-toned skin, these ones seemed to think they belonged here, too. They shrieked in falsetto, minced around calling each other "Miss Thing," and pretended to be faded divas I'd never heard of. The Beauties called them "Trolls" or "Old Queens." If one of them stared too long, or dared attempt conversing, we'd fly away, self-righteous and insulted.

At the time, clutching desperately to Beautyhood, I could hardly believe the two types had anything in common. Of course, I knew the Trolls had once been young. I just couldn't imagine the connection. I envisioned a sort of reverse metamorphosis that happened around, say, thirty. Beautiful hunky male butterflies would suddenly be overcome with this compulsion to spin cocoons, hibernate a season, and return transformed into — what? Worms? Lizards? Yeah, lizards with slimy tongues and beady, penetrating eyes. I was terrified of them, terrified of their soft touch and the bitter venom of their humor. I was terrified they'd reach out for my youth, taint it somehow, and snare me in their trap.

Ironically, at that point in my life I'd have given almost anything for the support and advice of an experienced Gay man. I longed for assurance and could have benefited immensely from even a little guidance about self-esteem, relationship, and how to be "out" in the world. Yet even though I was surrounded by older men who might have been able to help, my own fears kept me from connecting.

Why are Gay men so afraid of aging? Is it strictly physical? Do we fear infirmity and the loss of vigor? Do we measure our worth only by the number of reps we can do at the gym? Do we still give power to the old myth that says we need children to care for us in order to avoid sitting alone and unloved through our final, empty years? Must we fight time tooth and nail and let each birthday plunge us into gloomy defeat? Of course I'm exaggerating, but just the same, ask yourself — how much do **you** fear aging?

Part of the problem is cultural. In our society, youth has become a commodity. Advertisers spend billions to inundate us with images of "perfect" young bodies, each one posed seductively around some product we supposedly can't live without. From the look of many Gay publications, we seem to have bought it hook, line, and sinker. Thus, even with increasing Gay visibility, it is still very difficult to find positive images of healthy, older Gay men. Sure, we pay homage to icons like Walt Whitman, who stares across a century like a cross between God and Santa Claus, but while we can admire him from afar, very few of us would actually want to **be** him in this day and age. There are others — men like Malcolm Boyd, Harry Hay, John Burnside, and James Broughton — who offer us powerful and increasingly visible examples. Still, these men are exceptions. For the most part, a curtain of invisibility seems to drop over us at the age of fifty. No wonder we fear aging. The territory is unknown. We might as well fall off the edge of the Earth.

The only way to remedy the situation is for each of us to begin understanding the Elder in new ways. That's what you're about to do. By learning to connect with the positive aspects of the Elder inside you, you'll access a powerful source of inner guidance. By learning to embrace his wholeness, you'll deflate the fears that give power to his Troll-like Shadow. To open the door for his wisdom and support, your first step is to free your inner Elder from fears and misunderstanding that have kept him trapped.

The Troll and the Sage

Exercise

1.a. Title a new page in your journal, "The Troll."

As if you were describing him for an animated film, create a caricature of the Troll. Use words, or words and pictures, to make him embody all your worst fears about being old. Exaggerate. Is he a hairy-eared, slobbering hunchback who smells like pee? Is he a long-nosed cackling old queen who plays with himself in public by day and vampirizes tender-fleshed young men at night? Is he bitter? Alone? Pathetic? Evil? What parts of him do you find particularly offensive? Be creative. Make it a horror film. Give him warts and oozing sores.

How did that feel? Did you miss anything? If so, jot it into the margins now.

b. *Shake out your hands and start a new page. Call this one, "The Sage." Again, as if for a fairy tale, characterize the most ideal older man you can imagine. Give him the positive traits you admire in men you already know. Then exaggerate. Make him wiser than Merlin and as handsome as an aging Rhett Butler. Make him as strong as Samson and as connected as Zeus. Make him virile. Give him fifty willing lovers or just one special friend. Give him a hotline to the President. Let him be a wizard who can save the planet or guide the steps of one confused boy. Maybe he seems too good to be true, but hey, it's just a cartoon.*

How's that? Forget anything? Ask inside and jot down any additions. How was this in comparison to the Troll? Which was easier? Which gave you a more vivid picture?

c.   *Do a short movement meditation. As if you were auditioning for a play, act out the Troll. How does he stand? How does he walk? What's his voice like? What kind of things would he say? You're auditioning for a melodrama, so play it up!*

Once you're in character, go inside. What makes the Troll tick? How does he feel about himself? How does he feel about the world? about loving other men? about being old? Does he have friends? Jot down your insights.

d.   *Now, shake off and get into audition number two. This one is the Sage. The Sage is the good guy, the fairy godfather who makes everything turn out right. Act him out with your body. How does he stand? How does he walk? How does he speak? What's he say?*

Any good actor has to know what motivates his character. Where's the depth to the Sage? How does he feel about himself? How does he feel about his way of loving? About his place in the world? About being old? How does he interact with friends? Jot down whatever he tells you.

e.   Both these Elders are part of you, at least potentially. Your own inner Elder is probably some mixture of both. At times he may feel like a saint, at others an old fart. In reality, the two characters are opposite sides of the same construction. Let's do a little playacting and bring them together.

Close your eyes and imagine that you are the Sage. Take a moment to get back into the role. Feel how natural it is to share wisdom, clarity, and compassion.

As the Sage, notice that another figure is shuffling toward you. You recognize the Troll, acting like he needs something from you. As he gets closer, he pauses.

As the Sage, look into this other man's eyes. What can you see there? Is there fear? bitterness? Can you see the self-loathing of never daring to love the way he wanted? Can you see the pain of never taking his dreams seriously enough to go for them? Can you see neglect and isolation? What else?

As the Sage, how do you feel toward this other man? What would you tell him? Is there a part of you that can recognize him for what he is — a soul who is lonely and hurting? Can you look at him and see someone who could still discover his own worth? Is there a part of you that can offer him compassion?

f.   *Ask the Sage what he would do for the Troll. What could you tell him about himself? What insights might you give him? What could you do in your life now to help him? How might you apply the Sage's advice to yourself?*

When you finish, shake off all over and let both Troll and Sage go back into light.

RECONNECT WITH YOUR ELDER

Your Elder's in there. Actually, he's cared for you all your life. Even when you were very young, he supported you. He was there when your parents couldn't be, when you had to face the world on your own. He whispered strategies, deep inside, that helped you survive the challenges. Even if you didn't recognize him, he gave you enough trust in yourself to make it through. The fact that you're here proves he succeeded.

Even though the Elder is a strong figure, he can be wounded. For Gay men, one of the ways wounding shows up is that the Magic Boy and Elder trade places. Instead of enjoying childhood, many Gay boys act older than their years. Were you a boy who watched every step for fear that one slip of tongue or wrist would betray you? Did you hide your adolescence behind a wall of overachievement or give up your youth taking care of others? Many of us did.

For most of us, the stakes were high. Learning to be little adults enabled us to survive. But what was the cost? How much of your ability to play and explore did you barter? And later, when you came out, what happened? For myself, relaxing the vigil was like plunging over a dam. The walls of responsibility fell hard. How tempting to make up for lost time by diving into a sea of boyish hedonism. How strong the urge to fly forever, the eternal boy who won't grow up.

Health depends on balance. The Elder is your guardian and protector. Like a responsible parent, he sets boundaries that let the Boy in you play safely. Because the Elder provides a healthy structure, the Magic Boy can be spontaneous. Together in their rightful places, these two figures are very strong. Alone, neither lives a very satisfying existence.

Your Elder is a powerful ally. Having walked your path, he can guide you better than anyone else. He's patient when you're not. He offers companionship when you feel alone. His sense of perspective helps you lighten up and laugh at life's absurdity. He's loved you all along. Now, it's time to know him better.

Meet the Elder

2. For inner reality, time is irrelevant. Your Magic Boy, present self, and Elder exist all at once. Just as you can "go back" to heal the boy, you can easily "reach forward" to connect with the Elder.

How? First, trust that he exists. Your mind may want to cling to the old patterns by resisting the help that he offers. Like a three year old who wants to dress himself and throws a tantrum when you suggest boots instead of sandals for playing in the snow, your mind may want to struggle on alone. Give yourself the benefit of the doubt. If you open to him even a little, your Elder is a great source of support.

Parts a, b, and c offer you three very good techniques for meeting him. Pick one of them and enjoy yourself.

a. **Visualization**

• *Follow your breath to enter your Inner Council space. Feel the safety and protection of both Council and Tribe around you. Feel your connection with the Earth.*

When you're ready, ask your inner Elder to step from the Council into the center of the Circle.

Look at him. What's he wearing? How does he stand and move? How does he feel to you? Can you hear his voice? How does he speak? What are your general impressions?

Look into his eyes. What do you see there? Can you feel his strength and understanding? Can you sense his loving concern for you? It is all there. What else do you see?

• *When you feel comfortable with him, ask your Elder to remind you of the times he's helped you in the past. When has he been with you? Were you aware of him?*

Would he be willing to help you now? What would you like to know from him? Ask. Where in your life could you use his guidance? Ask.

Then listen. See what comes. There may be images, words, feelings. It may not be what you expect. You may get a great deal of clarity, or you may get nothing much at first. If it takes time for anything to come, relax. The door is open. More information will come when it's ready.

• *Ask the Elder how you can connect with him more fully. How can you call on him? How will you know when he's trying to get your attention? How can you communicate with each other more easily?*

If there's anything else you'd like to discuss, do so. Then, when you're finished, thank your Elder for being here and release him. Touch the Earth to release all the energy and record your impressions.

b. **Movement meditation**

• *With music, imagine standing in your Inner Council space. Feel the safety of Council and Tribe. Feel your breath in your body, your feet connected to Earth.*

When you're ready, ask your body, over and over, "Show me my Elder." Take your time. What shifts occur in your posture? How do you stand? How does your body feel different?

Take some time to move as the Elder. Feel how sure of himself he is. He's been through the situations you're facing now and can approach them with confidence.

• *Think of a situation in your life about which you'd like guidance. Ask your body first to show the situation. When you feel clear about it, ask your body to move as your inner Elder. Ask him to show you how he can help in this situation. Keep asking and see what comes. Is your body heavier? Lighter? Do you feel stronger, optimistic, or more centered? Whatever comes, just keep moving. Notice what the movements are showing you. Notice what insights or impressions come into your mind while you move. In light of these, what have you learned about the situation you asked about? Do you have any change in perspective?*

• *Tell your Elder you'd like to call on him again when you need his help. Ask him to give you a small gesture that will help you call on him. Ask your body and watch how it moves in response*

Then, thank your Elder for being with you. Let him go, shake off all over. Put your hands on the Earth and let yourself come back to normal. Record your impressions in your journal.

c. **Letters**

Another way to connect with your inner Elder is by writing letters. Here are two that will help.

• *First, write to your inner Elder. If you could meet him, what would you ask? Where do you need clarity or reassurance? Where could you use his perspective or his help?*

Ask him to remind you of times in the past when he was able to help you. Ask how to call on him in the future.

Make the letter as long as you like. Remember, he's been there with you for a long time. He'll know what you're talking about. He'll know how to help. When you're finished, sign the letter and read it aloud. As you do, know that your Elder hears every word.

• *Stand up, shake off, and get a new page. This time, write a letter from your Elder to yourself. Have him respond to all your questions. He'll tell you what he thinks of where you are and offer his guidance on the choices you face right now. Let him share whatever advice and support he has for you.*

If you'd like to go even more deeply, here's a technique you can try. Write the second letter with your non-dominant hand. If you're right-handed, write it with your left. The handwriting may not be too clear, but you will be surprised at what comes through. It will take a bit longer. Watch, though, and see what you learn. This is quite enjoyable.

Reclaim your Self

Exercise

3. **This exercise is very important. Don't skip it.**

Many times over the years, you reached out to older men for validation, encouragement, or help. Sometimes you got it. Sometimes you didn't. Right now, we're not going to be concerned about whether the job these men did was good or bad. Most likely, it was some mixture of both. Yet, whether your experiences were great or awful, the men in your life helped get you to this point. Now it's time for you to reclaim the Boy for yourself. It's time for you to take your role as his Elder and protector.

a. *Set aside time for a visualization. Go into your sacred Council Space. Breathe slowly and mindfully. Feel the safety and protection you enjoy here.*

When you feel aligned, put your hands on the center of your chest. Take a breath. Call forth your inner Elder. Have him stand with you in the center of the Council circle.

b. *With your Elder at your side, ask the Council to show you all the men you asked to take care of your little boy. Who comes? Maybe your father's there. Maybe a teacher you were close to or a grandfather who died before you knew him. Whoever comes, just watch.*

When they're all there, talk to them one by one. Your father first. Tell him, in your own words, "Dad, I gave you my little boy to take care of. I know that you did your best (even if I didn't always know it at the time). I'm here to tell you, Dad, that from now on, I'm going to take care of him myself. I release you from your duty totally. This boy is going with me from now on."

Imagine taking the boy from your father and bringing him into your own arms. Comfort him. Let him feel really secure with you and your Elder. Thank your father for whatever he did and then release him. Surround him with strong light as he fades away to where he came from.

c. *Repeat this process for each of the men you asked to care for your little boy. No matter what kind of job each one did, tell him it's your turn now. When you've spoken to all of them, your little boy will feel very present and safe with you and your Elder. Sit together for a few minutes in the center of your Inner Council.*

This exercise may bring up emotions. It may feel really good, or sad, or empowering, or scary. Sit with the feelings. Notice them. Share what your little boy feels. The more you claim him and his true feelings, the more whole you are.

When you feel centered again, ground the energy into the Earth, imagine the boy in your heart, and bring your awareness back to normal.

TRIBAL CONTINUITY

The Tribe of Gay Men did not spring forth from the Earth the night of the Stonewall riots. It did not start in the early fifties with Harry Hay's Mattachine Society. It did not even begin a century ago with Walt Whitman or Edward Carpenter. Our Tribe has been here as long as humanity. Even though most of our history has been suppressed or denied, we are the most recent generation in a long lineage of male lovers. Every generation of men-loving men can learn from those that walked the path earlier.

Nor do we stop here. Just as we've inherited the present state of Gay culture, we also create the inheritance of future generations. As long as there are humans, there will be men who love men. Not only do we share a debt to our ancestors, we also carry the responsibility for those to come. Each of us is called to share what he knows to ease the path of those who are just beginning to acknowledge and make peace with their own sexuality.

As much as we could all benefit, communication between men-loving men in different age groups tends to be limited. Especially in the cities, where a broader range of social outlets allows us to compartmentalize, the generation gap in Gay culture tends to be more pronounced than what we see in the rest of society. Conditions are changing so rapidly that men in one age group often have a hard time even understanding those just a few years older or younger. Men who came of age before 1970 or so were conditioned by the need to stay closeted in response to harsh societal persecution. Younger men, accustomed to visibility and freedom unimaginable before Stonewall, often operate from an entirely different frame of reference. In the same way, men who came out after the onset of AIDS can be hard pressed to understand the naïve sexual abandon of the 70's or to accept that the lessons of that era could possibly still be valid.

In addition, our society tends to discourage older Gay men from reaching out to younger ones who could benefit from their experience. Despite the need for competent, compassionate Gay mentors — a need underscored by disproportionately high rates of depression and suicide among Gay youth — older men are still reluctant to step forward. Surely, a great deal of this reluctance comes from fear. Much of society is still quick to condemn any contact whatsoever between Gay men and boys as recruitment, predation, or worse. The real need to protect boys from exploitation has been exaggerated and distorted until it kills almost any opportunity for positive mentoring. The pioneering programs that do pair Gay teens with older Gay men and Lesbians are still few and far between.

Tribal Elders are the rememberers of history, the keepers of our stories. Ideally, they keep sight of the bigger picture, reminding us of past progress as they guide us toward an empowered vision of the future. Your own Elder can help you now, as you turn your attention to the ongoing generations of the Tribe. He'll help you honor your Gay ancestors first, then guide you in considering how you could help those to come.

Honor the ancestors

Exercise

4. Tribal ancestors are all those men-loving men who have gone before us. Though they're usually not related in the traditional sense through bloodlines, your Tribal ancestors influenced you as surely as your own parents and grandparents.

You have a debt to these men. Most of the benefits we enjoy today — the freedom to live openly, to feel pride, to even consider civil rights, raising our own children, or serving in the military — are the legacy of many years of struggle. Many men fought hard for this liberation, men like Edward Carpenter, Oscar Wilde, Walt Whitman, Harvey Milk, and Magnus Hirshfield. These men, our ancestors, deserve honor and respect.

More personally, almost all of us have Gay brothers, friends, and lovers who are no longer here. These men, too, are part of the Tribe, ancestors now though we knew them in the flesh. They too, stand in your Tribal Circle as part of your "family in Spirit." With the other ancestors, they can be an important source of guidance and support.

It is important to honor these ancestors. How you do so is your choice. I invite you to create a ritual of your own. Use the guidelines we've explored to set up your sacred space. Be very clear as you call in your guides, your Inner Council, and the whole Gay Tribe. Feel them stand around you in a circle. Then, honor them in your own way.

• Tom wrote the names of his Gay ancestors, including those who had transitioned recently, on a paper scroll. He keeps it on his altar and reads the names from time to time in respect and remembrance.

• Samuel wrote all the names of Gay ancestors important to him on brightly colored ribbons. These he tied to the branches of a tree in his special place. He knows their voices come in the wind when he needs them.

• Jeffrey called the Tribal Council and spoke aloud all the names, thanking each one with a tone from his bell.

• William planted a flowering cherry tree in honor of all his ancestors. He mulched and watered and cared for it as a way to honor their memory.

• Mark spoke his gratitude to a silly totem — a gumby doll with a silver earring given him by a departed friend. He took the doll to a special place and left it as an offering of thanks.

• Harry spoke a prayer into each piece of wood he used to build a fire. As it burned, he sat and communed with all those who went before.

The honoring ritual empowers you. You are not alone and will never be. Your ancestors are now part of your Tribal Circle, where they share their collective wisdom and support with you always.

However you choose to structure your ritual, the closing is important. Honor the fact that your ancestors, however beloved, are now part of Spirit. Though you may hold their memories in your heart forever, it is time to release them.

To finish, release the ancestors you called up with a prayer of blessing. Even though you'll feel connected to them from time to time, let them all go back to Spirit now. Then place your hands on the Earth and let the energy you've raised flow into the ground. Release the Tribe, release the sacred circle, and let it go. You're complete when you feel centered again.

Honor those to come

Exercise

5. Tribal continuity works in both directions. You are an ancestor in the making. The choices you make now, and those we make together, lay the groundwork for generations to come. What kind of legacy will we leave them? What can you do? Can you maintain hope through the health crisis? Can you have the courage to live openly so it's easier for them to do so? Can you do your work with them in mind? Do you have the strength and foresight to honor them by being all you can right now? Any positive step you take helps.

The following exercises will help get you into this mode of living. Pick at least one that appeals to you.

a. **Legacy**
Think about your legacy. Imagine future generations of boys and men who love each other. What problems do we face today that will most affect them? What could be done today to help improve conditions for them? What are the most important things you could do personally to make their world better?

List five specific things that would help future generations.

- lobby for protection of Gay parents
- work to save the forests from destruction
- create a teen hot-line
- campaign for an end to employment discrimination
- what's important to you?

b. **History**
You are living the history of the future. If we don't tell our stories, how will our future generations know the truth of their history? Write one story from your own experience you think would be good for them to know.

- What was it like growing up Gay in your time?
- How did you come out?
- What was it like to have a lover in the present decade?
- What was your first reaction to hearing about AIDS?
- What is your story?

c. **Letter**
Write a letter to an imaginary Gay youth. Tell him what you've learned that could help him. You are the Elder here. Share your wisdom.

- "It's okay to be yourself, whatever anyone else says."

- "Don't waste time waiting for everyone else to approve of you. Not all of them ever will. Get on with your life."
- "Follow your dreams before it's too late."

d.   **Plant a tree**

As a final gesture, both in honor of ancestors and in recognition of future generations, do something truly lasting. Plant a tree and nurture it until it can sustain itself. Let its roots remind you of your own roots, your Tribal ancestors. Let the leaves, flowers, and fruit remind you of all the generations to come.

Plant a tree this year. Even better, plant one every year.

ELDERS IN TRAINING

Becoming an Elder is different than just getting older. Aging happens. No matter how much you kick and scream in denial, dye your hair, or pat your still almost-ripply stomach, you are going to age. Becoming an Elder is different. It involves the deepening of awareness that comes with experience. It includes a deep commitment to life, an understanding of priorities, and an honoring of self. Becoming Elder is the payoff to growing older.

Let's be real. Like every other age, being old brings challenges. Bodies change. Friends and lovers die or move on. Infirmity, mortality, and loneliness are very real issues. I remember hearing James Broughton speak several years ago. This man fairly sparkles with delight as he sings psalms to the joy of physical love among men. When I heard him, he was around 80 years old. "Don't romanticize old age," he said. "It's not all wonderful. I wake up in the morning and my joints hurt and my body's not what it used to be."

The wisdom of elderhood has its price. Some of life's lessons hurt. Some of the paradoxes of existence can't be resolved. There is no answer to death, to the loss of love, to the body's own aging. There is no way to go back and do it over. As we face these challenges, though, somehow we learn to stretch, to discover what's important and what isn't. There is no shortcut. The lessons of life come through the living.

There are things you can do that help. First, you can honor your own path. Every challenge you've faced has taught you something — from growing up different and finally coming out to breaking up with your first lover, being open at work, or dealing with HIV. Whatever your age in years, you have wisdom. This is especially true now when HIV has forced us to deal with issues around mortality that used to come much later in life. Every situation brings learning. Honor the lessons you've already received.

Second, you can embrace life as an ongoing process of deepening and becoming wiser. You don't wake up one morning and suddenly become an Elder. It starts the day you're born. As I write this in my 40's, I'd love to have the skinny muscular body I had at 20. I'd never trade it, though, for the self-esteem and awareness I've gained since then. I suspect most of us feel the same. Despite the trade-offs, the things that make life truly satisfying — self-acceptance, emotional stability, meaningful relationships — mostly get better. It's a healthy expectation to hold for the future.

Andrew Ramer likes to observe that we're all "Elders in training." Who you are as you age depends on who you are throughout your life. The kind of Elder you'll become depends on choices you make today. Think about it. If you'd like to be an eccentric, wise, interesting, and satisfied Elder, what would you do to cultivate those qualities right now?

Your Elder is not someone who lives far away in the future. He lives in you this very instant. His wisdom, strength, and insight are yours for the asking. What you make of him is up to you. Embrace him now, while you can. They say it's never too late to have a happy childhood. I say it's never too early to become a happy Elder.

Embrace the Elder

Exercise

Complete at least two of the following exercises.

6. *List ten positive qualities you admire in other people that have nothing to do with chronological age. What are they? How many of the same qualities can you see in yourself?*

7. *List five things you're better at now than you were 5 years ago. List five things you know about yourself you didn't know 5 years ago. List five things you can share now that you couldn't 5 years ago.*

8. *Give your Elder an hour — or an afternoon — of your time. Do a movement meditation in which you call him into your body. Then, while he's there, approach the world from his perspective.*

   Go where he likes. Do things he'd do. Take a walk. Sit and watch the ducks. Baby-sit a young child. Watch the sunset. Get together with your buddies. Whatever you do, let him lead you. You'll be surprised what you learn.

9. Priorities

   Part of the wisdom that comes with aging is a sense of appropriate priorities. You can get a feel for this yourself by completing the following exercise.

Close your eyes and go inside. In the sanctity of your Inner Council, ask yourself the following question: "If I had one year to live, what would be most important for me to do before I leave?". Listen carefully to what comes up and jot down your answers.

Repeat the question, changing it to, "What would be most important if I only had one month to live?". Do the answers change?

Ask a third time, "If I had only a single day left on this Earth, what would be the most important thing I could do?".

Ask one more question. "If my time were limited, which of the things that I do now would seem less important?".

Time is precious. Truth is, you never know how much is left. Look at what you've written. Think about what it would be like to live by the priorities you listed.

10. *Cultivate a relationship with someone older. Certainly, many older men and women in the community (Gay or not) would be grateful for your help. The concerns of seniors are generally very practical, tangible, and down to Earth. A little help goes a long way.*

Do you know someone who could use help shopping, or a companion once a week to fix lunch, cut the lawn, or put a few things into the attic? Is there someone you could visit from time to time just to talk? Is there an older man who might enjoy sharing his stories? If you're willing to look, opportunities are easy to find.

You'll discover that sharing usually works two ways. The effort you make for someone else comes back multiplied — initially as the simple satisfaction of helping, and then more strongly as a deepening of your own experience. You'll get to see the choices other people make when they face the challenges of aging. Your own fears will diminish as the unknown becomes more familiar. Your priorities may change as well, as you observe what lasts and what doesn't.

11. *List three ways someone like you might be able to help younger men come to terms with being Gay.*

Are there support services at the local Gay center? Is there a hotline that needs volunteers? Could you help create a support group for Gay teens at a local high school, church, or community center? Could you write about your own experiences or start a column in the newspaper? Even if you can't find opportunities to do anything directly, just living your own life openly and positively sets a powerful, helpful example.

12. *Place an object to represent your own empowered Elder on your altar.*

11 The Shaman/ Healer

THE POWER OF INTUITION

My friend Dominique tells a story of living with native people on the island of Tahiti. At times, she accompanied them on long hikes into the jungle. Even though dense foliage hid any landmarks for miles at a time, her companions always seemed to know the way home. When she asked how they did it, their response was simple: "The feet know the way." They showed her how they paused from time to time, "listened" to their feet, and then followed the footsteps that ensued.

From these same islands and elsewhere come reports of powerful healers who work in trance to improve the health of their patients, often without even touching them. Others are known to consult stones, "spirits," or their dreams for guidance that is amazingly accurate. Although many Westerners are quick to dismiss such stories as weird superstition or wishful thinking, phenomena like these are recognized in one form or another by almost every people on the planet.

How about you? How many times have you wished your feet could show you the way through the jungles of your own life? How many times have you wanted a guide to tell you which job to choose, which doctor could help you, or whether you'd prefer the Jumbo Caesar Salad or the Authentic Swedish Meatballs over at *Inga's Smorgasbord*? In fact, you already have such a guide, an inborn directional system called **intuition**. Even when your mind gets overwhelmed, intuition points the way to go any time you ask. The trick is to listen to what it tells you.

Almost every time I mention intuition, someone has a story about an instance where it helped them. Steve tells of meeting a guy several years ago who seemed just like "Mr. Right." After several dates, this man asked to move into the extra bedroom in Steve's house. Even though Steve was looking for a roommate to share expenses and this guy seemed too hot to be true, something underneath didn't feel right. Steve says, "For once I listened. Even though my mind said I was crazy, I told him, 'No.' Two months later, I found out this same guy had run up thousands on his last roommate's credit cards, then skipped out without paying a cent. Man, I'm glad I listened."

Gary tells about the conflicting advice his friends offered when he was dissatisfied with his job. One said to quit, another said to stick it out. A third said to go back to school, while a fourth advised that school would be the worst possible path this far into his career. Gary's mother told him just to work harder where he was. "Think of your retirement!" she cautioned. Gary himself could envision potential good — or potential disaster — in any choice he made. In the end, intuition came through. "I had a dream of being in school out on the West Coast. In the dream, I walked to the front of the classroom. Everyone started cheering for me. When I woke up, I felt so good, I knew I'd made my choice." Gary's intuition paid off. During the two years he spent at management school, he met a woman with similar interests. The two of them formed a consulting firm that has been quite successful.

Intuition bridges the gap between your mind and the rest of your being. It gathers information from many sources, then delivers its insights nonverbally through feelings, dreams, and flashes of understanding. Sometimes, intuition seems as mundane as following a hunch to carry your umbrella even though the sky is clear. At others, it taps the deepest sources of universal wisdom and delivers unexpected insights powerful enough to change your entire life.

Because it is subtle, intuition is easy to ignore. Our media-driven society inundates us with a daily flood of information and analysis that can easily overwhelm any sense of personal authenticity. Most people stay stuck in their minds, disconnected from deeper knowing, and therefore blown this way and that by prevailing public opinions. The only antidote is to learn to rely on your own built-in navigational system. Intuition, like radar, helps you get your bearings when your path appears cloudy or obscure. Of course, if you're used to depending solely on your logical mind, learning to trust intuitive knowing may take some time. It is, however, time well spent for it rewards you with a constant, reliable source of direction.

Thankfully, you have help. Deep inside, the Shaman/Healer stands ready to lead the way. This is an archetype that wears many names. In addition to Shaman and Healer, we could call him Priest, Diviner, Spiritual Intermediary, or a hundred other things. The terms we're using have very specific cultural connotations. Traditional shamans work in a state of altered consciousness in search of hidden, practical knowledge. To their peoples, they act as intermediaries between human and spirit. Healers access an inner blueprint, or pattern of wholeness, which they bring forth to promote health and balance. For our purposes, I use the terms generally, to denote someone who **taps inner wisdom to bring healing and transformation into the world.**

As a group, men who love men are quite adept at accessing this archetype. Indeed, the wisdom and power it gives are among our strongest Tribal gifts. At a personal level, the Shaman/Healer offers you a direct connection with inner knowing. As you discover your own way of accessing, interpreting, and using intuition, you'll gain confidence in your own judgment. You'll develop a sense of self-direction and be able to make important decisions with clarity. These are vital qualities for the spiritual Warrior. Clear direction is essential when you want to take strong, effective action. The guidance you access inside by connecting with the Shaman/Healer empowers you to act meaningfully and decisively outside in the world.

Learning to work with intuition is really a lifelong process. Every one of us accesses it in his own way. In this chapter you'll have a chance to explore several different modalities. Some will resonate for you more than others. To help you create your own path, I've included more exercises than you'll probably want to complete right away. Work with the ones that call you most strongly now. Leave the others for the time being. Give yourself the option to come back to them later when you want to deepen your experience. Also, feel free to experiment. After all, the exercises are just tools. Once you learn the ropes and get a feel for your own "radar," you'll move beyond them to receive your intuitive guidance directly and automatically.

 Tune in

Exercise

1.a. *Without even moving from where you are, take a moment to notice as much as you can about being here. What posture are you in? Where are you supported — seat? feet? back? Which parts of your body are comfortable? Which are not? What is the temperature of the air? Your skin? Can you feel your clothing? Do you notice any sounds? Any aromas? What is the texture of the light surrounding you? Does anything else here catch your attention?*

b. *When you've got a sense of yourself in relation to your surroundings, turn your attention inward. Listen to your heartbeat. Notice the rhythm of your breath. Do you notice any other internal sounds? Does any particular part of your body call you?*

c. *Next, watch the flow of thoughts. What do you notice right on the surface? What has your immediate attention? Then, listen more deeply and notice what lies beneath the surface. Are there worries about who you'll meet next Saturday? The grocery list? Don't try to change anything or take any action*

*right now. Your mind will do whatever it does. Just notice. Ask silently, "Are
there any other thoughts that would be helpful to notice right now?".
Then, listen.*

d.   *Do the same thing with your feelings. What are the big ones right on the
surface? Are they located somewhere specific in your body? What about
beneath the surface? Any back-burner anxiety? Excitement? Fear? Sadness?
Again, whatever you notice, just breathe and observe. Ask your body, "Is
there any other feeling that is important at this time?". Take a quiet
moment to pay attention.*

Tuning-in is about gathering information. Though it may take only a few seconds,
what you sense is vitally important. In any given moment, your body receives and
processes thousands of bits of information. Of necessity, it screens out the vast
majority, bringing to consciousness only the pieces that are related to survival — or
that you ask for directly. This subliminal river is always present and available. When you
take the time to consult it, it offers a rich source of intuitive guidance.

Tap in! Pay attention to the feelings, hunches, "synchronicities", and the faint
visions around the edges of your mind. With time, you'll get more proficient. What
seems almost impossibly subtle at first will grow stronger and clearer very quickly.
In the process, you'll learn to make sense of what you find and to distinguish real
intuition from speculation or daydreaming. With practice, tuning-in will become
natural. You'll get used to being in touch and your understanding of almost any
situation will be richer.

PERMEABLE BOUNDARIES

When you practice tuning-in, you bring to awareness the information gathered by
your five senses. And while sensory input is very important, it is still only a small part
of your total intuitive knowing. Let's go a step deeper by examining the realm of
energetics.

Every living being has a subtle body composed of energy that flows within and
around each cell. Although you can't usually see it, your energy body is as much a
part of you as your physical anatomy. Scholars in age-old systems of healing,
including Chinese and Ayurvedic (Indian) medicine, have described energetic
anatomy in great detail. These doctors teach that the condition of your energy body
is vital to health. If your energy flows strongly and in balance, you stay healthy. If it
is blocked or out of balance, problems develop. A complete study of energetic
healing would be fascinating and valuable, but it's far beyond the scope of our
exploration here. For, now let's just look at it generally, to see the extent to which
energy affects your health and colors your interactions with other people.

Your body senses energy intuitively. Surely, you've had the experience of reacting strongly to someone you meet for the very first time. Even though you may know nothing at all about this person, you intuitively feel a strong attraction or repulsion. Sensing energies, your body knows something your mind doesn't. Likewise, consider how many times you've been driving and noticed someone attractive in the next car — only to have him turn to look at you just as if he "felt" your gaze?

Energetic connections are tangible and real. You can learn to feel them consciously quite easily. All it takes is to pay attention. The next exercises will give you some practice. Do at least the first part and then as much of the rest as you'd like.

➤ Feel energy

Exercise

2.a. *Rub your hands together lightly. When they feel warm, hold them a few inches apart, palms facing each other. Be sure to keep your shoulders and arms relaxed. Take a few easy breaths and notice what you feel with your hands. Everyone senses energy differently. You may notice a slight tingling, or warmth, or coolness, or nothing at all. Stay relaxed and observe.*

Try moving your hands, slowly and gently, farther apart and closer together. Do you notice any changes? Is there any resistance to the movement? Some people report that their hands feel like magnets, gently attracting or repelling each other. Others say the warmth or tingling increases or decreases as they move.

What you're sensing is very subtle. You may need some time to get used to it. If you're not feeling anything at all, relax and be patient. Usually, a little practice is all it takes. Be sure your body is relaxed, that you're breathing gently, and that your hands are fairly close together. In a short time, you'll probably find that this is simple and easy.

b. *Once you get used to feeling energy with your hands, deepen your experience by trying to describe it. Though none of the following terms may be accurate literally, they will help you hone your energy-sensing skill. As you feel the energy of a particular object, ask yourself the following questions:*

- *If I could see the energy, what color would it be?*
- *What "texture" does it have?*
- *Is it hot, cool, warm, cold?*
- *Is it static? Does it pulse?*
- *Does it seem to move in a certain direction?*
- *What else do I notice about this energy?*

c. *Experiment with feeling the energy of various things around you. One of the easiest ways to begin is with a tree. Rub your hands together, then bring your palms slowly closer to the trunk. You'll probably feel greater "density" a few inches from the bark. Hold your hands there and go through the questions from part b. Then, bring your hands all the way to the trunk and hold them there lightly. Notice any changes in your sensations as you do so.*

d. *Try the same procedure with other things,*
- *a stone or rock*
- *a table, chair, or other piece of furniture*
- *houseplants*
- *an apple, banana, or other type of food*
- *a cat, dog, or other small animal*
- *whatever else calls you*

If this is entirely new to you, you may be surprised at what you find. Try to keep your mind from judging or attempting to explain away what you're feeling. Record your impressions and let your experiences speak for themselves.

Once you recognize that every person and object has an energetic body, the implications are far-reaching. Think about how the following statements apply to your own experience.

First, **we are all interconnected**. Because your energy extends beyond the limits of your skin, you are continually in touch with everyone and everything around you. Your environment affects you. The people around you affect you, and you affect them, whether you know them casually, intimately, or not at all. Of course, when you interact intimately and/or sexually with someone, the energy exchange is much greater.

Second, **emotions affect your energy**. We recognize this instinctively through our language, when we speak of emotions in energetic terms like "red-hot anger" or "feeling blue." Blocked emotions can lead to energetic imbalances that directly affect your health.

Not only do emotions affect your own energy, they also color the energy you share with others. My friend James remarked that he never got through a meeting with his ex-boss without a fight. Even when he had the best intentions, things almost always degenerated. After looking deeply at his own motives, James realized that he was really angry about having to work at all. No matter how nicely he phrased his thoughts, his boss responded to the underlying anger. Once James resolved the issue (by realizing that working was his own choice, not something forced on him), his energy shifted. He did change jobs soon after, but the move was graceful and without a fight.

Energetic sharing works two ways. Just as your energy touches others, you're also affected quite strongly by your energetic environment. Have you ever noticed feeling exhausted after visiting a medical office, hospital, courtroom, or other place where people tend to be stressed out? Even if you're not directly involved, you can pick up the distress, fear, and anxiety of the people around you. This can be quite dramatic if you spend a lot of time with people in crisis. I noticed it personally when I first started working as a massage therapist. Because I was so intent on helping my clients feel better, and also had relatively little understanding of keeping myself clear, I picked up energy all the time. Believe me, it was not subtle. I knew something was going on when I'd spend an hour relieving someone's stiff neck and then develop an identical stiffness two hours later in my own. I'd work the pain out of someone's right knee, then be stuck in a chair that night with a pain in my own right — not left — knee. Obviously, I had to learn to ground and clear myself in order to continue working.

The third implication relates to **intention**. Whenever you touch someone else, your intention directly colors the energy you share. If you're with a friend who is ill, a simple touch can communicate all the concern, support, and love you want to share, often better than words. If you spend time with someone with whom you have an unresolved issue, notice how that energy permeates your exchange, no matter what you say or do. If you interact sexually with someone, the underlying intentions directly influence the quality of your sharing. The next set of exercises will help you get a stronger feel for how energy colors your interactions with other people and your environment. Again, complete the first one, and then whichever of the others call you.

Connections

Exercise

3.   *Clear your energy body*

Whenever you are with someone, you connect energetically. Learning to stay clear helps you maintain a stronger connection with your intuition. The act of clearing your energy field doesn't mean that other people's energy is bad. It just means that the energy you pick up isn't your own and can take you off center.

The following visualization is very powerful. At first, set aside time to explore it quietly and alone. Later, you'll be able to do it quickly and silently in any place or situation.

a.   *Imagine standing on the Earth. As you breathe, feel giant roots, like those of a redwood, sink from the base of your spine through your feet deep into the Earth. From the top of your head, feel a bright, white light that flows downward, easily and gently, washing through you like a stream of crystal clear water. Let the light pick up any negativity, blockages, or concerns you might have and wash them into the Earth.*

Let this cleansing river flow through you, warm and easy. If there is any person or situation around which you feel special concern, imagine the light flowing there as well, dissolving connections and washing you totally clean. You'll begin to feel lighter and softer, as if all the muddy spots inside you were being scoured away. Know that everything you release into the Earth is transformed, like compost, and its energy released in a form that brings forth new life.

b.   *When you feel clean and bright, imagine a deep green light that flows upward from the Earth, supporting, healing, and reinvigorating your body. Feel strong life force pulse upward like a fountain through your feet, your legs, your spine, and your whole body. Let it flow up and out through your head and hands. Feel as if you were sprouting branches far into the sky, branches that support you and help make you strong and light.*

c.   *As the flow of green light continues to strengthen and vitalize, imagine another light, this one deep violet, that flows outward from the center of your being. Feel this violet light bathe and surround you until it creates a strong, protective ball.*

As you continue to breathe, feel all three lights flow strongly. The white washes downward from your crown through your roots into Earth. The green pulses upward from Earth through your branches into Sky. The violet glows outward to surround you in protection. Know that these lights are with you. Then, when you are ready, return to normal awareness.

The energy cleansing visualization can help you in almost any situation. As you practice, you'll begin to feel actual physical changes that indicate you're being successful. You can also use this visualization any time you're entering a stressful situation. For example, if you're going to visit someone in the hospital, imagine your roots and branches bringing energy from below and above. You'll stay clearer and stronger than if you depend only on the energy of the hospital environment.

If your mind is very literal, this may take a bit of faith. Understand that your body knows very well how to stay clear and grounded. With a visualization, you use symbols to communicate your intention. Try it with an open mind. Once you know that visualization works, your mind will probably need less of an explanation.

4.   **Check out your surroundings**

To discover just how much they affect you, try an experiment. Take yourself to two or three of the following environments (or choose your own):

- a crowded bar or party, with lots of lights, sound, music, smoke, and so forth
- somewhere quiet and outdoors — a beach, park, woods, or just a neighborhood with lots of old trees
- an urban street, full of people, traffic, and concrete
- a shopping mall
- a hospital, doctor's, or dentist's waiting room

In each environment you choose, do the tune-in exercise. What is your level of comfort here? How does your body feel? What are your thoughts and feelings? How open or relaxed are you? How connected do you feel with yourself?

Without judging, compare your responses from place to place. Though there are appropriate times to visit each of these places, knowing how their energy interacts with your own will help you make conscious choices to take care of yourself.

5.   **Share energy**

For the next three exercises, you'll need a partner. Find someone who is open and willing to experiment, since having to counter someone else's skepticism will get in your way.

a.   *Rub your hands together, until they feel warm and sensitive. Then, slowly bring them toward your partner's chest, just as you did with the tree. What do you notice? Where do you begin to feel your partner's energy body? What does it feel like? Can you characterize it (color, texture, etc.)? Can s/he feel your hands as they get closer? Bring your hands forward until they rest lightly on your partner's clothing. What sensations do you notice?*

b.   *With your partner sitting or lying comfortably, move your hands lightly and slowly over various parts of his/her body. Notice any variations in your sensations from one place to another. Can you quantify these? Does the energy feel stronger or weaker, outgoing or ingoing, warmer or cooler, moving or still? What else do you notice from place to place? Does your partner feel anything from your hands?*

Scanning this way is an important component of energetic healing. For now, what you're feeling is informational only. Don't try to interpret or change anything. While you're working, be very conscious of your intent. The fact that you're touching this person's energetic body with honor and respect is very healing. Often, you'll feel the energy flow get smoother as you continue to scan. Your partner may feel very relaxed. As you explore, be sure to remember your own roots, follow your breath, and just observe.

c.　*Gently massage your partner's hand with both of your own. Use a little oil or lotion if you like. Don't worry about technique. Trust your hands to know what feels good — and ask your partner to tell you if something doesn't.*

Continue the massage as you try a little experiment. Tell your partner that you're going to start thinking of an emotion, but don't say what it is. Then, doing your very best not to change what your hands are doing, think about something that makes you very angry, or sad, or happy, or joyful, or horny, or bored. So your expressions don't give you away, turn so that your partner doesn't see your face. Get as much into the feelings as possible, but don't change the movements of your hands. Switch hands from time to time if you like.

Take a few minutes with each emotion, choosing them in whatever order suits you. Ask your partner what s/he notices, if anything, about the quality of the massage. Do feelings come up? What do you notice? How do you feel? What does this experiment show you about intention?

You may sense a great deal right away, or you may feel very little. Don't push yourself. Practice. Try the same thing in a few weeks and see what has changed.

Be sure to finish with a few minutes of very intentional soothing and easing of your partner's hands, so that everything feels good when you stop. Wash your own hands when you finish.

CONSCIOUS DREAMING

If you want to know yourself, know your dreams. The conscious mind, self-important as it can be, is no more than the slender beam of a flashlight lighting up one small corner of your totality. Most of the action takes place below the surface. Your subconscious mind stores emotions, processes experiences, and sifts the day-to-day content of your life for meaning. Usually, all you catch are glimpses of these processes, bits of insight and intuition that seem to come mysteriously out of nowhere. One way to create a more direct link to this inner awareness is to begin to work with your dreams.

Like other ways of accessing intuition, dreamwork is a long-term process that will come in and out of focus over the course of years. Each section of this discussion represents a different level of interaction. Only work with the sections that relate to where you are in your own exploration. If you don't remember your dreams at all, work with the first part. If you'd like to interpret what you do remember, go a step further. To take a more active role, complete the sections on induction and active imagination.

Dream recall

To work with dreams, you have to remember them in the first place. Everyone has dreams, but not everyone is used to recalling them in detail. Dreams are ephemeral. Like dew, their lives are short once the day begins. Unless you take direct steps to preserve them, the images fade quickly, making way for the concerns of the day.

To remember your dreams, write them down. Put a pen, notebook, and flashlight in easy reach of your bed. As soon as you wake up, jot down whatever dreams you remember. Even if you only recall a few images, write whatever you have. Often, the very act of writing jogs your memory and other bits come through with the flow.

Get the dreams into your notebook as quickly and accurately as you can. Don't be concerned about analyzing or understanding them. That comes later. For now, you're just gathering raw material. As with any endeavor, dream recall improves with practice. The more you write your dreams, the more you'll remember. The more you remember, the more your subconscious will use this channel to communicate with you.

Dream interpretation

Once you save your dreams, how do you decipher their meaning? Dreams speak in symbols and often on several levels at once. What you see first is rarely the whole message. While many books and traditions deal with dream interpretation — some even to the point of offering extensive dictionaries of the "true" meanings of various symbols — in the end, your exploration will be highly personal. Though books may be helpful, what they tell you varies greatly from one to the next. Ultimately, your dreams are the product of your own subconscious. As you pay attention, you'll develop a working vocabulary of your own dream symbols and begin an inner dialog that shifts and deepens with time. In the final analysis, your dreams mean what they mean to **you**.

Let's look at a few techniques to help your interpretations. First, ask direct questions immediately after you write down your dream. I like to set up a written interview with an imaginary part of my subconscious I call, "Dream Guides." Here's how it works.

Let's say you wrote down the following dream:

"I'm in my living room and hear the doorbell. Three people are there, people I know but whose names I can't remember. They say I invited them for a visit. They sit on the sofa while I make coffee in the kitchen, but they get angry when I give it to them. In desperation, I find some milk in the fridge and serve that to them with cookies. Immediately they turn into children I knew in kindergarten, and start playing dress-up and charades."

Your interview might go something like this....

Question:	Dear Dream Guides, Who are these people?
Response:	Old friends you forgot about.
Question:	Actual people?
Response:	Remember those promises you made to yourself in college, about being creative?
Question:	When I said I'd be a dancer whatever else happened, even if I couldn't make money?
Response:	Yes.
Question:	What do they want?
Response:	To visit.
Question:	What does coffee mean?
Response:	Adult conversation. See, it doesn't work. You have to treat them like children.
Question:	What are they telling me to do?
Response:	Play. Pay attention to yourself and your old dreams.

This exercise can help you get beneath the surface of a dream to understand some of its deeper meanings. Remember, though, that dreams can be ambiguous. Their content comes from many sources, some as meaningless as a rehash of the day's events or images from a movie you watched and some as profound as intuitive guidance, prediction of events, soul-level healing, or collective mythology. The rub is that you never know exactly which level you're dealing with.

In dreams, things are rarely as they appear. Your subconscious distorts, exaggerates, and alters imagery shamelessly. For example, a minor irritation with a co-worker during the day might come back as bloody murder the next night. A small attraction toward one person might lead to steamy dream sex with someone else. Steamy sex might mean something entirely different, like it's time to fertilize the garden or you're bored with life and need some action in your dreams. Marriage might mean a death, a careening truck might be telling you something about your body, and a church service could mean peace, quiet, or war. Be patient. With time, you'll understand more and more of your own symbology and your dreams will become an active part of your intuitive guidance.

Sometimes, it is helpful to regard every character in a dream, even people you recognize from waking life, as symbols for parts of yourself. Viewed in this light, dreams are an active monitor of your own inner dynamics. For example, I often dream of my sister or my high school girlfriend. Usually, when these women come up, they bring the message that it's time to pay attention to my own feminine side.

Pay attention to the feelings in dreams. They can be an important clue to deeper meanings. Pay attention also to the actual words you use to record them. Often, dreams speak in puns — a dream in which you buy a bag of "flour" might tell you it's time to cheer yourself up with a bouquet of daisies. Two slices of stale "bread" in the fridge might reflect your hidden fears about money. Be creative. How "accurate" your interpretations are is really measured in terms of how useful they are to you.

Dream induction

With a little practice, you can ask your dreams for guidance on specific issues. This technique, called **dream induction,** focuses the creative power of your own imagination. Before you go to sleep, spend some time thinking about the issue in question. Picture yourself in the situation. Imagine as many specific details as you can and phrase your questions clearly. Stay with the images until you fall asleep, then record whatever dreams you remember as soon as you wake up. Often, your dreams will give you insight on the questions you asked. If not, keep paying attention. Your answers may come at a later time or in a different way. Whatever you ask, your subconscious always addresses the issues that are really on your mind.

Speaking of induction, watch the extent to which your activities immediately before going to sleep affect your dreams. You can easily induce specific types of dreams without intending to. Do you fall asleep watching the news or reading the paper? Do you collapse from serious work right into bed? I don't recommend either, since they'll both tend to make you tense all night. Instead, try ending your day with a quiet walk around the block, a bit of stretching, or another activity that is relaxed and non-mental. Your dreams will reflect your relaxation by following channels that are much more useful and pleasant.

Active imagination

The place between waking and sleep is a deeply creative zone of consciousness. Dreams give you a way to work with this place, a bridge to your own creativity that can yield tangible, practical results. The process of **active imagination** uses dream images as the raw material for creative visualization. By consciously manipulating the symbols, you can often gain powerful resolution to issues that have been bothering you. Let's see how it works.

Return to the dream we discussed above. To work with it actively, close your eyes and imagine yourself back in the dream. Once there, ask your guidance what each character or major object represents. This is important. If some of the dream characters are people you know in waking life, work with them only as symbols for parts of yourself. Since we've established the major characters in this dream, let's move on to the next step.

Figure out the main dynamic. In this case, an old dream of being a dancer has come back to demand your attention. You try to talk to it as an adult, mentally buying it off, which doesn't work. When you offer milk, a fairly universal symbol for nurturing, the characters turn into children who begin playing. Your imagination process might go like this ...

> You ask the children if you can play with them. They say yes, but one of them says he thinks you might not be able to do it right. So you ask him to show you how.

> Immediately, they all start acting out a scene. One of them gets very stiff, like an adult, and the others run around screaming and laughing. With this setup, you imagine yourself coming into their play, taking the "adult" and spinning him around in a circle until all four of you fall on the floor laughing. Then, the children give you a costume and you all dance together.

You'll probably feel good after this process. You can do the same thing with any dream. If there are scary characters, ask them what they represent. If there are monsters, ask them what they want. Usually, these figures are parts of yourself that have become frightening in an attempt to get your attention. Once you listen to them, you'll be surprised at how much they tell you about yourself and your inner feelings.

At times, active imagination can be the start of an ongoing dialog. You might have further dreams on the same subject. You might find that your behavior shifts in some part of your life. In the case above, having imagined yourself being less serious might make it easier to enroll in a continuing education dance class or take yourself more lightly in other areas.

Dreamwork is an open-ended, ongoing exploration. It may extend from childhood to old age, getting richer all the time. If you let them, your dreams will become a deeply meaningful part of your daily experience. You'll come to value them as friends, guides, and partners on your path.

Conscious dreaming

Exercise

6. Pick whichever of the following exercises represent the level of dreamwork you feel comfortable exploring at present.

a.   Claim your dreams as the valuable gift and tool that they are. Get yourself a dream notebook and begin to record whatever you remember. Try working with the ones that seem most complete, or those most charged with feeling or energy.

b.   What dreams can you remember from earlier in your life? Were there any recurring nightmares in your childhood? Any images that you can remember particularly strongly? Are you aware of recurring themes or situations in your dreams? Have you ever had any that felt predictive, or that were helpful in showing you something going on that had been hidden?

c.   Experiment with interpretation by setting up the dream guide dialog and active imagination. Pick dreams that grab your interest or that feel especially strong. Write out your tentative conclusions and see what they might be telling you. If you like, start to compile your own dictionary of personal dream symbology.

d.   Experiment with dream induction. Think of an issue that concerns you a lot. Before you sleep, ask for guidance and information on that issue. Be as specific as you can, taking yourself into the situation as you drift off. Record any dreams you have as soon as you wake. If you can't remember any in the morning, set the alarm for some time during the night, or drink a lot of water so your bladder wakes you up. Usually, your intention to remember will get the process rolling on its own.

e.   Pick a dream that seems puzzling or particularly interesting. Experiment with active imagination by going into the dream and taking it in a direction that feels positive and empowering. Let your intuition guide you, write down your experiences, and see where they take you.

f.   If you have someone else in your life who is interested in dreams, try to dream about the same subject. Decide what you'll focus on, set up an induction process and follow it for a period of time. When you check back in, compare notes on the dreams you had. You may be surprised at the similarities and parallels. This is a good introduction to the work you'll explore later with the "Lodge of Dreams" visualization in Chapter 16.

Ask the Right Questions

Through intuition, you access many, varied sources of inner guidance. You've already explored some of them, including body awareness, the wisdom of your Elder, and the spontaneous feelings of your Magic Boy. Beyond these. a broad range of paths, beliefs, and traditions can help you. Some men access intuition by connecting with the world's great teachers — Buddha, Mohammed, Jesus, and others. Some turn to ancestors, to angels, the "Higher Self," the Earth, or the conscious forces of the natural world. Whatever your path, whether you follow a specific tradition or none at all, the Shaman/Healer will help.

A large part of his job is to give direction. At any given moment, you have access to a vast pool of potentially interesting sensations and information. Though all of it might be helpful, some pieces are more pertinent to a given situation than others. The Shaman/Healer helps bring these pieces to awareness by guiding your subconscious search. He does this by helping you to pose appropriate questions. Any time you look for an answer, whether from your inner Shaman/Healer or the local librarian, you can only get what you ask for. If you're not getting the answers you want in life, start asking different questions. Let's see how it works.

Inherent in any question is a set of presuppositions. These represent attitudes or beliefs implicit in the way you state the question. See if you can determine the presuppositions in the following:

> *"Why don't people like me?"*
>
> *"Why can't I find happiness?"*
>
> *"Why can't I attract a lover?"*

Did you find them? Each of the questions implies that something is wrong with the person asking it. Perhaps it's easier to see if we rephrase them.

> *"People don't like me. Why?"*
>
> *"I can't find happiness. Why?"*
>
> *"I can't attract a lover. Why?"*

Every statement, even when posed as a question, is actually an affirmation. Positive or negative, affirmations seek fulfillment. The questions we just looked at actually reinforce the problems they were intended to solve. In response to them, your intuition will give you lists of data that support the negative statements. It will say that people don't like you because your skin is bad, you're too self-centered, or you don't go to the right gym. You'll never be happy because you don't remember jokes or can't dance a two-step. You can't find a lover because you have bad breath. The lists could go on and on and not once would you get the answers you really want.

To change your answers and the results they create, change the questions. Look at the list again. How might you reframe these questions so that they work for you instead of against you? Try asking them this way:

"How can I enjoy people and have them like me?"

"What can I do to create good relationships?"

"What can I explore in order to be happy?"

Look at the presuppositions in these questions. Each one is positive. You **can** enjoy people. They **can** like you. You **can** create good relationships and you **can** be happy. Asking this way affirms your positive qualities and opens the intuitive door to constructive answers. Changing the way you look at the issues in your life is a giant step toward empowering yourself to heal them.

➤ Questions

Exercise

7.a   *Just for practice, write five or ten questions you have right now about your life. For each one, write out the statements inherent in the question. For example, "Why am I sick?" contains the statement, "I am sick."*

To set the stage for the answers you really want, be sure each question is in the most affirmative form possible. The question we just asked could become, "What can I do to feel better" or, "How can I best support my health?""

b.   *Review the goals you outlined in Chapter 2 (page 30). Rewrite as many as you can into positive, empowering questions. Does your perspective shift when you do this? Do you feel any differently about your goals now?*

PUT IT ALL TOGETHER

Because an effective Warrior needs strong guidance, your work with the Shaman/Healer provides a strong foundation for making positive changes in your life. To get where you want, practice working with intuition as often as you can. At first, you may need to set aside a chunk of time for visualization and meditation. After a while, though, you'll learn to call the Shaman/Healer quickly and easily. You can still use the longer sessions to work in greater depth, but for most everyday situations you'll find short-cuts. If you find that you're stuck, remind yourself of the following three points.

First, **intuition works best when your mind is quiet**. If you have a strong expectation or opinion about what your intuition **should** say, you'll probably overrule the quieter voice inside. "Of course I can have the Extra-hot Thai Chicken, it looks so good." If your mind is overpowering your intuition, you'll usually know it — first by the feeling of unease or bravado with which you make the choice and then by regrets next morning. "Why didn't I listen to myself? Ow, ow, ow. I should've had the Veggie Deluxe."

Second, **intuition works on its own time schedule**. While some answers come right away, others take a bit longer. Pushing the process only gets in the way. If you ask, "Is this the guy for me?" and nothing comes, continue to pay attention. It may be too soon for an answer. You may need time to reflect, gather more information, or get quiet enough to hear. The insight you're seeking may pop into your mind when you're driving, daydreaming, or vacuuming the living room. It may come in your dreams the next night or from somewhere entirely unexpected. Even though staying patient can seem like the hardest thing in the world, it helps.

Third, **ask appropriate questions**. Be absolutely sure you ask for what you want, because you will get what you ask for. Now, keep these ideas in mind as you learn to embody your own expression of the Shaman/Healer.

Embody the Shaman/Healer

Exercise

8.   For the following visualization, set aside 10 to 15 minutes in which you won't be disturbed. Work either with silence, quiet music, or repetitive drumming that you play quietly in the background.

Before you begin, think of one question you'd like to ask your intuition. Make it as tangible as possible, and also state it as positively as you can.

a.   When you're ready, close your eyes and follow your breath into your sacred Council Space. Feel yourself rooted here and call forth the members of your Inner Council. When you feel their protection around you, along with that of the Tribe of Men Who Love Men, ask to meet your inner Shaman/Healer.

First, look at him. Who do you see? Is he familiar to you? What does he wear? How does he carry himself? When you feel that he's fully present, ask the Shaman/Healer to help you get in touch with your intuition. When he tells you he's ready, prepare for a short journey.

b.   Follow your Shaman/Healer as he guides you to the place where he consults with intuition. Watch what happens. Perhaps he leads you through a tunnel into a dark cave. Maybe he leads you along a path to the top of a mountain or even through the air to another place. As your guide, he will lead you on a good path. Know that you are safe with him as you follow wherever he leads.

When you reach your destination, watch as he shows you what he does to call forth answers. Perhaps he sits by a shallow pool of water, reading *answers in the reflections. Perhaps he reads the starry sky or looks deep into a stone or crystal. Maybe he consults a special book, a plant, an animal, angel, or teacher. Watch as he shows you.*

c. *When you've seen how to ask, repeat the same actions yourself. In the appropriate manner, state your question and ask for clear guidance. Then, wait quietly for the answer. Since it may come in any number of ways, be open to whatever happens. Watch for feelings or sensations in your body. Listen for words in your mind. Watch for images. See if you go on another journey, or if hints come in any other way. Sometimes, your answer will come to you very quickly and clearly. Other times, it will take a little interpretation. Be patient.*

If you receive a clear answer right away, remember it. If what you receive isn't clear, ask for clarification. If nothing seems to come at all yet, don't worry. Your response will come in its own time. The fact that you've posed the question here will help you get clear on the answer whenever and however it comes.

d. *When you're ready, follow the Shaman/Healer back to your Inner Council circle. Thank him for his help. Remember that you can call him at any time and then let him return to his place in your Inner Council. Gently release him and the Council, and follow your breath back to normal awareness. When you're ready, record your impressions in your notebook.*

9. If you'd like, guide yourself through a movement meditation in which you embody the Shaman Healer as you've learned to do with the other archetypes on your journey.

a. *Create your sacred space and play appropriate music. Call on your Inner Council and the protection of the Tribe. Then, ask your Shaman/Healer to come into your body. Invite him to move your face and limbs. Let your body show you through its movements how it feels to embody this archetype. Feel his confidence and patience. Feel the power he receives from listening deep within himself.*

b. *Ask him to show you, through movement, the answer to a question that has been on your mind. Ask to see the situation first, as you move, and then any insights he has to share with you about it. Take the time you need to experiment. Be sure to let your body and not your mind direct the movement.*

c. *When you feel complete but before you return to normal awareness, ask your Shaman/Healer for a gesture that you can use to call on him in any situation. Your body will show you. Whatever comes, remember it. Later, when you want to call on him, you can do so by starting the process with this same gesture.*

d. *Thank the Shaman/Healer for his help, then allow him to return to his place in your Inner Council. Release the Council and the Tribe, then follow your breath back to normal awareness. Ground any extra energy into the Earth and record your impressions in your journal.*

10. *Place an object on your altar to remind you of the transformative power of the Shaman/Healer in you.*

11. Optional Exercises.

Once you've learned to call on your Shaman/Healer, you can work with him in many different ways. The following exercises will give you further practice in calling on his guidance.

As usual, keep an open mind. Your rational mind, wanting everything to be neat and literal — i.e. under its control — may try to rebel. "This is dumb. Rocks can't talk!" In its way, your mind is right. At the same time, it's not. Consciousness manifests in many ways. Suspend your rationality for the time being and approach these exercises as a way to attune with non-linear parts of your own awareness. When you do, you'll teach your mind something new and wonderful.

a. **Consultation**

Think of a series of questions. Take each one to the place the Shaman/Healer showed you in Exercise 8 and follow the process he demonstrated to seek answers. Do it either as a visualization or as a movement meditation. Watch what comes up.

b. **Medicine walk**

To use a "medicine walk" as a way to receive guidance on a particular issue, go to a natural place like a park, beach, or woods. When you arrive, call upon the wisdom of your inner guidance and the wisdom of the Nature realm.

Formulate your question as clearly as possible, then ask the Shaman/Healer to guide your steps as you take a walk or hike. Follow the turns your feet show you and observe where they lead. Pay attention to anything unusual. Listen to the water, the sound of wind in trees, the song of birds. Watch the animals around you. Listen with your whole being. Even if the answers don't come in words, you may be surprised at how much clarity you have by the end of your walk.

Before you leave, be sure to thank everyone who helped you — including your own guidance, as well as birds, trees, sky, and whatever else you noticed.

c. Natural guides

As a further experiment, meditate with a stone, flower, or tree. This is a technique used by people in many cultures. If you let it, it will work well for you, too.

With a question in mind, look for a natural object that calls you. Approach the object you've chosen with respect, as if it were alive and conscious. Touch it, or hold it your hand as you focus your intention with the following short meditation.

Close your eyes. Follow your breath for a few moments and let yourself grow calm. Imagine yourself growing as quiet as the object in your hand. Turn your eyes inward and notice what part of your body resonates most fully with this object. Surely some part of you feels just a little quieter, a bit more still. Imagine yourself looking at the object and see what colors are inside it. Listen for the sound or tone it makes.

Focusing on your question, ask the awareness associated with your object if it has anything to share with you. If it could talk, what words would it use? Notice any images or feelings that come to you. Let it clarify your own intuition as you become aware of the answers.

When you've finished, thank the guidance for coming through and put the object back where you found it. Jot down in your notebook any impressions you received.

In time, you'll get more adept at making sense of this type of input. If you like the process, try it with a different object and see if you notice any differences. You could adapt this same exercise to work with a mountain, the ocean, a star, or the consciousness of Nature in general. Let your own creativity guide you.

d. Health questions

Your inner Shaman/Healer is also a powerful ally around health issues. If you ask inside, your body will tell you the best way to support your health at any time.

To focus on health issues, formulate your questions carefully. "How can I support myself best in the present situation?"

"Which doctor could help me the most here?" "Do I feel good with this treatment?" Use the techniques you've already learned to tune in to your own guidance. What does your body tell you? What images or sensations come?

A word of caution. If you are dealing with a serious medical condition, do **not use this process in place of a doctor.** In the face of health challenges, it is often difficult to know whether or not your guidance is clear. Always listen to the opinion of your health care professional.

At the same time, understand that medical opinions are often just that — opinions. Check what you're told against your own intuition. If something doesn't feel right to you, ask questions. Let your mind and your intuition work together. Take responsibility. Do some homework. Read up on the subject. Get a second opinion, or a third. Do whatever you need until you feel good with the course of treatment you're following.

12 The Warrior

CREATE YOUR OWN LIFE

With all the nastier misconceptions pushed on us in the name of religion, the story of Creation seems pretty innocuous. You know the standard version — God created the world in six days, finished, and then rested on the seventh. As stories go, this one doesn't seem all that bad. It's even sort of sweet, really. Very few of us take it literally. Yet, the story has a couple of major flaws. First, it makes Creation a done deal, a single event somewhere in the past. And second, it gives someone else — in this case, God — all the responsibility.

Creation is a process, not an event. It is an ongoing part of being alive and every single person is involved. Even as you read these words, **you** are creating the world, along with the rest of us, through your choices, attitudes, and actions. You create **your** world each time you choose to go left instead of right, speak your truth instead of staying silent, or have the ham salad instead of the chicken. You create your world by saying "Yes" to that job you wanted at the bookstore, "No" to the salesman hawking life insurance, "I'm willing" or "I'm too scared" to the man who's offering you love. Whether or not you hold a supreme being as its ultimate source, the power to create rests squarely in your own two hands. You were born to use it.

To create the life you want, you have to learn to act with integrity in the world. Up to this point, the focus of your empowerment journey has been almost entirely internal. Every exercise has been designed to help you get clear and aligned within yourself. Now, you've reached the point of bringing it all together. You're ready to turn your focus outward and begin taking steps to make your dreams real. Your ally in this part of your process is the Warrior.

In our society, the Warrior is easily the most misunderstood of all the archetypes. For most of us, the word probably conjures up images of green-clad Rambos or ruthless, gun-slinging cowboys. In truth, these images say more about the skewed values of our society than about the real energy of the Warrior.

In essence, warriorship is a highly evolved state. At the level of day to day activity, it empowers you to act in alignment with your convictions. When you call on him, the Warrior helps you take specific, directed steps toward realizing the goals that are important to you. His strength and integrity support your making immediate, powerful changes in the way you interact with other people and the world.

In its fullest definition, though, warriorship goes much further. The Warrior is a spiritual master who acts from a place of balance, conviction, and alignment. His training is long and its focus is internal rather than external, because an effective Warrior understands that his greatest battles are most often within himself. His actions in the world are the result of crystal clear intention combined with patience, restraint, and a strong vision of his desired results. Ideally, warriorship becomes a way of living every moment in alignment with the highest spiritual principles.

As an ideal, the Warrior is universal. Warrior trainees in diversely different societies — from the Japanese Samurai to the Lakota warrior clans — aspired to ideals that are remarkably similar. How, though, does he look in **your** life? I can hear minds clicking. Imagine, a Gay Warrior! Sounds like the ultimate fantasy, doesn't it, or the perfect plot for a porn flick. Can't you just see yourself, working one more night at that sleazy restaurant, balancing four dirty plates in your left hand, two coffee pots in your right, and listening to another irate customer who thinks his two-bit tip makes him your master. Suddenly, the front door smashes open and a lusty knight in torn leather — who just happens to look a lot like that new guy at the gym — scoops you up with muscular arms onto the back of his enormous Clydesdale, sending lettuce, coffee, and three or four customers flying. Without a backward glance, he carries you off to the mountains for a whole weekend of delicious pleasure. Gay Warrior, indeed!

I won't destroy your fantasies, but the real Gay Warrior looks even better. Look in a mirror. Look at the men around you. The Warrior is there, every day. His actions don't need to be bigger than life. He's there whenever you stand up for yourself or take a step toward one of your goals. You felt the Warrior the first time you framed the words "I'm Gay" or "I love you" to another man. You know him now, when you finally register for that voice class you've wanted to take for years, and later, when you get up the courage to audition for the local men's chorus. He helps you pick up the phone and call that guy you met last Wednesday, even though you're scared to death he'll say "No." The Warrior's there again, helping you stand tall when you ask for a promotion or call to interview for a better job. Whatever your goals, the Warrior helps you bring them into your life.

In the Gay community, the Warrior is alive and well. You hear him in the voices of men who chant and shout at Gay Pride marches. You see him in the faces of those who take a stand against prejudice in the military. He's there in the letter you write to a Congressman protesting funding cuts for social services. You know him in each man who gives his time to raise money in the annual AIDS walk or donates two hours a week to feed those who are ill. The Gay Warrior has fought hard to bring us this far. He offers the power to get us wherever we want to go.

The focus of this chapter is to bring him fully into your life.

Changes

Exercise

1. Outline your goals

    The Warrior is most effective when you give him a focus. His strength is best used in service to goals that help you achieve personal satisfaction and fulfillment. As you prepare to call him, think for a moment about where you could use his help. What part of your life isn't working as well as you'd like? Where do you feel the greatest constraint, limitation, pain, or fear? What are the issues that really stump you, the ones that come up when you say, "My life would be great except for ..."?

    a. *Make a list of five to ten changes you'd like to make in your life. These could be big, long-term goals or short-term concerns that you want to resolve quickly. You could use the goals you outlined in Chapter 2 or pick others that seem more pertinent right now. List goals that really matter to you.*

    b. *Notice the feelings these goals bring up. Do they make you feel hopeful? sad? defeated? excited? anxious? frustrated? judgmental? Whatever you notice, don't try to change it. Just observe. Any response is valid.*

    c. *When you complete your list, prioritize. Which issue would you like to clear up first? Does one seem to underlie the others or carry a greater emotional charge than the rest? Pick one issue to focus on for the rest of this chapter. Once you've learned the principles, you'll go back and apply them to the other goals on your list.*

Now get more specific. Your Warrior gives you only what you ask for. The clarity of your original request is what determines how well you fulfill it. This means translating your goal into tangible, measurable outcomes. If your original request is nebulous or unclear, you'll have trouble fulfilling it. You might not even know if you have fulfilled it or not.

Let's look at an example. Maybe your goal is the same as Roger's — "I want a relationship." Though you might think you know just what you mean, the way the request is stated makes a it pretty broad. In answering it, your Warrior has a lot of leeway. He might bring a new co-worker to share your office, nosy new neighbors who move in next door, or a new beau who just wants to fight all the time. He might bring you a puppy, or a pushy telephone solicitor who calls twice a day begging for donations to save endangered rhinos. Technically, all these possibilities answer your request for a relationship. And not one, I'm sure, is the relationship that you or Roger had in mind.

To get the relationship you want, ask for it. The clearer the question, the clearer the results.

- *"I'd like to meet a man to share my life, live with me, and love me all the time."*
- *"I'd like a loving partner to help me raise my son."*
- *"I'd like a satisfying, loving, sexual relationship with a man independent enough to have his own life."*

Now these are goals your Warrior can work with!

▶ Refine your goal

2.a. *Look at the goal you chose in Exercise 1. Rewrite it as clearly, concretely, and tangibly as possible. How will it look and feel? How will you know when you've accomplished it? Even if you don't know all the exact details yet, get as close as you can, especially in terms of the qualities you're seeking. Though it might not matter if your partner is blonde or bald, it is important that he be open, loving, and playful. That's what to put on your list.*

b. *Double check. Make sure you support this goal with your whole being. Be honest. Is there any part of it that feels wrong or "funny"? Is there any underlying negativity in your motivation? Do you really want happiness for yourself and another man, or are you trying to find a new lover to make your ex feel jealous? Do you feel guilty taking a new job because it would mean moving away from your ailing parents? Does your goal really benefit everyone involved?*

If anything feels amiss, redefine the goal until you feel good about it. That will help you to act toward creating it much more clearly and effectively.

SHADOW: THE BLOCKED WARRIOR

If your Warrior were fully empowered right now, you'd reach for your goals easily and quickly. Unfortunately, in most of us, he gets blocked in one way or another. Fear can keep him silent and paralyzed. Negative personas like the Victim, Saboteur, or Tough may hold him hostage. Old beliefs, negative self-worth, or internalized homophobia can convince you that there's no point in trying. In order to reclaim your power to create, you first have to break the chains that have held the Warrior hostage. You can do it, especially if you deal with the blockages one at a time.

Let's start with fear. Fear has many forms and disguises. Recognize any of these?

Fear of taking action or making waves —
- "What will people say?"
- "It would kill my mother if she found out!"

Fear of repercussions or backfire —
- "What if he fires me for requesting a raise?"
- "What if I get punched in the face for coming out?"

Fear of failure —
- "I'll screw it up."
- "It's no use. I'll never be good enough."

Fear of rejection —
- "He'll never like me."
- "I'd die of embarrassment if he said "No"."

Fear of the unknown or unfamiliar —
- "Where would I live if I left him?"
- "At least I get paid, even if I hate the job."

Fear of success —
- "What if I get the job and everyone hates me."
- "It'll never last. As soon as I fall in love, he'll leave."

Fear, per se, is not bad. It's a healthy, natural response to new situations. It carries a highly adaptive message from the body — "Caution! Pay attention! There's something here!" In stressful or dangerous circumstances, fear is an important ally. Is it wrong to fear an out-of-control truck in your lane of traffic? Is it stupid to be afraid of an abusive partner or a gang of fag-bashing teens? Hardly. In fact, it would be foolish not to. In these cases, fear signals the need for appropriate action.

In other cases, though, fear gets in the way. Fears that are unfounded or out of proportion to a situation can block you from taking any action at all. Until you take back your power, fears like these become a chronic drain on your energy. They hang out just beneath the surface of your awareness, doing their best to hold you paralyzed with vague forebodings and hard-to-define anxieties. Remember that fears, like all other thoughts, are highly creative. Big or small, reasonable or irrational, conscious or hidden, your subconscious mind treats them all alike. The only way to free yourself is to look inside, see what's there, and then haul it out into the daylight where you can deal with it directly. Then, you're starting to take charge of your own life. Let's see how it works.

➤ Deal with fear

3.   Unmask and evaluate

a.   *Copy your goal at the top of a new page. Beneath it, create three columns. In the left-hand column, list all the fears you find in yourself about this issue. Don't edit. Put down everything, no matter how inconsequential or stupid it seems. Here's an example:*

GOAL: GET A JOB WHERE I CAN BE OPEN ABOUT WHO I AM.		
FEARS		
• I won't like it		
• Won't pay enough		
• Resumé out of date		
• Bad economy, no one's hiring		
• I'll lose this job if they find out I want a new one		
• Boss will find out about my piercings		

Is that all? Go back and add any other little fears you think of, no matter how stupid or minor they seem.

b.   *In column two, classify each fear you listed according to the following categories:*

   • **reasonable** — you can do something about it and need to take it into account
   • **unreasonable** — you can't do anything about it or it's based on fears from the past that don't apply here
   • **silly** — pure conjecture, a bogey man under the bed

c.   *In the third column, list outcomes.*

- For reasonable fears, list one or two possible actions you could take to address the situation.
- For unreasonable ones, rewrite it as a positive affirmation that you now choose to believe.
- For silly fears, laugh.

Continuing the example:

GOAL: GET A JOB WHERE I CAN BE OPEN ABOUT WHO I AM.

FEARS	TYPE	ACTION
• I won't like it	unreasonable	I'll only take a job that is satisfactory
• Won't pay enough	unreasonable	I'll only take a job that is satisfactory
• Resumé out of date	reasonable	update it
• Bad economy, no one's hiring	unreasonable	there are always jobs, I'll do my best
• I'll lose this job if they find out I want a new one	reasonable	be discreet and don't tell anyone
• Boss will find out about my piercings	silly	he may like them, hire me and ask me out too

You can apply this exercise to any area of your life. It's a great way to get hidden fears out into the open where you can defang them and move on.

4. Movement: The freak out

Analyzing fears rationally is important and helpful. Sometimes though, especially when fears are unreasonable, silly, or paralyzing, a more visceral response is called for. Dance them out!

Get some fast, frenetic music. Before you turn it on, take a moment to breathe and tune in to your body. When you feel aligned, ask your body to bring up all the fears it carries about your particular situation.

Turn on the music and shake out the fears. Begin by shaking your hands, as if you were throwing off drops of water. Let the movements get bigger, however they want to. Soon, you'll feel them take on a life of their own. Bring up as much fear as you can and shake it out of your body.

Play with it! Exaggerate! Shout, moan, scream! Carry on until you've exhausted the fear. Your heart will be beating. Your breath will be full. You'll feel lighter. When you're ready, bring the movement to a gentle close.

I recommend freak out dancing whenever fear starts to get the upper hand. Though the Unmasking exercise is better for finding creative solutions, this one clears your body. Instead of feeling paralyzed, you'll probably feel energized and ready for action. Your relationship with the fears will change. You'll see them in a different perspective. They may seem funny, irrelevant, or at least not so strong as before.

NEGATIVE PERSONAS

Archetypal energies **always** find a way to express. If your Warrior can't find a positive expression, he'll come through in his darker incarnations. When this happens, rather than empowering you to reach your goals, your Warrior's strength becomes distorted and acts to limit or block your power.

What does a blocked Warrior look like? You can probably imagine. All of us have ways to avoid taking action, to hide from difficult issues, or keep ourselves from power. We'll look here at three faces of the Shadow Warrior — Victim, Saboteur, and Tough. Though they are composites drawn from many personal styles, most of us resonate with one or more of them. As you read, notice if you recognize any of your own patterns.

A word of caution. Don't use this as a chance to beat yourself up. Recognizing negative patterns is necessary to healing them. Do your best to detach from the judgement, be honest with yourself, and open to the healing that comes with recognition.

In the same vein, it is really easy — and a cheap shot — to call other people's trips. "Oh, look at Blanche, acting out the Victim again. Doesn't she know the play's already been cast?" While it may bring a malicious smile, judging others misses the point — which is to recognize the same tendencies in your own behavior. You can approach negative personas with more compassion by realizing that all three are symptoms of the same wounding we've dealt with all along. Look beneath the surface. Apply the techniques you've learned to heal the underlying hurts. Then, you make room for the healthy Warrior.

Victim

The Victim has given up responsibility for his own life. "I'm this way because society doesn't accept Gay men," he says. "They (parents, teachers, the Church, whoever) did this to me and I'll be miserable forever." The Victim blames everyone else for the parts of his life that don't work. He's quick to play "woe is me" and "misery loves company." Because he's so comfortable in the role of underdog, the Victim is usually loathe to change. His oppression and the injustice that caused it have become too big a part of his own identity. If you dare suggest ways he might improve his lot, he's quick to counter with a list of reasons why they'd never work.

There's a difference between speaking the truth about difficult situations and playing Victim. In fact, abuse, oppression, homophobia, prejudice, and a host of other evils are very much part of life. Every one of us has been hurt. As you've already seen, to acknowledge realistically where you've been wounded is an essential part of healing. That's what we've done in almost every chapter of this workbook. The problem with the Victim is that he becomes lost in the old hurts and doesn't know how to get beyond them. Ultimately, his wounds become an excuse to abdicate responsibility for his own life.

Gay men, like members of any other stigmatized group, need to pay special attention to this issue. It's tricky. Pointing out the truth of prejudice is important in raising the understanding of the political mainstream. Yet, if oppression becomes too strong a part of our self-definition, we risk giving up the power to make meaningful changes. Ultimately, to heal the Victim, we need to treat our wounding as a starting place for further action.

How can you do that? First, recognize that **everyone on the planet**, Gay and otherwise, has experienced pain and suffering. Whatever form it takes, being wounded is part of being human. Each of us has to learn to deal with it. Second, realize that while it wasn't your fault that you were hurt in the first place, what you do with it now is your own responsibility. Either you can stay stuck and let what happened ruin the rest of your life, or you can take steps to heal it and move on.

A good first step is to call on the Shaman/Healer. Ask him to help you find new ways to look at the old wounds. If you've done the ground work of acknowledging the hurts and processing the feelings associated with them, he'll help you find a new filter. You can do this by asking different questions. Instead of staying stuck with "How did these people wreck my life," try a more productive line of inquiry — "What have I learned from this situation? What new strengths did I gain in the process? How did it help me to grow? What can I do to move on?"

Just as with the forgiveness process, reframing the way you look at old wounds doesn't mean you're condoning the actions that hurt you. It doesn't negate the grief and pain you suffered. It does, however, offer a sort of redemption by helping you take back control of your life. It helps you reclaim the reins of your own creative power. Since there's no changing what happened in the past, why not embrace the lessons and move on?

I've seen it work over and over. The Gay and Bisexual men I lead through this process rarely have trouble listing the many ways they were hurt growing up "different." Most have a list half a mile long of the things they considered wrong with themselves. "Threw like a girl," one will say, while others chime in with things like "too shy, too nerdy, too nelly, stuck in books, afraid of the other boys, hated myself." No surprises here. Nor are there many when we look at where the hurts came from. "Father. Teachers. Parents. The other boys. My grandfather. Our minister. Every jock on the planet." You've already made the same kinds of lists yourself.

The surprises come when we start changing the questions. "I learned I could survive on my own if I had to." "I learned how to have a sense of humor." "When I really thought about it, it made me question everything I was told. I learned to think for myself." "I got stronger because I learned to stick together with the few friends I did have." "I got good at understanding other people because I had to look inside myself so much." Almost always, these statements come forth in a tone of wonder. Most of us have never thought about our lives this way.

You'll have a chance to do the same thing yourself in the next set of exercises. For now, if you recognize aspects of the Victim in yourself, be gentle. Acknowledge what you're seeing — because that's already 90% of the healing — and then give yourself permission to experiment with new ways of looking at the situations involved. In time, shifting your perspective even a little has the power to transform the way you approach your life.

Saboteur

Like the Victim, the Saboteur never seems to quite make it. On the surface, he intends well and tries very hard. He may spend long hours at his job, take all the right classes, polish his attitudes, and dress for success, yet his life never gets a whole lot better. Something always comes along at the last minute to trip things up. The job falls through, the apartment is rented to someone else, or the new boyfriend turns out to be married. The Saboteur runs on a treadmill, a day late and a dollar short, with whatever goals he desires held just out of reach.

The Saboteur is sneaky. Despite the good face he puts on — even to himself — he's trapped in a pattern of his own making. He courts defeat. Whatever comes along, he's too afraid to change the status quo. On the verge of a new relationship, he'll panic and bolt. At the point of finishing a long-term project, he'll suddenly lose interest or find a reason to think it wasn't important to begin with. At the cut for a new job, he'll seize up and throw the interview.

Look deep. If you recognize parts of the Saboteur in yourself, realize that though the problems may seem to come from outside, the key to healing them lies inside you. It's not that you're bad or inadequate in any way. The sabotage comes from old beliefs you're probably not even aware of. As with the Victim, Saboteur behavior is a response to wounding. For Gay men, it often stems from subconsciously buying into the false stereotype that says we're ineffectual sissies incapable of succeeding in the "world of men." Even when we're highly qualified, we fear exposure as fakes, think we don't deserve success, or fear attack if we do break the mold by achieving our goals.

Again, be gentle with yourself here. You can start to heal the Saboteur with the tools to uncover and reframe negative beliefs that you learned in Chapter 3. Repeat a statement that affirms your power to achieve your goals and see what negatives come up in the back of your mind. Do a ritual to release these negatives, then reprogram your subconscious mind with positive affirmations. You have the power to change whatever beliefs you want.

Tough

The Tough is a character who'd never even want to hear about wounding. His whole approach to the world is one of defensive hostility. This is the man who attacks the world with fists clenched and tongue set on "shred". You know the type — chip on shoulder, always ready to take offense or pick a fight. The Tough seems to think that whoever yells the most, or has the most sarcastic tongue, wins the point — and he goes out of his way to win as many as possible.

The Tough is a caricature. He wears a number of masks. You might see him in the defiant swagger and exaggerated belligerence of the short-guy Marine wanna-be. You might see him in the tough-as-nails drag queen who thrives on put-downs and never misses a chance to skewer someone else. Though he has no problem taking action, the Tough rarely accomplishes much of value. Since he doesn't know the meaning of forethought, he doesn't call his own shots. Most often, he's responding to someone else, and the very fact that he's so obnoxious tends to create resistance to whatever he says. Even if he calls a situation right on the mark, no one gets past his tone to hear the words. In the end, all he does is create a lot of negative attention and piss off everyone else.

Of course, he's bluffing. The Tough is wounded like the rest of us and all his posturing is pure overcompensation. It's all a smokescreen, the desperate attempt of a scared little boy who feels totally powerless. At the core, it's himself that he's trying to impress. It's himself he needs to convince that he's strong and doesn't care about being alone. For all his activity, the Tough — like the Victim and Saboteur — ends up supporting the *status quo*. Even if he rails against it, he feels safer with the way things have always been.

It's hard to see the Tough in yourself. It may be even harder to give him the nurturing touch he needs. If you recognize some of his patterns in your life, acknowledge the places you hurt inside. Recognizing the pain and isolation you've felt is half the battle toward ending them. Realize that admitting you've been hurt doesn't mean you're weak. It's actually a sign of great strength. If you need help in learning to nurture yourself, get it. As you continue with this process, you'll find ways to express your Warrior nature that are much more effective and satisfying than the old overcompensation.

PAYOFFS

You were born to be creative and powerful. You were born to reach your goals, achieve your highest dreams, and make great contributions in the world. You know this with every cell in your body. When negative personas and old beliefs keep you from fulfilling your potential, what happens is that you feel pain. No matter how much you put on a happy face or try to tell yourself it doesn't matter, staying disempowered carries feelings of loss, discouragement, and failure. Even though every one of us has the power to change, many of us spend years and years stuck in the same painful place. Why? Because the payoffs to staying stuck seem better than the benefits of moving onward.

It's a simple balance sheet. Even though pain comes up strongly in the liability column, something on the other side comes up even stronger. Yet what could possibly be worth living with so much repressed pain? Though different men come up with different answers, most of them boil down to two basics — **security** and **ease.**

For most of us, what we know — even when it's unpleasant — feels infinitely safer and more comfortable than what we don't. The blocked Warrior feels safe because he knows where he stands. His place in life is secure, even if it's at the bottom. Thus, fear of the unknown feeds the negative personas until they become rigid and self-perpetuating. The Warrior uses all his power to maintain the status quo, even if that means convincing you and everyone around you that you're essentially powerless.

There's another payoff that you might not think of right away. In addition to false security, staying stuck in old wounds is often a backward way to achieve a sense of intimacy. For all the talk about love, society really gives us very few models for being truly intimate. All the words are about sex, which may or may not have anything to do with sharing real feelings. This isn't just a Gay issue, though we get a strong dose. All around us, people are groping for ways to fight the overbearing sense of personal isolation. One of the few answers we've found is to tell each other where we've been hurt.

Do you know what I mean? How many daytime TV shows do you see that are full of people exposing their deepest secrets? How many people do you know whose main source of intimacy is a support group based on where they were wounded? How many do you know whose whole identity is tied up with old hurts? "I'm an incest survivor. I'm an alcoholic. My father wasn't responsive, so I'm afraid to commit." When we don't know any other way to let people in, our wounds become precious. We'll do almost anything to avoid giving them up.

Don't get me wrong. I'm not against support groups, nor do I encourage pretending that wounding never happened. The path to empowerment, though, means using these as tools to achieve healing and then moving on. It means changing scripts and refusing to play "misery loves company" any more. It means finding the courage to take steps on your own and searching for different ways to be intimate with others.

To break the hold of negative personas, first be honest with yourself. Without judging, identify where you've been blocking your power. What are the payoffs?

> *"By not getting a new job, I can coast along in this one I already know. I don't have to risk failing at something I'm not already good at. I don't have to put forth the effort to learn new skills."*

> *"By staying single, even though I'd rather not be, I can get lots of sympathy for being lonely. I don't have to risk being hurt again. I don't have to share the bed or deal with anyone else's schedule in the morning."*

Instead of numbing yourself, get in touch with all the feelings you have about being blocked. **Feel** the fear that you won't ever change. **Feel** the pain of not getting what you want. **Feel** the discouragement of being stuck in a job or relationship that doesn't meet your needs.

Then, be willing to risk that the benefits of changing outweigh the payoffs of staying stuck. In fact, they do. You'll gain self-confidence and discover pride in the effort you're making. You'll find that swimming through life feels better than just drifting. Even if you make mistakes, you'll learn from them better ways to achieve your goals. You'll welcome increased vitality and excitement as you relate to people from a place of power and strength. What do you have to lose? Nothing but your pain.

Want to try? Looking at negative personas and the payoffs of staying stuck doesn't need to take a long time. It is, however, a vital step toward accessing the power of your inner Warrior. For the next exercise, keep your focus on the goal you've chosen. The way you approach it is most likely the same way you approach anything else in your life that is important.

Again, beware of your Inner Critic. This is an easy place for him to get out of hand. Don't let him. You're looking at patterns of behavior that everyone shares. Acknowledge what comes up and keep moving. Getting into self-judgement is just another way to keep yourself stuck.

Unblock the Warrior

Exercise

5.   *Write out the goal you've chosen to focus on — the same one you used in Exercises 1–4.*

a.   *Rephrase the goal into a sentence that goes like this — "**I can have (the goal)** _____ **right now."** For example, for the goal we've been using, you'd write "**I can have a job where I'm openly myself right now."***

As a way to activate your own habitual defenses towards change, repeat the new sentence over and over to yourself out loud. As you do, imagine that you're actually accomplishing it and get into the feelings of leaving behind your present situation.

Keep going as you listen in the back of your mind. What objections start coming up? Can you hear the voice of your Inner Critic? Can you hear the list of reasons why you won't make the change? Jot these down and continue repeating the statement for a few more minutes. Jot down every feeling that comes up, no matter how insignificant it may seem.

You may feel that nothing negative at all came up. Maybe there's nothing there to discover. Understand, though, that there must be some reason why you haven't yet achieved this goal. If nothing comes after you have tried for a while, proceed with the rest of the exercise anyway. See what the next parts trigger.

b.   *Using what you just wrote down, list all the payoffs you get from having things the way they are right now. What are the benefits to you of NOT achieving your goal?*

c.   *Do any of the feelings or objections that came up remind you of one or more of the negative personas? (Careful, no judgment!) If so, jot a note to yourself as to how the pattern fits. Does it remind you of other situations in your life, or times in the past that you were wounded or felt you'd failed?*

d. *To look at the other side of the balance sheet, list the benefits you could expect from achieving the goal you've chosen. How would you expect to feel? How would you expect your life to change? How might you start to view yourself and your place in the world?*

Before you stop, list the benefits you'd receive even if your efforts don't achieve the results you hope for. Even if you had to adjust in mid-course, how would it feel to begin taking charge of your own life? How would it feel to know you support yourself enough to go for what you desire?

On your mental balance sheet, do the old payoffs of staying stuck still outweigh the benefits of taking action?

CLAIM THE WARRIOR

You already have the power of the Warrior. All along, anywhere you've been blocked, you were using his energy to keep yourself stuck, based on the old belief that being safe meant never changing. What you're doing now is reassigning his energy. By inviting the Warrior to become an active, vital part of your life, you choose growth over stagnation and healing over wounding.

Calling the Warrior is relatively simple. You've already completed the groundwork. All that remains is to bring him into your body. The next exercise will take you there. Because it consists of several steps, be sure to read through the whole process first, then take the time you need to complete each part. Once you understand the nature of the energy you're calling on, especially in Part b., you won't need to reread the entire description to call it into your body.

Do your best to get into each part of the exercise **bodily**. Because the Warrior's realm is action, just reading through the steps or letting your mind give you the answers won't take you where you want to go. The process has to be physical. Though it takes a little time at first, with a little practice you'll soon be able to apply the process quickly and easily to any situation that calls for action.

Warrior

6.a. *Set the stage. Set aside about 15 minutes in which you won't be disturbed. Give yourself enough space to move freely and have your movement music ready. Use music that has a good beat, but not so frenetic as what you used for the freak out dance.*

When you're ready, close your eyes and call forth your Inner Council and the Circle of the Tribe. As you feel them around you, pay attention to your

Exercise

breath. Let it take you deep inside. When you feel safe, aligned, and centered, turn on the music and begin.

b.   *As you start moving, ask your body to show the part of you that has enabled you to take every important step of your life. Repeat the request over and over in your mind — "Show me. Show me." Let your body, not your mind, lead the movements.*

This is the part that carried you from the dark safety of the womb into the bright unknown world. It's the part that has supported you every time you've taken a step since that first moment of your life. Whatever those steps were for you, let them come through in your movements. Remember that despite any fears or doubts you may have felt, at every step you had the power to act anyway. This part of you was stronger than anything that stood in your way. It got you through! Feel its strength as it moves in your body.

This is the part that stood by you those first days at school, the first time you went somewhere by yourself, the first time you stayed at home alone. This is the part that supported you when you stood at bat, auditioned for the band, or faced a hundred other challenges. This is the part that healed your cells when you fought to recover from illness or injury. It got you through all the hurts of growing up. It empowers you to claim who you are, to come out first to yourself and then to others. It's the part that has carried you through your entire Gay Spirit Journey, all the way to the present moment. This part is stronger than anything the world has ever thrown at you. You're still here!

Continue moving. Keep asking to feel the strength inside you. Enjoy its power. Express it even more fully. Give it your breath. Give it your feet and legs, arms and hands. Give it your heart, your back, your organs, your face, even your mind. Express this energy with your whole being.

*When you feel that it is fully present, ask your body to show you a single gesture — a single, small movement — that sums up this energy for you. Just ask and see what comes. When it does, repeat it several times until you're sure you remember it. Call this gesture, "**empowered.**" It represents all the energy of your inner Warrior.*

Then, shake off all over and come to a quiet resting place. Breathe for a few moments until you feel strongly centered. Then, proceed.

c.   *Focus on the goal you chose at the beginning of the chapter. Ask your body to show you — **by moving** — how it feels to be blocked from reaching this goal. Repeat the request in your mind, over and over, as you watch the way* *your body moves. Let it show you the fear, hurt, pain, sadness, or other feelings associated with not achieving your goals. Make the movements a little bigger. Exaggerate a little more. Keep breathing, moving, and observing until the feelings are expressed in every part of your body.*

Then, ask for a single posture to come through you that represents all the blockage. Hold that posture for a few moments and notice how it feels. Call this posture "blocked." Remember it. Then release it and relax. Breathe a few moments until you feel centered.

d. *Resume your **blocked** position for about a minute. Really feel again what it's like to be here. Imagine all the fears and doubts you've carried about this issue, as if they were materialized into a wall, right there in front of you. Feel how it is to be blocked in the face of all that resistance.*

Now, right there in front of all the fears and doubts, use the "empowered" gesture to call on your inner strength. Feel what happens as this strength comes into your body. Feel how it empowers you, even though the fears and doubts are still right there in front of you. Using the empowered gesture, ask your body to express all the power you felt before, right here in the blocked situation. Feel how you can breathe! Feel how you move!

When you're ready, take small steps and move right through the wall of fear and doubt. For however long it takes, let the power carry you through that wall to the other side, to the completion of your goal. Feel how it is to move forward even when doubt and fear are present. Feel how it is to face your challenges head on.

When you reach the other side of the wall, ask your body to show you the part that got you through. You took action! You were stronger than the fears and doubts! Move your power. Move your strength. This is your Warrior.

e. *Move in honor of the Warrior for a few minutes. Feel him in every cell of your body. Watch what he shows you. Watch how you feel.*

Then, when you've experienced him fully, gently thank the Warrior for his help, release him for now, and breathe yourself back to center. Let your movements get quiet. Bring yourself back to normal awareness, let all the energy flow into the Earth, and relax.

f. *You've just completed a very powerful piece of inner work. Congratulate yourself. Have a drink of water. Write down in your journal any insights you want to record from the process. Then, rest a little if you need it.*

EFFECTIVE ACTION

Now that you've empowered him, the Warrior's job is to take action. No matter how much you think and process, the only way you'll finally resolve challenges and move toward your goals is to act. In any situation, some actions are more appropriate than others. For your Warrior to be truly effective, he needs to act in concert with the rest of your being. **You** have to be the one to chart the course he'll take. This is a good time to review a few points about making your actions as effective as possible. Consider the following questions:

- *Am I clear? Am I connected with inner guidance?*
- *What are my choices?*
- *What is my desired outcome?*
- *Is the timing appropriate?*
- *How can I map out an action plan?*
- *Am I committed?*

Let's look at these in more detail.

Am I clear? Am I connected with inner guidance?

As an effective Warrior, you'll rarely act without consulting the wisdom and insight of your Inner Council. Very few situations call for an immediate, unthinking response. In those that do, trust your instincts first, then analyze later. Almost always, though, you have at least a moment to breathe, get calm, and ask your intuition, "What do I do now?". Then, **listen for the answer**.

If you have more time, you can work with the exercises we've already explored. Consult your inner Elder. Ask the Shaman/Healer to connect you with your inner knowing. Do a movement meditation to ask your body for guidance. Ask your Magic Boy what his feelings are. However you access it, intuition gives you effective guidance even if your mind is confused or overwhelmed. When you act from a place of inner alignment, you have a much greater chance of achieving the results you want.

What are my choices?

However stuck or trapped a situation makes you feel, you almost always have more than one way to approach it. Examine all your options. Sometimes your first impulse is the best course to follow. Sometimes it's not. Brainstorm. Write down all the alternatives you can think of. For example, suppose your boss yells at you for making a mistake. Your immediate response might be to leave the office in a huff, slamming the door so hard behind you the glass breaks. That might feel good. It might even be the best response. Before you burn bridges, though, look at a few other options. You could ...

- punch him out,
- wait till the end of the day when you've both cooled down, then tell him how you feel,
- call **his** superior and file a complaint,
- let it go for now, but commit to spending time each day looking for a better job,
- call him at home at 4 a.m., then hang up each time he answers,
- forget about it.

Obviously, some responses are more effective than others. Which you choose depends on what you really want to accomplish.

What is my desired outcome?

It's usually not hard to project the results you'll get from a specific action. Always ask yourself if the action you're planning moves you toward the goal you actually desire. If not, you need to refigure.

Check your motivation. Strong feelings like frustration, anger, and hurt often come up in difficult situations. Acknowledge them. Share them if it feels appropriate. Don't let them, however, determine the course of action you follow. Even though it might feel good to punch your boss in the face, that probably wouldn't get you what you want in the long run.

Reflect a little. What is it that you really want out of this situation? A new job? A raise? Revenge? Once you're clear about where you want your actions to take you, then you can decide what to do with the feelings. If it's not appropriate to share them with the other person, process them yourself. You might adapt the freak out dance to release the anger physically, or write a venting letter like you did in Chapter 7. Feelings contain energy. Don't spend all yours in one great explosion that goes nowhere. Instead, figure out what your real goals are and use the emotional energy to spur you on toward achieving them. You'll be much more satisfied in the long run.

Is my timing appropriate?

Choosing **when** to act is often as important as the action itself. Acting too early can be as harmful as putting something off until your opportunity is gone. Telling your boss that you have another job offer when all you really have is an interview could backfire. Telling your folks you're leaving home before you have anywhere else to go could be disastrous. Whenever you're deciding on a course of action, ask yourself, "When is the best time to put this into effect?" Act right away if that seems the best course. If it doesn't, remind yourself that choosing **not** to act until the time is right is the mark of a powerful Warrior. You'll get where you want to go much more effectively.

How can I map out an action plan?

If you're dealing with big or long term goals, break them down into smaller steps. One of the easiest ways to sabotage yourself is to make a goal overwhelmingly large or to demand big, dramatic actions you're not yet ready to make.

Make an actual map of your strategy. What would be a good first step toward your goal? How could you follow that step with others that would lead to successful completion? Be realistic. Make your steps concrete and easily achievable. Be flexible. Remember that your plan may change in response to unforeseen circumstances. Change it as you need. Even if following a plan seems to take a long time, you'll get where you're going more quickly this way than if you stay paralyzed because the task you've chosen is too big to handle.

You may need further information. If you're looking for a job, do you know where to look? Do you know what's out there? Do you need further training? Answering these questions has to be part of your strategy. Include information gathering among the proposed steps toward your goal. "Go to the library. Read the want-ads each Sunday. Write to schools that offer programs in the areas I like."

Each time you complete a step, *acknowledge your power to act*. No matter how small or insignificant it seems, each action is an important part of your empowerment. Congratulate yourself verbally. "I talked to so and so and it was good." "I revised my resume and I feel more prepared."

Personally, I like acknowledgment that's even more visceral. I keep a list over my desk where I write down each task I complete. Beside each one, I put a bright gold star. My adult self thinks the list is sort of silly, but it's still the best response I've found to that critical inner voice that says, "You can't do this, you never do anything!" Now I say, "You're wrong. See, look at all the gold stars on this list! I can accomplish my goals!"

Am I committed?

This is your final step. All the talk in the world isn't worth a dime if you don't actually take the actions you decide on. Commitment helps you put your money where your mouth is. When you choose your course of action, make a commitment to yourself to actually complete it. Set a date. Be sure the proposed action and time frame are realistic. Then, just do it.

Making commitments and taking actions, even if they seem very small, can be radically transformative. Both in your own life and in the world outside you, it's easy to get depressed or overwhelmed by the scope of the changes that need to be made. Always remember that *actions antidote despair*. They don't even need to be big and dramatic. Small acts are just fine, because they add up. Try it. Next time you feel stuck in your life, do one small thing to change it. Make a call to inquire about a new job. Call a friend who's taken a class you might like. Have lunch with someone you can talk to. Try the same thing out in the world. Next time you're angry about the politics of the radical right, write a letter to your Congressman. Next time you're upset about how quickly we're losing the rain forests, plant a tree in your neighborhood. Pissed about prejudice against PWA's? Go visit someone who's sick. Then see how you feel.

Even if taking one small action doesn't fix the entire world, it does change you. You'll feel your own power. You'll find the next step just a little easier to take. As you continue to act, one step at a time, you **will** make a difference. Actions add up. Not only do they help you solve problems directly, they also help indirectly as other people see your example. Some will join you in your efforts. Others will turn in different directions and take steps on their own. Both ways, your actions count.

Every journey begins with one small step. Set your course, call on your Warrior, and take that step. Now.

Action

Exercise

7.a. *Call your Inner Council to be with you. Use the "empowered" gesture you discovered in Exercise 6 to call your Warrior into your body.*

b. *With the help of Warrior and Council, create an action plan for completing the goal you've been focusing on. Ask them, either through visualization or by movement, what would be a good first step toward completing your goal. How would you start? What would you do next?*

Write out your action plan, one step at a time. Make each step small. Set a realistic time frame for completion. Remember to be flexible.

c. *When you have your plan, write out a commitment to yourself.*

"I, _____, commit to (step 1) _____, by (date) _____. I commit to take this step and then continue taking each consecutive step in a timely manner, until I complete my goal. I will be flexible and supportive of myself as I do this."

Then sign it.

d. *Post the action plan and your commitment where you'll see them. If you want, buy a box of gold stars to mark the map each time you complete a step. Otherwise, mark each one off with a colored pencil. Then, do the first step.*

8. *Place an object on your altar to represent the power, strength, and integrity of your Warrior.*

9. *Sometime this week, go through the entire Warrior process with your focus on a different goal. Choose the goal. Refine it and be sure you can commit to completing it. Work with your fears. Examine the payoffs to staying stuck. Call your Warrior and create an action plan. Each time you work with your Warrior, it gets easier.*

    Practice calling your Warrior. Practice taking action. Practice feeling empowered. Go ahead. Dare to change your life!

.

13 The Explorer

PASSION = LIFE

When my friend Bobby dances, the world gets bright. His body, which is actually pretty small, seems to grow until it threatens to burst out of his clothes. His movements take on a sinewy wildness that makes me think of jungles and windswept mountaintops. As he gives himself all the way to his dance, Bobby's whole being shines. You can hear his breath sounding hot, as if it were erupting straight from the Earth. His eyes focus upward and his look makes you wonder at the miracles he must be witnessing. His enthusiasm is contagious. People with him when he dances inevitably end up smiling.

Bobby didn't always dance. In fact, when I first met him, he moved like a stick. "I'm a klutz," he'd say with a sigh, "Can't dance, don't want to." At the time, Bobby worked in a bookstore. When he talked, his tone was flat. He didn't seem to have much energy for anything. A few years ago, just to please a man he liked, Bobby went to a country dancing class at one of the bars. To his surprise, he liked it. He went back with his friend week after week. When the friend went away, Bobby kept going on his own. From two-step, his style expanded into something uniquely personal. Elsewhere in his life, Bobby's transformation was astonishing. Suddenly, he came alive. He seems taller now and his voice is charged with enthusiasm. For Bobby, dancing was the door to **passion**.

Passion is the realm of the Explorer. It's a shimmering, shining part of you that makes all of life worth living. Each of us follows a different route to find it. Bobby found it dancing. Steve finds passion hiking in the wilderness with nothing but a backpack and camera. Jim writes detective stories. Chester explores erotic massage. Joe says his passion is watching old movies. I believe him — you can tell by the enthusiasm in his voice when he talks about them.

Where's your passion? When was the last time you were really excited about living? Can you describe your daily existence as a brilliant, exciting adventure? Do you jump out of bed each morning eager to explore all the fascinating challenges of the coming day? If you're answering "Here! Now! Yes! Yes!" you may not need this chapter. Your Explorer self is fully alive and active. Most of us, though, probably respond along the lines of, "Well, maybe I'm excited sometimes, but you know, I gotta work, gotta make a living. And it's not all fun and games."

It can be. Now that you've claimed the power of the Warrior, you can call on him to help you create the life you choose. Why not choose excitement, passion, and vitality? Why not make your work into play? Why not put your energy into activities that feed your sense of adventure? By aligning your Warrior with the passion of the Explorer inside you, you can break out of conformity and start to set your own agenda. You can reclaim your dreams, live with purpose, and bring the brilliant colors of your soul out to shine in the sunlight.

That's a big order. How do you start? Most of us love the *idea* of passion, but few of us have a very clear picture of where to find it in ourselves. Somehow, it got buried a long time ago under the more pressing concerns of surviving, fitting in, and making it in the world. Although it's surely alive and well somewhere deep inside, bringing it to the surface usually involves a little digging. So that's where you're going to start. With the help of the Warrior, let's backtrack a bit and return to the time in your life when your dreams and passion were much more immediate.

RECOVER THE EXCITEMENT

You came into this life as a full-fledged Explorer. Your first years were a constant adventure as you learned about the world and your place in it. You drank in all the wonders with bright-eyed curiosity. You spouted an unending fountain of questions:

> *"What color is the sky?"*
> *"Why does electricity come out of the wall?"*
> *"Look at my penis, it gets longer sometimes! Why?"*
> *"Why do bunnies like to eat carrots?"*
> *"Where did the snow go?"*
> *"Why do boys wear pants and girls wear dresses?"*

Can you remember the enthusiasm that came with being a boy? In this first exercise, ask the Magic Boy to remind you.

Magic Boy

Exercise

1.a. As you begin the following movement meditation, take a few moments to get centered in your body. With quiet music, create sacred space, call your Inner Council, and feel the Tribal Circle around you. Breathe into your body until you feel safe and aligned.

When you're ready, call your Magic Boy into the circle with you. See how he looks now. Let him know you're glad to see him again. Let him stand with you in the circle, and then invite him to dance inside your body.

Move freely as the Magic Boy for a few minutes. Let him remind you how he feels, how he moves, and how it is to be him. Notice if calling on him now feels different than it did the first times back in Chapter 7. Is he easier to access now? Are you more relaxed than you were then?

b. *Ask your Magic Boy for help in answering a few questions. When he agrees, bring your body to rest and sit with your journal. Let him guide your responses to complete at least 3 of the following exercises. Answer quickly, before your adult mind has time to edit.*

• *What did you like to do the most as a boy? Make a list of at least ten things you loved.*

• *When you were a boy, what activity could you do for hours, so engrossed you forgot the time? What would you have done all day every day if you'd had the chance? Was there one activity? More? Ask inside.*

• *What were you **not** supposed to do as a boy that you liked so much you did anyway? List five things if you can.*

• *What were your favorite stories, movies, or TV shows? What sorts of things were they about? Who were your favorite characters?*

• *What were you going to be when you grew up?*

Thank your Magic Boy for being with you. Release him for now, but remember that you can be with him at any time just by calling him. You may enjoy comparing your answers here with those you came up with in Chapter 7.

As a little boy, your questions were endless. Somewhere in the middle years, though, your curiosity got dulled. Some of the answers weren't very pleasant.

"Boys don't play with dolls."
"Don't touch yourself there, that's bad."
"Don't be so sensitive. Big boys don't cry."
"People laugh at you if you talk funny."
"If you don't act right, you'll get hurt."

You weren't the only one. Peer pressure, parental pressure, religious pressure, and our own desire to be accepted made most of us clamp down. We learned — sometimes the hard way — how to fit in and not make waves. We learned to compromise, to pretend, and to hide our difference however we could. While this is true for everyone, for Gay kids it is a fundamental fact of life.

Shutting down your inherent sense of adventure and wonder takes away your joy. Every time you believe that part of you isn't acceptable, you close it off. If you look at them one at a time, the compromises might not seem so great. Okay, you don't play guitar any more because you weren't as good as Jimi Hendrix. You can live without it. You don't adopt stray puppies, either, because they make messes in the house. You can live without that, too. And you don't roll down hills, make paper kites, or skip, because those aren't adult activities. I guess you can live without those as well, but be careful. Every time you shut down even a little, some of your sparkle goes away.

Closing down is a path that ultimately makes you bored, dull, depressed, and bitter. You can follow that path if you like, but you don't have to. If you want, you can turn it around right now by choosing to open doors instead of closing them and deciding to follow your heart instead of pretending it doesn't exist. The best way to begin is to find out where you shut down in the first place. By uncovering the hidden beliefs and agreements by which you gave away your passion, you're already well on the way to reclaiming it.

Break the chains

Exercise

2.a. **Attitudes**

You already know how to listen to subconscious chatter. Here, you'll use the familiar techniques to uproot attitudes that keep you away from your own passion.

*Draw a line down the center of a new page in your notebook. On the right side of the page, quickly copy the following sentence twenty times, "**It is safe and healthy to explore everything that calls me.**"*

As you write, listen to any objections that come up in the back of your mind. Listen any time you hear the word "except ..." or "not...". Whatever comes up, jot it down on the left side of the page. Just write, don't think.

b. *Complete at least one exercise in each of the following categories:*

• **Expectations**
Who was most influential in your early life? For the one(s) that influenced you the most, copy the following statement 10 - 15 times, filling in the blank with whatever comes to you. Do it quickly and without editing.
*"**My (mother, father, whoever) expects me to** _____."*

• **Fears**
Complete the following 10-15 times.
*"**I'd love to** _____, **but men don't do that.**"*
*"**Because I'm an adult, I can't** _____."*

• **Judgments**

Complete one of the following sentences 10-15 times.

"If I weren't Gay, I could _____**."**

"The worst thing about being Gay is _____**."**

c. What came up? Review the negatives you discovered in parts a. and b. Which of these seem to have the most charge? Which came up over and over? Which would you definitely like to get rid of right now?

As you learned to do earlier, release all the negative statements with a ritual gesture — burning, flushing, or whatever works for you.

Then, turn the negatives you discovered into positive affirmations.

"People won't like me" becomes "I like myself more when I express myself fully."

"My father expects me to get married" changes dramatically when you add, "but I can do what I choose."

"I would learn to sew, but men don't do that" becomes "I enrich my life each time I learn something new."

Enjoy this one. The more fun you have at it, the more you bring in the energy you're trying to encourage.

TELL YOUR STORIES

Whatever specific beliefs you came up with to block your Explorer, they all stemmed from a single core negative — you believed that something inside you was unacceptable. Was it your attraction to other men? Was it your sensitivity? Was it the fact that you wanted to cook while other boys wanted to play football? Or maybe that you wanted to play football naked and so you took up cooking to keep anybody from finding out? The specific details are less important than the fact that the core negative belief — "This part of me isn't good" — put various paths off limits to exploration. Your world got smaller, more prescribed, and less interesting.

To broaden your horizons again, reclaim the details of your life. You can do this easily by turning the significant moments into your own special stories. Telling your stories affirms who you are. When you honor the path you've traversed, you'll be surprised at the richness of feeling, humor, and insight you discover. You'll laugh at the irony of situations that used to terrify you. You'll validate old urges you once clamped down on with the ferocity of the Inquisition. Charting the road you've traveled to get this far will help you appreciate just how far you have come. In the process, you'll go a long way toward recovering the curiosity and enthusiasm you gave up along the way.

Once you get going, writing your stories is easy and fun. You'll get to claim the secret joys and fears you've hidden for years —

"I've always liked to watch men's forearms. Something about the way the veins make maps under the skin is really sexy."

You'll have an opportunity to acknowledge things you're proud of that didn't get recognized the first time around —

"When I was ten, I climbed up the mountain behind my grandparents' farm. It was over 3000 feet up and I did it in a morning. At the top, I saw an eagle! When I got back, Papa was so mad I'd gone off without telling him, he grounded me. I never got to tell him about the eagle."

You'll get to put difficult moments into a better perspective —

"I thought I'd die the time my father caught me and Jerry in the bushes playing doctor. I was giving him an "examination" when Daddy found us. Daddy was pretty cool about it, but I could tell from the way he told us to put our clothes on that he was really upset."

You can let go of the secrets you've carried too long —

"When I was seven, I peeked through the bathroom keyhole and watched my mom get undressed. I ran away before anyone saw me, but I felt really guilty for a long time."

Natalie Goldberg, a wonderfully inspiring teacher, speaks about writing meditation. She suggests setting a timer for a specific interval, say 20 minutes, and writing on your chosen subject until it goes off. Your intention is to get to the core of your experience — what she calls "first thoughts" — without editing or interpretation. Keep the pen moving. Let your mind go where it will. Don't cross anything out. Be specific — use names, details, and descriptions. Go for broke — put down whatever holds the most energy and explore it for all its worth.

One memory will stimulate others. Keep a list in the back of your notebook of topics you'd like to explore later. To jog your memory, try her suggestion of beginning a meditation with the words, "I remember ... ". Whenever you get stuck, just go back to "I remember ... " and take a new tack. The same exercise works very well with "I don't remember." You'll be amazed at what comes up.

Writing your stories provides a good structure for ongoing self-exploration. First and foremost, write for yourself. By claiming the freedom to write without an audience, you'll go deeper and avoid the temptation to slant things so that they look more presentable. Experiment. Play. Reading the stories will bring you satisfaction, perspective, and a renewed appreciation of your own worth. If you decide later that you want to share what you've written, that's fine. For now, though, just enjoy the process and receive whatever comes through as a special gift to yourself.

Stories

Exercise

3.a. *Either use your journal or get a special notebook for stories. Start wherever you feel the urge. Write about people who were important to you, activities you liked to do, adventures you always wanted to have.*

- Who was your first "crush"?
- When was the first time you had sex with another man?
- When did you first know you were Gay?
- What were your parents like, and your grandparents?
- What was the funniest incident you ever experienced?
- When was the first time someone you loved died?

Wherever you start, let the story flow along whatever channels it likes. Don't edit. Don't try to dress it up and make it more dramatic, more politically correct, or funnier than it was. Just tell it.

b. *After each story, ask yourself if it brings up anything you'd like to explore further. Does it remind you of a something you'd like to reclaim? Does it remind you of any activities you used to like that you stopped doing? Could you find any way to explore the same types of activities today?*

LOOK IN THE MIRROR

Another way to rediscover hidden parts of yourself is to notice where you see them reflected in the world. Remember projection? Whenever you notice something over and over in the people around you, there's a very good chance you're really seeing a part of **you**. We've already looked at projection several times. Now, let's play with it again as a way to recover your sense of creativity and adventure.

Who attracts you? Who do you bring into your life? Do you, who are sure you can't dance your way out of a paper bag, count 25 dancers among your closest friends? Ever ask yourself why? Do you keep attracting sexy men in black leather, even though the thought of being with them makes you nervous? Do you spend all your time watching cooking programs on TV, even though you've never dared make anything more than a three-minute egg? You can learn a lot about yourself by noticing who catches your attention.

You can also learn a lot by observing what bugs you. Who do you envy? Whose success makes you feel jealous? Is it your writer friend who just published his third popular novel? the Gay doctor whose practice is booming? your downstairs neighbor who just joined a nudist club? your friend who works as a flight attendant and gets to travel all the time? Maybe if we asked you, your initial response would be defensive, "What, me jealous? How ridiculous. I never wanted to be a doctor." But look deeper. If these people weren't reflecting something in you, their accomplishments wouldn't bother you at all.

Turn the situation to your advantage. Instead of envying talent and success in the people around you, let them steer you toward your own. Where do they remind you of dreams you abandoned? Can you dare to imagine that you, too, could be a doctor, a successful writer, or someone who travels for a living? The first step toward reclaiming your dreams is to admit to yourself that you still hold them.

As you complete the following exercise, you may discover some old feelings that aren't so pleasant. It hurts to give up your dreams. It hurts to abandon your aspirations. If feelings like these come up, stay present. They may actually indicate that you're on the right track. You're doing exactly what you need to heal them. When you allow yourself to honor them, they'll propel you into new explorations. Once you begin taking action to recover your dreams, the joy and satisfaction you feel will far outweigh anything else.

➤ Mirrors

Exercise

4.a. *List the people you admire the most. What about them appeals to you? Is it what they do? How they do it? List any qualities these people seem to have in common.*

b.   *List the people toward whom you feel jealousy or envy. Be honest. This list is for you — you won't need to share it. What about these people really catches your attention? What really bugs you about each one? Do they have anything in common?*

c.   *Here's the mirror. Where do you see parts of yourself reflected in the people you listed above? Write down what you see.*

Be easy on yourself. This isn't about judgment. If people around you have already achieved things you'd like for yourself, that doesn't make them better than you. It just means they're on a different schedule. Likewise, if you're feeling envy, turn it around. Once you admit it to yourself, you're on the way to manifesting what you want and the jealousy won't have any reason to hang around.

d.   *Acknowledge your feelings. How does it feel to admit that you've wanted something you thought you couldn't have? How does it feel to begin thinking about going for it now?*

FOLLOW YOUR BLISS

The well known mythologist and teacher, Joseph Campbell, advised over and over, "Follow your bliss." If you seek the path of greatest personal satisfaction, he said, it will always lead toward your soul. "Great advice," I thought when I heard it, "but how do I follow something I'm not even sure exists? What the hell is my 'bliss' anyway?"

When you've lived in compromise for so long, it's often hard to figure out what's underneath it. Hopefully, by this point you're starting to get an inkling. Now it's time to take the exploration a full step further. You're about to recover possibilities you once gave up and to experience the Explorer in all his glory. These are exercises you should approach with great lightness. Follow the processes and enjoy what you find!

 The Explorer

Exercise

5.   *Recover possibilities. Answer at least three of the following questions as spontaneously as possible. Write first. Analyze later.*

a.   *If you had all the money you ever needed, what would you do? Fly around the world? Buy a ranch? Visit Rio? Own an ice cream company? Parachute into the outback? Star in a comedy film?*

   List ten things you'd love to do if money were no object.

b.   *If you had to go back to school, tuition free, and could take any courses you wanted, what would you choose? Dog grooming? Conversational Swahili? House renovation? Japanese flower arranging? Twirling?*

   List at least five things you'd love to study.

c.   *Where in your life now do you feel most creative? What can you trance out on for hours? Your job? Cooking? Painting? Making love? Cutting the lawn?*

   List five of your favorite activities.

d.   *What do you like to do on weekends, when nothing else is scheduled? If you could take a vacation for 6 weeks, what would you do? How about if you had a year to play?*

   Enjoy brainstorming ideas for adventures and activities.

e.   *If you knew you had 6 months left to live, what would you feel you had to do before you left?*

f.   *What do you want to be when you grow up?*

6.   **Movement meditation.**

a.   Like the Warrior movement, this will take a bit of time. Give yourself enough so that you don't have to hurry. Pause between sections, without breaking the energy, if there's anything you'd like to jot down in your journal. As you become more familiar with his energy, you'll be able to call on the Explorer easily and quickly.

Center yourself by following your breath into the core of your being. Create your sacred space and when you're ready, call your Inner Council and the Tribal Circle to be with you. When you feel immersed in their protection and guidance, start your music and call your Explorer into the center of the Council space.

Look at him first. Take in his appearance. What's he look like? How does he stand? What does he wear? How does he move? What do you see when you look into his eyes?

Ask your Explorer to help you, then invite him into your body. Make the request, over and over silently, "Show me my Explorer." Let yourself move. Feel what comes through, how it is to be the Explorer. Move for several minutes, getting used to him.

b.   *Ask your Explorer to show you where you already express his energy. What activities does he inspire in you now? Where in your life do you already embody him easily? Remember what he shows you.*

c.   *Ask your Explorer to take you on a short journey. Imagine climbing with him to the top of a high mountain. The air is cool here and the sun warm. Below you, many valleys spread forth in different directions. Each valley represents one of the many dreams you have an opportunity to explore. Let your body move gently as you imagine surveying the different valleys, looking and noticing what they feel like. You'll know right away what some of them represent. Others may give you feelings or images that are less specific. Don't worry about details for the time being, just observe.*

From your vantage atop the mountain, you have the freedom to explore any or all of these valleys. What does it feel like to embrace all the potential in your life? "Show me how it feels to open to all my potential." Ask your body, and then move in response for a few minutes. When you've got the feeling all over, let your movement come to a gentle pause and then go on to the next step.

With all that potential present, ask the Explorer to show you, through movement, which of the dreams is most appropriate to explore right now.

As you move, imagine that you're still on the mountaintop, looking down at all the dreams. Notice which one calls your attention. Even if you don't know all the details yet, work with this for the rest of the process.

Continuing to move, ask to see and feel how it would be to explore this dream. What would the details be? What would be involved? Where would be the best place to start?

You may get very specific images. If not, ask for more clarity.

Finally, ask the Explorer to show you the very first step you can take on this exploration. Get a very specific action you can take, just as you did when you consulted the Warrior. Look and remember.

e.   *When you're ready, let your Explorer guide you back down the mountain and into the center of your Council space. Thank him for his help, release him from your body, and let him return to his place in the Council.*

Ground all the energy by placing your hands on the Earth. Let yourself come back to normal awareness and record your impressions in your journal, taking special note of the first step in your exploration.

LIVE THE EXPLORER

In the first part of this chapter, you focused on how you compromised your dreams in the past. That's not really the end of the story. The very same forces are still alive today. There is *always* pressure to conform. Every one of us wants to be accepted by the people important to us, and so we're tempted to be what *they* want instead of following what really calls us from inside. There's always a temptation to give ourselves the short end of the stick. We open up a little bit — just enough to relieve some of the internal pressure and convince ourselves that we're actually doing something — and then ignore the inner voice again, as if it had only one thing to say in our whole lives.

Just like "coming out" really means "living out", opening to the Explorer is an ongoing adventure. At times it can be subtle, at times dramatic. How do you embrace passion fully? Honor it every single day. Push limits. Be suspicious of habit. Shake yourself out of ruts and refuse to do things just because that's how they've always been done. Wring every bit of curiosity for all it's worth. Honor your questions and give yourself permission to change them daily. Pay attention to your urges, for they represent the voice of your soul calling you home to yourself. Listen. Heed their call to life.

When the Explorer sets out on a new quest, you're never quite sure where he'll take you. There's a point at which you have to let go of destinations and trust in the sheer joy of the exploration. Some trails lead nowhere special. Others offer unexpected bonanzas. You never know which until you try them. As an example, let me tell you about my friend, Jack.

Jack spent twelve years in a very closed relationship. As a recovering alcoholic, he enjoyed the security of depending on his partner for almost everything. Most of the time, he wouldn't even drive. Though they were happy enough, neither man grew very much. Four years ago, they decided they'd outgrown the relationship. Though it terrified him at times, Jack began to do things by himself. He mastered his fear of people by going out again, even though he fled after only two minutes the first time. He learned to two-step, something he'd never even considered, and got up the courage to attend Gay rodeos — first with friends, then by himself. He started to date again occasionally. Resisting the temptation to get too sheltered within his new circle of "cowboy" friends, Jack listened to the call to keep moving. He swallowed his fear and began to explore the spiritual aspects of S/M sexuality, which led to a new relationship. Now, Jack and his new partner are finding different ways to express intimacy and achieve satisfaction.

Jack learned to honor his Explorer and bring him into a strong, healthy relationship with the Warrior. Taking one step at a time — many of which terrified him — he pushed his limits and allowed himself a degree of freedom he'd never thought possible. He had no idea when he set forth where the trail would lead. He just followed the call of his own inner desires. The path he followed certainly isn't for everyone — each of us has to discover his own — yet the health and vitality he's achieved are truly inspiring.

How can you make the Explorer an ongoing part of your own life? Let's have a look.

Exploration as a way of life

Exercise

7.   *There are thousands of ways to honor the Explorer in your day to day life. The following are a few suggestions. Experiment with as many of them as you like right now, and then remember where to find them for future reference. These exercises are tools you can use whenever you want to stimulate changes in your life.*

a.   *This week, break routines. Find new routes as you drive to work, to the store, or wherever else you go regularly. Go by bicycle or walk instead of driving on short trips.*

b.   *Switch sides of the bed.*

c.   *Rearrange the furniture. Find new places for things. Clean out closets. Reorganize your files and toss out anything you no longer need.*

d. Pick three pieces of music you'd never think to dance to — classical? country/western? jazz? bluegrass? Ask your body to move to them. Don't judge what comes out, just enjoy it!

e. Begin a new activity that looks like fun but that you've never let yourself try before. Release your expectations and enjoy it.

f. Pretend that you're a tourist in your own town. What are the sights here? What is there to see? Where could you go that you haven't ever gone?

g. Have lunch or dinner at a new restaurant. Find an ethnic grocery. Try eating something you've never had before.

h. Volunteer for an organization that appeals to you. Meet new people. Join a club. Join a gym. Check out the art museum or zoo.

8. Part of giving yourself permission to explore new activities is to take your energy back from old ones that no longer give you what you want. Here's how to begin.

a. Make a list of five activities you do often — party hearty at the bar, eat out five nights a week, see every movie that comes to town, and so on.

b. Beside each activity, write down your reasons for doing it. For example, your reason for partying at the bar every night might be to meet people and relax.

c. On a scale of 1-10 (10 being the highest), how much does each activity fulfill your goals? Maybe your goal for eating at restaurants is to enjoy good meals and you realize it works about half the time. Give it a 5.

d. For anything that came out less than 10, brainstorm. How could you alter the activity to fulfill your goals more satisfactorily? Go out less and cook at home? Invite friends to your house some nights? Join a dining club to meet people with similar interests?

Play a little here and see what you come up with. Remember, you're under no obligation other than to find better ways to make yourself happy.

9. In your journal, read the first step your Explorer showed you in the movement meditation (Exercise 6). Take it.

10. The Artist Date

I'm thankful to Julia Cameron for describing this exercise in The Artist's Way. It works!

Once a week, make a date with yourself to spend two hours doing something that seems like it would be fun. It might be something spur of the moment or something that you've wanted to do for a long time.

An Artist Date is a gift to your Explorer, a chance to feed your creativity and nourish your soul in small, ordinary ways. One of my favorites has been to explore the Indian, Hispanic, and oriental groceries dotted around the city. Once, I found a sari shop and spent an hour enjoying the textures and colors of the fabrics. Try checking out the latest blooms at the botanical garden, scanning the recent acquisitions shelf at the library, or shopping for a new set of refrigerator magnets. Whatever you choose, enjoy it.

Artist dates are easy to resist. Because they're not directly "productive", lots of people put them so far down their list of priorities that they never get to them. In fact, because they feed you, they make the "productive" times better. It's also easy to resist going alone. "Isn't it more fun with someone else?" Sure it's good to do things with other people. I encourage it. Your artist date, though, is for you, without the compromise of trying to please anyone else. You deserve the gift of your own undivided attention!

Make a commitment to do one Artist Date a week for the next month. See what you come up with. Then, do it!

11.   *Honor yourself as Explorer by placing something on your altar to represent all his spontaneity, joy, and sense of adventure.*

THE EXPLORER AS CONSCIOUSNESS SCOUT

Not only is the Explorer a vital part of your own self-empowerment, he also carries an important piece of healing for the entire Tribe. As you express your new sense of discovery and adventure, the significance of your actions goes far beyond the personal. In many ways, the Explorer holds the key to our Tribe's healthy placement within society as a whole. Let me share with you a vision of Men who Love Men as Explorers for humanity.

The bulk of a People always moves slowly. Imagine a tribe of nomads trekking across the valleys and passes of time. At the front and rear stride tall protective warriors. In the center walks the great mass of humanity — quiet elders, mothers carrying babies, playful children, artisans, workers, and the rest. Among them, they carry an accumulation of goods necessary for survival and cultural continuity. The path they follow is wide, chosen with care for maximum ease and safety.

Around the edges, ranging far ahead and in all directions, run the scouts. Singly and in pairs, these individuals serve as eyes and ears for the slowly moving column.

Unencumbered, they move quickly, exploring a wider reach of terrain, sniffing the winds for hints of change. Their reports are vital to the welfare of the whole People. *"Three valleys west, sweet water, plenty for all." "Two days east, a settlement whose people are friendly, eager to trade." "Prepare to take cover, storms threaten just beyond the far horizon."*

In our culture, Gay people have always acted as scouts of a different kind. Andrew Ramer calls us "consciousness scouts." Instead of physical terrain, we explore the realm of creativity, bringing forth new ideas and perspectives to enrich social awareness all around. As artists, writers, designers, composers, and people "on the fringe," we explore the unknown, unfolding edges of consciousness. In the process, we perform a unique and valuable service to the whole.

In Gay circles, it's almost cliché to observe that we set the trends. From fashion to behavior, what we do among ourselves is often what everyone else does a few years later. When we're acting as trendsetters, we walk a step or two ahead — more colorful and less conformist than the mainstream. Our observations are diverse and touch many areas of society —

> *"See, families can be made by choice, based on love and not just on blood relation."*
> *"How 'bout it, sex can be healthy and liberating!"*
> *"You men would be happier if you quit the silly posturing and showed your real feelings."*
> *"Listen, you don't have to fit the old molds. Be happy whoever you are!"*
> *"You know, Girlfriend, your hair would look a lot better if you wore it up."*

Along with other groups of outsiders, Gay men act as the cultural yeast that keeps things bubbling and developing. We're not alone out here, but what we share is important and unique.

We need both parts. Faced with the need to provide security for developing offspring, the mainstream of any society is essentially conservative. In order to ensure stability, most social institutions reinforce tradition and maintain the status quo. Conservatism, though, (and don't we all know it!) can be carried too far. Resistance to change enhances stability, but when it squelches innovation altogether, it becomes lethal. Because external conditions shift continually, the fundamental rule of all life is "Adapt or die."

In a healthy society, conservatism and innovation live in balance. Understanding this, many peoples have honored the gifts of individuals who were different. Too many people within our own, unfortunately, seem to fear the very elements that keep us alive and vital. In times like these, when old ways are breaking down, conservatism fails. It's time for alternatives. Coming up with new ideas is the job of scouts.

Each of us has to make his own choices. As individuals, we all walk at different places within the Tribe. Some of us are pretty mainstream. Others explore terrain farther out. Wherever we walk as individuals, though, Gay people as a group are perceived to be "different." Like it or not, we are not part of the social mainstream. We've been pushed into the wilderness beyond the dominant paradigms and no amount of trying to fit in has changed that fact. We have a choice. On one hand, we could rail against society, isolate ourselves further, and feed our image as victims of social injustice. On the other, we could turn the tables, claim this place as our own, and enjoy the freedom and power it offers.

What to do? ***Embrace your differences!*** Your mission, should you choose to accept, is to make the Explorer a major part of your life. You're here to observe society from a different vantage point, discover the limits of the status quo, try alternatives, and then report back to the whole. Your visions, dreams, and sensibilities are a gift from Creator. Denying yourself by trying to meet the expectations of others negates the very gifts you were born to share. The role of Explorer and scout is yours. Claim it with enthusiasm and vigor!

Part 3
TAKE YOUR PLACE

14 Sustain Yourself in the World

Welcome to the final stretch of your journey! Since the point when you turned inward in Chapter 2, you've made major steps toward empowerment. You've faced fears, reframed negative beliefs, and learned to access powerful inner allies. With only a little more to go, you've already completed the hardest parts of the path.

In fact, you've come full circle. In order to keep your process safe, up to this point you stayed within the boundaries of your Inner Council. You kept your explorations private and focused primarily on yourself. This final leg of your quest is about re-entering the world. Your new attitudes and understanding can now support you on a broader stage. You're ready to step out and call into action all the strengths your newly-empowered allies — from Magic Boy to Explorer — have to offer.

In order to get to know them, you approached the archetypes one at a time. Actually, though, they don't exist as separate, isolated entities. The only way they can ever come into the world is through **you**. And no matter how much you empower each one individually, they can only express within the context of **your** personality, perspective, and identity. You are a unique and special individual. These final chapters are dedicated to helping you live in the world with your greatest satisfaction and fulfillment.

First, you'll examine how to support yourself by reclaiming your own connection with Spirit. With that support in place, you'll move on to discover what calls you into the world and create a vision of the future you want. Both of these explorations are important steps. As you complete them, you'll bring yourself to a point where you can continue exploring on your own. This phase of your empowerment journey will be complete and your gifts free to come forth in full measure.

RECLAIM YOUR SPIRITUALITY

Sunday mornings are often the spiritual high point of my week. Church? Hardly. Roller blading! Whenever I can swing it, I get up early, stretch, and strap on the blades. For a few hours, while everyone else is home with the paper or safely parked at church, I own the roads. I enjoy the sunshine on my skin, the fresh breeze in my lungs. I love the way my muscles dance — pumping hard up the hills, then balancing for the slide back down. Zooming across the pavements, I feel like a hawk, one with the world and full of life.

Blading is great exercise, but that's only one of the reasons I love it. I value it even more because of what it does inside. Blading washes away the tensions of the week. My mind forgets its habitual chatter and I find myself becoming clear and calm. Gifts of insight seem to jump out of nowhere, fully formed in my head. I'll think of the perfect response to someone who called with a problem last Thursday, or a new angle on a situation I'd been fretting about for weeks. After a mile or so, I start feeling connected all over — not only to my body, but also to people I pass, to oak trees, wandering dogs, the sky, the Earth. When I finish, I'm full of energy and ready to tackle the next round of living.

I particularly enjoy blading past the churches. Looking at all the parked cars, or maybe hearing a bit of sermon float out through an open window, it's hard not to feel just a little smug. I remember how I used to feel as a boy, dutifully attending our local Presbyterian church. Back then, I knew that church was supposed to be something very special. What I felt, though, was quite different. Mostly, I felt bored. Nothing in church seemed to have any life at all. Sometimes, I felt guilty. Guilt seemed to be part of the teaching. Mine came from knowing that God loved everyone else, "even the smallest sparrow," but not me, because I was sinful and didn't fit His mold. Sometimes I just felt itchy. I think my Mom had read somewhere that little boys need heavy wool pants in order to get to Heaven. When I compare all that yuck with the vitality and connection I feel blading, I can't help but smile. How different my conception of spirituality is now from what it was then!

For men who love men, "spirituality" is a loaded topic. A lot of us cringe — or turn off entirely — as soon as the term comes up. So much of our wounding was inflicted in the name of "God" and religion that, in defense, we reject spirituality altogether. This response is understandable, yet it's based on a fundamental misconception that religion and spirituality are the same thing. In fact, they are not. Religion comes from outside, through other people. Spirituality, on the other hand, comes from within. It's a part of your being as basic as the ability to eat or to breathe. To reject your spiritual nature for any reason is to rob yourself of wholeness.

In its essence, spirituality has absolutely nothing to do with any particular creed or dogma. Instead, it represents your innate ability to live with connection and alignment. To live spiritually is to recognize your place within the sacred circle of all life. It is to know beyond doubt that your existence has meaning, value, and purpose. It is to live in accord with your own truths and to embrace the full measure of your inborn potential. No matter who tells you otherwise, spirituality is your birthright.

In our Western, compartmentalized way of thinking, we commonly draw distinctions between activities we consider "spiritual" and those we don't. *"I'm spiritual from 10 to 11:30 on Sunday mornings and for fifteen minutes each night when I meditate."* In this view, some parts of life are more "spiritual" than others. Attendance at religious ceremonies, meditation, service to others, and volunteering usually get high marks. Baser activities like doing housework, having sex, or enjoying a good time get put down. Yet, compartmentalizing misses the point. Spirituality is a way of living that encompasses every part of your life. **What** you do matters much less than **how** you do it. Wherever you are, whatever you do, you can approach your life as a path to greater awareness.

Inevitably, life provides you with raw material through the situations and events of everyday living. How you use them is entirely up to you. If you choose to do so, any activity or condition can become a path to raise your spiritual consciousness. Oppression can be a path, and so can privilege. Poverty can, and so can wealth. So can sex, celibacy, doing drag, S/M ritual, raising children, being in a relationship, being single, having HIV, not having HIV, being openly Gay, staying closeted, living, or dying. If your intention is to live in alignment, even the most mundane activities can be intensely fulfilling. Conversely, the most dramatic works, if done without heart, are empty and meaningless.

When I mention spirituality to other men, some come back with "Why bother? Isn't all this talk of spirituality just some irrelevant exercise dreamed up by navel-watchers with nothing better to do?" If you're feeling skeptical, bear with me. In fact, honoring your spiritual connections is one of the healthiest, most relevant and practical steps you'll ever make. In the end, it will allow you to take care of business in every part of your life with greater intention and clarity. It will improve your relationships, give life meaning, and help you achieve tangible results whenever you take action. We'll just have to find a way that works for you.

Your relation with Spirit

Even in a single language, Spirit has many names — Higher Power, God, Goddess, All That Is, Creator, Source, Infinite Being, Universal Light, and hundreds of others. In fact, except for sex and money, this is probably the most talked about concept on the planet. People get very serious about it. Countless wars have been fought, innumerable people killed as one group tried to make its definition prevail over others'. Ironically and tragically, we're all probably talking about the same thing — and in the end, it's something we can't really define anyway.

Spirit is beyond form or definition. Human comprehension is firmly based in material reality, and so our ability to perceive what lies beyond this plane is limited. All our attempts to contain Spirit are as doomed to failure as trying to catch the wind with a gauze net. Spirit **IS**. All the rest is just words.

I think about my own definitions over the years. When I was very young, God was that white-haired patriarch seated on a giant marble throne like the one at the Lincoln Memorial. He knew me personally and, like Santa Claus, sat in judgment over every thought and action. *"John,"* He'd frown, *"if you listen to your mother, eat your beans, and brush your teeth every day, you're good. If not, though, if you hit your sister or touch yourself 'down there', I'll smite you with boils."*

As I grew older, new definitions layered themselves on top of the old one. When I was in tenth grade, God did a stint as an Ayn Rand super-capitalist. Later, when I became a scientist and "existentialist," He didn't exist for a while. When I discovered the Goddess, "He" became "She" and lived in Nature like Bambi. For a while after that, I thought I couldn't know God without a guru to take me there. And so it's gone through one exploration after another and another.

I'm sure I could find people to call me flighty, sinful, or worse for questioning who or what God might be. Actually, my fumbling, meandering search has taught me a lot. First, I know that Spirit exists, and continues to exist, whatever I happen to believe about the subject. I've learned that we can conceive of the Inconceivable in an almost infinite number of ways. None of these are mutually exclusive, nor is any one of them ultimately more "right" than another. In fact, each of the definitions I used worked well enough at the time. Each one gave me pieces that continue to be useful. And I can see the same principle for different peoples and beliefs all around the globe.

I suggest you view your own definitions of Spirit as tentative, working hypotheses. Give them room to grow and evolve as your understanding does. Give yourself space to shift your beliefs when you find ones that work better. Instead of accepting on pure faith what other people tell you, try measuring your ideas against more practical criteria — "Does this idea work? Does it help me live with greater satisfaction and power?" If you answer "yes," use it. If not, discard it and keep looking.

Spiritual evolution

Exercise

1. *In your journal, write a short definition of God/Spirit/Higher Power as you understand it. How would you define it? What terminology makes you the most comfortable? How would you describe Spirit to someone who's never heard of the concept (an unlikely situation, given that almost everyone has pretty definite ideas on the subject!)?*

2. *Take a few minutes to review your own spiritual evolution. As a child, what were you taught about God (or whatever name you used)? Have your beliefs and concepts changed over the years? How? What did each belief tell you about yourself? When you review your definition from the first exercise, how does it feel to you now? Are you still satisfied with it?*

SPIRITUALITY AND RELIGION

You have a direct connection with Spirit. Everyone does. If you let it, that connection will sustain you every moment of your life. It gives you inner peace and the power to heal. It gives you direct inner guidance, a realization of your oneness with every part of being, and the ability to achieve exalted, ecstatic states of awareness. These abilities are inherent in every human being. Get that? **Every** human being. We're **all** part of Spirit.

Ideally, the goal of any path is to help you make spirituality a functional, rewarding part of life. Every religion on the planet was probably built around a core of beliefs and procedures that actually served to meet this goal. Unfortunately, for many of them that core has been warped, interpreted, and obscured until very little of the original remains. Far too many religions have become instruments of separation, confusion, and disempowerment.

For Gay people, one of the most insidious and harmful manifestations of religious disempowerment is the belief that Creator has rejected us. It's as if we've been cast into a sort of limbo outside the rest of humanity. Though it may be deeply buried, this belief is widely held among men who love men. Its effects are pervasive — it makes us doubt our right to be happy, to partake of anything spiritual, and by implication, even to exist.

If you look at it logically, this belief is ridiculous. Why would Creator bring us forth in the first place — and continue to do so — if not intentionally? How could anyone be separate from the rest of Creation, anyway? Until you really look at it, though, and intentionally cast it out, this hidden demon saps your health and keeps you in a state of perpetual disempowerment. It's time to reclaim your right to belong — to family, tribe, nation, and humanity — by recognizing that the judgments you heard as a child came not from God, but from people.

Religions are run by people. Even religious leaders with the best of intentions make mistakes, and others with less integrity lie, swindle, and suck up power — your power — in direct contradiction to their own words. Like anything else in the hands of people, religion is a two-edged sword. It has been used to help as well as hurt, save as well as torture, heal as well as murder millions upon millions of people. Religion tends to have a lot of clout because it usually speaks in bold capital letters: "THE WORD OF GOD". Religious pronouncements are often considered by the speaker to be above examination. Not true.

Spirit is beyond form. Anyone who receives spiritual illumination has to work through his or her own beliefs, outlook, and language (did you think God just spoke English?). Any word received from "God" has come through a human filter and is thus subject to interpretation. When you hear someone claim to speak for God, take it with a grain of salt. There are many truths. Never accept someone else's until you measure it against your own knowing. If it rings true, good. If not, find another truth that does.

This is not to say that all religious traditions are bad. Many of them offer powerful, relevant teachings. You just have to make your own decisions. You were born with a natural and vital connection to your own Source. If a particular teaching or religious tradition helps you get in touch with that Source, go with it. Still, don't be afraid to ask questions. Beware especially of any system that requires you to cut off part of yourself (like the way you love) in order to belong, or that shuts down your inherent flow of joyful expression. It is not for you.

It takes guts to follow your own path. It takes guts to connect directly with Spirit and to stand in your own truth. Are you worth anything less? Overcome your resistance and reclaim your spirituality from those who would deny it. Then, you are on the path to full empowerment.

Claim your own spirituality

Exercise

3. *Choose one of the following exercises to uproot hidden negative beliefs. Use whatever name for Spirit carries the most energy for you.*

a. **Affirmations**

    Which of the following statements touches you the most deeply?

- I am one with all Being.
- God loves me just the way I am.
- I was created for a reason.
- I belong here.
- I am worthy of God's love.
- I am a deeply spiritual person.

Use the statement that calls you as an affirmation. Copy it twenty times quickly and jot down beside it any negative chatter that comes up in the back of your mind. If you don't get a lot to work with, repeat the exercise with the next statement on your list.

Rewrite any of the negatives as positive affirmations. Work with them over the next few weeks to make them part of your consciousness. Release the negatives ritually as you learned in Chapter 3.

b.   **Religious biography**

Outline your own religious biography. Were you raised to follow a certain religion? Has that changed over the years? What did each set of teachings contribute to the evolution of your personal spirituality? Where are you now? For each stage in your outline, consider the following questions:

- *What did this belief system tell you about yourself as a man who loves men?*
- *What did it tell you about yourself in relation to other people, and about Creation in general?*
- *How helpful was it in meeting your spiritual needs at the time?*
- *Did it teach you to accept yourself as you are or require you to change yourself in order to be acceptable?*

c.   **Story**

Write a story in which the main characters are a boy and God. Begin with what God tells the boy about himself early in his life (i.e. what you were told). Then write whatever story it takes for the boy to be welcomed by God into Creation, into the Garden of Eden, at the head of the family, or whatever other scenario makes you feel fully connected, worthy, and empowered. Have fun with this. Use it to make yourself feel really good.

SPIRIT LIVES WITHIN YOU

So where is Spirit? Most of the time, we talk as if we have to go somewhere else to find it. It's only in church or at the synagogue. It's up in Heaven, at the top of a holy mountain, or somewhere else out in Nature. In fact, we tend to look for Spirit everywhere except where it really lives. The way to reach Spirit is not to look outside yourself, but to shift your focus, get quiet, and go deeper within.

Spirit lives in you now and always as the irrefutable core of your being. Like everything else in this realm, this inner Divinity goes by many names — "Higher Self," "Soul," "Spirit," "the still small voice within." You've met him already in your journey, as the "Self Who Knows," the first time you called on your Inner Council. Whatever you call him, this is the part of you that brings all the rest together.

The good news is that you don't have to actually do anything to activate him. He already exists, fully formed and operating within you. Most of the time, though, we get so distracted by all the hyperactivity of the world that we forget this part even exists. Our challenge, then, is to calm the mind enough to let that divine Self come forth. For most of the rest of the chapter, we'll look at ways to cultivate inner stillness. First, though, let's take a moment to meet your divine Self more directly.

The Self Who Knows

Exercise

4. Read through the following visualization once or twice. When you can remember the general outline, close your eyes and let it guide your inner journey.

a. Follow your breath for a few minutes. Focus your attention on the inhale ... exhale ... inhale ... exhale ... until you feel yourself become more centered inside.

When you're ready, call your Inner Council. Imagine all the parts of you surrounding, supporting, and holding this safe, sacred space. This is where you'll meet your deepest Self.

b. Quietly, ask this part of you to come forth. Call him the "Self Who Knows" if you like - or any other name that feels right. Just sit quietly in the center of the Council circle and observe whatever sensations or images come to you.

At first, opening to the Self Who Knows may seem much like tuning in to your intuition. As you let it evolve, though, the experience goes much deeper.

The Self Who Knows is like a tone at the center of your being. He is the one who carries your identity through every change and transformation in your entire life. He existed in you already as you were born — and before. He is the Self who made you yourself as an infant, as a boy, as an adolescent. He's the Self that knows you as yourself now, even though you look and feel entirely different than at those other times in your life. This Self maintains your integrity each day as you grow and change in mind, body, and heart.

This Self will be with you as you grow older, approach death, and even make your transition. He exists behind all the physical appearances, the changes, the relationships, the events. He lives at your core, every moment of your life.

Of course, this Self may feel quite familiar to you. After all, you know him better than any one else in your life. Let him come in. Let him fill you up with a sense of your own essence. There may be words, there may be images, there may be feelings, or there may be nothing very tangible at all.

Whatever comes is fine.

c. *Whenever you want, you can deepen the experience by repeating the request, "Show me my essence. Show me my Self Who Knows." Let yourself follow your breath farther inside.*

This is the Self who connects with All of Being, the One you've been seeking whenever you were looking outside yourself for peace. He is the core and the goal of all your spiritual striving. Let him be there, supporting you now.

If you like, you can ask specific questions of your Self. If you like, you can share gratitude, joy, or other feelings.

If you like, just let his energy fill you with a sense of support and well being. You are never alone, really. You are always connected with All of Being, right here inside yourself.

d. *Stay with the exploration for as long as it feels good, then gently bring yourself back to normal awareness. Ground the energy you've raised and record any observations in your journal.*

SPIRITUAL PRACTICE

"Before enlightenment, chop wood, carry water,
After enlightenment, chop wood, carry water."
— *Buddhist saying*

Wouldn't it be nice to feel the clear support of the Self Who Knows all the time! Mostly, we're not even aware that he exists. Instead of being centered and calm, we spend our days dealing with one distraction after another. Think about all the conflicts and dramas that demand **your** attention. Will you make enough to cover the bills? Will you get along with the new guy at the store? Will your folks invite your lover to come home with you for the holidays or do they expect you to be alone again? On and on it goes, until you're swept away in a flood of conflicting voices, demands, and claims.

In a society addicted to busy-ness, the quiet voice of Spirit can seem subtle and easily overwhelmed. In order to maintain any sense of Self, you need a way to still the voices and reconnect with your own quiet center. How do you do that? The key is to cultivate a habit of tuning in regularly, no matter what else is going on. This is the basis of **spiritual practice.**

Though it can be relatively simple, spiritual practice is something that you have to develop yourself. I wish I could make it really easy and hand you a set of exercises to transform your life, cookbook style, with one simple, infallible recipe for eternal bliss:

> *"Take twenty deep breaths. Add four yoga postures, six rebirthings, and half an hour of tantra. Beat well. Add a dash of compassion, 4 sprigs of joy, half a tsp. of humility, three Hail Mary's and an affirmation or two. Don't stir. Let rise for three days, then bake in a meditative oven until done to perfection."*

I used to think things worked that way. When I began this journey, my expectations were naïvely high. "Wow!" I'd think, "This is the one. _____ is gonna change my life! From now on, I'll have all I need, no more pain, no more problems. I'll like myself, get laid daily, and win the lottery." I filled in the blank with the latest new class or discovery — yoga, meditation, EST, metaphysics, religious science, and on and on.

It didn't work. Even though each step brought insights or helpful techniques, ongoing bliss was elusive. I still had to get up each day and work to pay the bills. The dishes didn't suddenly start washing themselves. People around me still got sick. Some of them died. The world didn't change just because I was now meditating, or speaking positively, or whatever. In time, I learned that living in alignment isn't supposed to make life go away. Spiritual practice won't make you immune to pain or free from fear or challenge. If anything, it makes the experiences deeper and more present. However, spiritual practice does foster a shift in perspective that lets you deal with the challenges in ways that are more effective and meaningful.

No one can tell you which practice will work best for you. Different men are called to different spiritual techniques. Alan found that meditating regularly lets him function more effectively in his job as a lawyer. Martin sketches three times a week and swears it makes everything else fall into place. Joe does running meditation to feel centered and calm. Jimmy uses yoga to get over the stress of working as a critical care nurse. Andy finds his inspiration with a friendly congregation each Sunday. What works for you depends on your own sensibilities.

The basis of any spiritual practice is to quiet the mind. Let's return to the simple tuning-in exercise you've already used, just to help you remember what it feels like.

Come into the moment

Exercise

5. *Sit comfortably. For the next five minutes, keep your attention on your breath. Set a timer or sit where you can see a clock. Breathe in, then out. On the inhale, mentally say the word, "In." On the exhale, "Out." In. Out. In. Out. "Boring," you say? Of course it is. It's supposed to be. Just keep going. Once your logical, linear mind gets bored enough, it stops trying to run things and you begin to see what's going on underneath.*

What do you notice? Does your mind keep distracting you? Back hurt? Gotta do something right now? Your mind will do almost anything to avoid stillness. Whatever comes up, just keep returning your attention to the breath. Even if you forget the "In, Out," just resume it as soon as you remember.

After five minutes, how do you feel?

Spirit infuses the ordinary details of life. Conscious breathing brings you into the moment, where they live. Try watching your breath the next time you eat dinner, jog around the block, or vacuum the living room. Get out of your head. Pay attention to textures. Smell the air. Feel warm sunshine, cool rain, hot flesh. Try it next time you visit a sick friend. If there's pain, stay present. If you're uncomfortable, breathe in, and out. Next time you're making love, or dancing, or cooking, let go of theories about how life **should** be and notice how it really **is**. Don't look to heaven for permission to live. Live now. Then, Spirit comes to you.

Living in the moment brings understanding and joy you used to overlook. You feel the breeze on your face while you're walking to your car or catch a bit of song from that mockingbird in the hedge. You hear pain beneath the cheerful words of a friend and can pause to share a reassuring hug. You remember bits of a dream from last night, or take a moment to jot down the words to a poem that just flitted through your mind. You realize that your ego's not really in charge and understand that whatever drama is consuming you this moment won't last forever. Quietly and subtly, your life becomes richer in texture and detail. Even without any dramatic, transformative incident, you begin to feel more satisfied and alive.

HOW TO CHOOSE A SPIRITUAL PRACTICE

The only way to know if a particular technique or spiritual tradition meets your needs is to try it. Fortunately, if you're serious about looking, your chances of finding something that works for you are very good. There are thousands of techniques to choose from — and you can adapt any of them to suit your own inclinations. Let's go over a few guidelines that will help you make clearer choices.

In choosing a practice, honor your own path. Techniques that work for someone else might not do a thing for **you**. Be suspicious if there's too much hype around some spiritual group or if a particular guru or class is touted as **the** answer for everyone. Also, look very closely if the spiritual lessons end up costing an arm and a leg. Though a fair exchange of energy, including money, is appropriate for spiritual teaching, when the balance shifts too far toward expensive, you might wonder about motives and integrity. No matter how insistently someone tries to sell you on a particular path, trust yourself to make the final decision.

Trust yourself around **timing** as well. Your spiritual path is constantly evolving. What is entirely appropriate at one point in your journey might not work at all later. Don't be afraid to keep moving, to let go of any practice that seems outdated, and find something else that more closely addresses your present needs.

Practice, as the word implies, is something you do regularly. Just like brushing your teeth, eating well, or exercising, spiritual practice is an ongoing commitment to quality living. One trip to the gym may feel good, but it changes very little unless you make it part of a regular program. In the same way, doing spiritual practice once can feel satisfying, but the true value lies in doing it again and again. At first, staying with it takes effort. Once you get used to the structure, though, practice becomes a sort of inner gyroscope that stabilizes you through the ups, downs, twists, and turns of living in the world. In time, it will become so natural you'd never even consider doing without it.

It takes time to reap the benefits. If you're called to a specific technique or path, give yourself a chance to really experience it. When you're learning something new, it might feel dramatic and powerful right off, or it might feel too hard, too easy, or simply boring. Trust your intuition. Unless the practice feels harmful — in which case you should stop immediately — hold off a while before you make a judgment. It might take several weeks or even months to determine whether this practice works for you. Be patient.

Bottom line, spiritual practice works. When you practice regularly to cultivate "quiet mind", you create a space in your life for Spirit. Spirit **will** respond. Support will come. The tricky part is that you never know just how or when. Spirit follows its own rhythms. Instead of trying to force it to do what you want — which is impossible in any case — open to the even greater reward of ongoing alignment.

The rest of this chapter is a survey of simple centering techniques. Obviously there are too many for you to try right now. Read through them lightly to get an idea of possibilities. If any of the techniques seems particularly appealing, experiment. Let the suggestions presented here inspire you to create your own personal brand of spiritual support.

BODY CENTERED PRACTICE

Sitting meditation

This is a well-established practice in many traditions. You've already tried it several times when you used your breath to tune in to deeper levels of awareness. There are many schools of meditation, some with very involved or deliberate guidelines. If sitting meditation appeals to you, formal instruction in one of these traditions might be quite beneficial. You have nothing to lose, however, in trying it on your own.

Sitting meditation uses many of the same techniques you've already experienced. Your eyes can be closed or partly open and focused softly on a candle, a flower, some meaningful image, or nothing at all. Follow the breath. To still the mind, you could repeat "In/Out" as you did earlier, repeat an affirmation, or count to ten over and over.

One way to steer your mind onto a good track is to prime the pump with a bit of inspiration. Many books offer inspirational prayers, quotes, and meditations. Choose one that appeals to you and read a short section each day to set the tone for your reflection.

To make sitting meditation into ongoing practice, make a commitment to sit each day for a specific time. Sometimes it will feel wonderful. Sometimes it won't. What matters is that you continue. Make a date with yourself to meditate and keep it, no matter how you feel. At first, your mind will resist with every trick it knows. When it's time to sit, you'll have an unbearable urge to clip your fingernails, clean all the old issues of *Undergear* out of your closet, call your ex, or scrub the tub. Don't give in. In time, you'll enjoy the quiet centering that meditation brings and your practice will get easier.

Walking meditation

In Golden Gate Park, I once watched an old Asian man walking very slowly and deliberately. Each step inscribed a perfect arc. The foot seemed to rise automatically, float a moment, then return to the Earth in front of the other. His head was still, eyes open but focused inward. Several minutes later, a couple of other men joined in two steps behind him. In ten minutes, there was a line of twenty people slowly crossing the green grass. When the first man paused, bowed slowly and left the line, the others continued walking. I was entranced. Even though I hadn't a clue about what was going on, the day had become peaceful and serene. Later, I learned that these people were practicing walking meditation.

In the Buddhist tradition, walking meditation is used to encourage alignment with self and the Earth. The principles are the same as with sitting meditation except that you walk — slowly, quietly, and deliberately. Each step takes an entire breath. The slowness can feel exquisite — or excruciating — as it forces you to let go of where you're going and come fully into where you are. Repeating a mantra — a short, inspirational statement — with each step helps calm the mind further. One of my favorites, taught by Joan Halifax, is "For the green Earth." Others are "Right here, right now," "We are all One," "I support all Life," or whatever appeals to you.

Movement meditation

The movement meditations you've explored on this journey can form the basis of a very satisfying practice. Review the techniques you learned in Chapter Four or adapt any of the others you explored to suit your needs. Use whatever music calls you and take as long as you like. By moving every day or so, you invite your body to become an equal partner on your spiritual journey. The following instructions will serve as a good beginning.

In a quiet space, playing music you like, close your eyes and focus your attention on your breath. Let it lead you inward, starting with your head, down through your neck, shoulders, spine, and so on until you feel your whole body in alignment. Let your awareness move all the way through your feet and into the Earth. Feel how you can breathe with your whole body.

When you're ready, ask your body, "Show me how I feel right now." Repeat the request in your mind as you let your body move. Start small at first and follow the motion with your breath. Let it lead you wherever it likes. This could be the whole meditation.

If you have specific questions, situations, or issues you'd like to deal with, address them the same way you did in earlier exercises. Repeat "Show me ..." over and over as you let your body respond.

For greater clarity, call your archetypal allies. Call the Magic Boy, Elder, Lover, and Shaman. Call the Warrior. Call the Explorer. Call on Spirit or the Self Who Knows. Let them clarify your questions and help you resolve challenging situations. Be patient and imaginative. Enjoy yourself.

When you feel complete, gently bring your body to stillness. Follow the breath through every part of your body. Notice how your feelings have shifted. When you're ready, open your eyes.

Athletic practice

With intention, **any** physical activity can become spiritual practice. Anyone who has trained seriously in athletics understands that the "inner game" is usually more important than the outer one. The same outlook that helps you master a physical skill also helps you master your mind.

If you participate in a regular program of physical training, you already have the beginnings of spiritual practice. Activities that are most conducive involve aerobic, repetitive movement in which your attention is focused inward rather than on other people. Walking, jogging, bicycling, swimming, weight training and dancing are excellent meditative vehicles.

Use the techniques we've been discussing to quiet the mind. Focus on your breath and the rhythm of the movement. Give your mind something to do by repeating an affirmation or a simple count. When I do repetitive exercise, I like to use affirmations instead of counting. I choose something simple like "I-am-strength-and-I-am-health-I-love-my-bo-dy-and-my-self-(pause)." Because I know that this statement represents 16 beats, I use it to keep track of how many reps I've done. Keeping your focus in your body, instead of replaying last night's argument with your lover over and over, helps you be clear, centered, and aligned.

CREATIVITY AS PRACTICE

Joy journal

Writing in your journal enriches your life with insight and stability. All it takes to turn it into spiritual practice is the commitment to write regularly. Give yourself twenty minutes, or three to four pages, each morning to clear your mind and set your goals for the day. If you'd rather, give yourself time before bed to record the insights and gems of the day's experience.

Several years ago, I had the pleasure of taking a journal-making workshop with a delightful artist named Paulus Berensohn. Punctuating the class with outbursts of poetry and outrageous stories, he exhorted us to keep what he called a "Joy Journal." "There's enough pain and grief in the world. Do yourself a favor. Save and savor every bit of joy! This is what feeds you."

Paulus demonstrated his own daily meditation process. Each morning he turns to a new, empty double page in his journal. Opening to Spirit, he then fills the pages with whatever gives him joy. He showed us poems he'd copied, pictures, anecdotes, and bits of wisdom with which he'd filled the pages. The joy that shows in this man's lined, smiling face and the vitality in his body were enough to convince me that he knows exactly what he's talking about.

Try it. You might begin with a sketch of the first daffodil you saw after a winter of snow, or a photo of gray thunderheads illuminated by the golden sunset last Wednesday. It might be a picture of the first man who ever held you tenderly or a recipe for the fabulous peach and raspberry pie your friend Brian brought to dinner. It might be three whiskers from the cat who sleeps with you or a drawing sent by your favorite niece. You might put a gold star on one page with a note reminding you of the project you finished successfully at work. However you do it, focusing on the positive parts of your life keeps them alive and also creates an opening for more to come in.

Creative practice

My grandmother used to knit for hours. A seemingly endless stream of afghans, blankets, sweaters, and scarves flowed from her couch onto the backs and beds of her growing family. She never paid much attention to the knitting. Her needles seemed to have a mind of their own. When I asked her once why she didn't rest, since we could obviously afford to buy all the woolen goods we needed, she looked at me like she didn't understand the question. Then, she just laughed and said, "It keeps my hands happy." Though she'd never have called it that, my grandmother knew the secret of creative spiritual practice.

Ask any artist. Creativity is a powerful tool for centering the mind. When you make creative activity the focus of spiritual practice, your goal is the mental stillness it fosters rather than a finished product or work of art. You don't need artistic skill nor any particular talent. All you need is your own permission to immerse fully in the process.

Choose any creative activity you enjoy — dance, pottery, weaving, writing, painting, collage, sculpture, or whatever. As you begin, center your mind with the techniques we've discussed. Later, you probably won't need them. Creative process has a way of drawing you in and capturing your attention until you're fully engaged in the moment.

What makes creative practice work is your willingness to let go of where it takes you. Keep your attention on the process and let it lead wherever it will. Sometimes you'll end up with a finished product that delights you. Sometimes you'll uncover ideas for further exploration. Sometimes you won't come up with anything useable at all. None of that matters. Just stay with the process.

Writing meditation

We discussed writing meditation in Chapter 13 (page 216). To make it into practice, make a commitment to write for a specific length of time each day, or at least several times a week. By choosing a subject and agreeing to write continually until your time is up, you'll enter deeply into the creative void. As you let the writing lead you, you'll feel as if you're mining your subconscious. It takes a whole lot of digging, one word, one breath at a time. Every now and then, somewhere in the enormous pile of dirt, a true gem of insight will sparkle in the light of your attention. These occasions are an extra benefit. Most of the time, you'll be rewarded with deep, calm satisfaction.

Spiritual retreat

Does your life ever feel too fast, like an endless rat-race of bills, demands, and meaningless tasks? Do you feel like you never have time even to think? If so, you're a perfect candidate for spiritual retreat.

Retreat is an age-old tool that helps you step out of your normal routines and touch back into wholeness. Depending on your needs, it can mean a five minute dance break between clients, a brisk walk around the block, a weekend at a lakeside cabin, or three months of silence at a monastery. Often, a small bit of "down" time to regroup, refocus, and gather your wits makes your "up" time a hundred percent more rewarding and productive.

Be creative. Give yourself spontaneous breaks from routine. Gift yourself with an unstructured weekend at the beach or ten minutes in the rocker on the front porch. Sit in a dark field and watch the stars move across the sky or watch your breath steam in the cold air on the way to work. Your rewards will be a sense of revitalization, deeper clarity, and profound connection.

Retreat in a natural setting is particularly effective. All our vitality comes from the Earth. When we learn to distrust our bodies, when we live in artificial environments on artificial schedules, our connections with the planet are severely threatened. Any steps you make, even very small ones, toward reclaiming these connections are amazingly revitalizing. Stand outside in the fresh air. Watch a sunrise. Immerse yourself in the ocean. Find the trees that live even in the heart of the densest city. Explore the life around you. Your own life depends on it.

CREATE YOUR OWN RITUALS

Life is a string of moments, some special, but most pretty ordinary. Throughout history, virtually every people has marked significant moments with ceremony and celebration. You can do the same by learning to create and practice simple rituals.

A ritual doesn't have to be a major event. A single action can add great depth and meaning to your life. You could:

- Clean out the old ashes and burn a bit of sage to start the first fire of the year in your fireplace.

- Mark the changes of seasons by spending time outside.

- Hold hands with your partner for a moment at the start of each meal. Look in each other's eyes and remember why you're together.

- Light a candle when someone you know is sick or makes his transition, just to send a prayer of support.

- Invite a group of friends to your garden in honor of the first flower of Spring.

- Take a cleansing bath on each new moon, just to remind yourself that you can turn over a new leaf at any time.

- Go dancing or serve a meal for friends at the full moon, just because you appreciate them.

Be creative. Marking the small and large passages in your life enriches your experience and makes you aware of your place within the larger cycles of all being.

Try it!

Exercise

6. *Practice*

Just by doing the exercises on this empowerment journey at a regular pace, you've already been engaging in a sort of spiritual practice. You can continue that as your practice until you finish.

If you'd like to try another type of spiritual practice in addition to these exercises, choose one from the suggestions here or from other practices you're familiar with. Write a commitment to practice that activity each day for the next few weeks. You won't need a lot of time — 10-20 minutes a day would be plenty. In fact, it's better to aim low and complete what you say you'll do, rather than overcommit and get discouraged.

Figure out exactly what you'll need to do to get started — buy a notebook, rearrange your schedule, get out your running shoes, find a cushion to sit on, whatever. Do this the first day.

In your journal, draw a calendar of the next three weeks. Each day when you finish your period of practice, mark off that day in your journal. By encouraging yourself to stay at it, you'll get a better idea of how this practice works for you. If you skip a day, don't beat yourself up. Just continue the next day.

At the end of three weeks, take stock. How do you feel? Did you practice each day? Did you notice any difference in the way you feel, or in how you relate to life? Did you receive any insights? Would you like to continue this practice for another month? Could you revise it to suit your needs better? Is there something else you'd like to try?

7.   **Joy**

What gives you joy? For me, it's hiking to a waterfall, digging a new bed in my garden, hanging out the laundry on a breezy afternoon. My friend Jim loves renovating houses. He's happiest with a hammer in his hand, bubbling over with ideas, projects, and half a dozen color chips for paint. Monty gets off on designing wigs and dreaming up costumes for theater. Rob gets ecstatic writing smart-ass dialog. Bob does woodwork. Marguerite paints. John dances.

Any activity that makes you joyful is a spiritual tonic. List five of yours. Then list ten more. Finding the joy in your life is one of the best spiritual practices going. Then, go enjoy them!

15

Live in the World

RETURN HOME

You have been on a journey through the wilderness, a journey that began long before you picked up this book. It started, really, at the moment years ago when you first realized you were different, that you didn't fit into "normal" society. A part of you went into exile then, into a wasteland as dark and fearsome as that faced by any young hero of mythology. You wandered through strange lands on a path that brought suffering, danger, and isolation. You'd probably never have chosen this journey consciously, and might have done anything you could to avoid it, yet all in all it has been far from fruitless.

You survived. You are no longer the youth who set forth. You've grown. You've explored the depths of your soul and gained new understanding, perspectives, and beliefs. You've met powerful allies. You've grown in stature and wisdom to become a man who can hold his own in the world. Now at the culmination of your journey, it is time to return home.

You stand at the threshold. Your hero's journey comes to completion with this final passage — return to the society that you left so long ago. Returning, you redeem the journey by claiming it as your own. You move beyond the pain and wounding by integrating the lessons they brought you. Returning, you step forth to demand your rightful place as an active, empowered, and fully contributing member of society.

Why would you want to do that? For one thing, it feels great! The talents, gifts, and power that live in you become most fully yours when you share them with others. Have you ever helped a child, or an old person, or a sick friend who needed assistance? Have you ever planted a tree and watched year after year as it spread green branches toward the sky? Have you ever made someone laugh, offered comfort to a grieving relative, or shared your song with a group of friends? If you have, you know the simple, profound satisfaction of helping others. It feels good to share.

In the second place, your gifts are desperately needed. You're not alone here, not an independent agent, no matter how isolated you've felt. You are inseparably part of society, humanity, and the planetary being. Like it or not, we sink or swim together. Right now, we stand at the precipice of global crisis. You know the problems without my listing them. You personally hold pieces of the healing. Your figurative journey through the wilderness has equipped you with tools that can fight humanity's collective disease. The very fact that you hold them gives you the responsibility to use them.

Where can **you** make a difference? Anywhere that calls you. Can you, who understand it so well, fight homophobia by teaching other people to look beyond differences? Can you help provide support for the men and women who suffer not only from AIDS, but from all kinds of disease? Can you help combat the apathy that plagues our political system or the greed and misplaced priorities that contribute to starvation, poverty, and environmental degradation? Whoever you are, there is a need in the world that cries out for your attention. There is a niche that only you can fill —and your filling it brings you satisfaction as it helps the world. When you share with the world, you share with yourself.

Maybe you're already sharing. Maybe you haven't a clue where to start. Wherever you are, this chapter will help you recognize and deepen your connections with society and the world.

AFFILIATIONS

Can you think of one living thing on Earth that exists in a vacuum — a single tree perhaps, or a mouse, or bacterium? You can't, I'm sure of it, because nothing lives alone. Even men walking over two hundred thousand miles away on the moon were supported by a cast of thousands. Even the tiny creatures inhabiting deep-sea trenches six miles from sunshine depend on each other and all the creatures above them for food. **All** life is interdependent and interconnected. Every single being draws from and contributes to the whole. That includes you.

Throughout this book, we've talked about the Tribe of Men who Love Men as if it were a discrete, separate entity. That's not entirely accurate. Membership here is not exclusive. In fact, one of the strengths of our Tribe is that we come from every people and society on the planet. We are born to families. We have ethnic roots. We belong to religious, community, social, and political groups. We are citizens of neighborhoods, communities, cities, states, nations, and planet. We are multifaceted beings within an ever-changing landscape of affiliations.

No matter how independent or reliant, isolated or connected you feel, you depend on and respond to other people every day. They, in turn, are affected by you. Just as every cell in your body is part of tissues, organs, and systems, you live within the interconnected network of all life. Like any cell, you were born to fulfill certain tasks that affect the functioning of the whole organism. Like any cell, your own health and well-being are inseparably linked to the health and well-being of the whole. Ultimately, it is impossible to consider one part without the other.

Affiliation comes in many different forms. Some connections feel intimate, like those with family, lovers, and close friends. Others are more casual, like your relationships with co-workers, fellow dancers at the bar on Saturday night, or people who shop in the same stores as you. Some feel positive and harmonious, others not. Some you may not even be aware of. Each one has its own parameters. Each one presents challenges, offers benefits, and demands responsibilities. All of these connections are important. The next exercise will help you recognize just how extensive your own network of connections really is.

Your connection network

Exercise

1.   **Personal connections**

a.   *Make a list of ten groups with which you feel actively affiliated. Leave a line or two after each one for comments. List familial, social, professional, religious, political, and interest-based organizations to which you belong. List relevant associations based on where you live — condo, neighborhood, etc. — or your various levels of citizenship — city, state, national, planetary.*

Some of your affiliations will be actual organizations. Others may be less formal, such as people concerned about the environment, interested in astrology, dealing with HIV, and so forth.

Describe yourself and your major affiliations in a single sentence. "I'm a 35 year old bisexual Jewish-American accountant who cooks and belongs to a bicycle club." "I'm a second generation Dutch immigrant queer New York leather queen who raises dachshunds."

b.   *Beside each affiliation on the list, jot down the major benefits you get from it — sharing love, professional support, enjoyable companionship of people interested in the same things as you, and so on.*

c.   *Jot down the contributions you make to each group. Do you provide leadership for your neighbors who are meeting to deal with rising crime? Are you an enthusiastic uncle who takes the kids to the beach on weekends? Do you enrich the support group at the hospital with your sense of humor and compassion? Acknowledge the gifts you share.*

d.   *Being part of a group also involves challenges and responsibilities. What are these? Citizenship, for example, involves paying taxes, voting, and staying informed on issues. The bicycle club requires $10 a year in dues, and sometimes you have to avoid the guy in the chartreuse spandex who wants more of your time.*

2.   Energetic connections

Some connections are less apparent. Energetically, you're connected with any individual or group with which you carry unresolved business. This type of connection takes many forms. Michael found that his family still played a major part in his life, even though they had broken off contact with him years ago. The hurt, anger, and resentment he felt toward them still influenced his behavior very strongly. Willie discovered similar feelings in relation to the church that had excommunicated him for being Gay. He realized that he still had some business to attend to there, and that until he did, he was still connected.

a.   *How about you? Are there people, groups, or organizations that you feel strongly about, even though you may not be physically connected? The key here is to notice the level of energy. List only people or groups about which you still feel a large amount of energy (anger, resentment, sadness, longing, or whatever).*

b.   *If you'd like to look deeper, do a short movement meditation, in which you request of your body, "Show me who I'm connected to energetically."*

The point here is to acknowledge where you have connections. Don't try to do anything about them just yet. You'll use them later as a guide for potential areas of action.

3.   Connections with the world

Take a moment to acknowledge your connections on a broader scale.

Think about the food you've eaten today. Where did it come from? Who was involved in growing, processing, distributing and preparing it? How does your purchasing and eating that food affect them?

Think about the water you drink. Where does it come from? Where does wastewater go? What affects the quality of your water supply?

Air is your most basic commodity. Who has shared the air that made up your last breath? Who shares it when you're done with it?

Think about any action you take and notice how it affects other living things — people, plants, animals, etc.

Remember "six degrees of separation," the concept that any two individuals on this planet are connected by a chain of associations averaging only six individuals? Pick any living thing on the planet — from a bacterium in Saudi Arabia, a sperm whale in the South Pacific, or a cute young daddy in northern Australia — and trace the hypothetical chain of associations that leads to you. For example, the bacterium lives in the soil that grows food eaten by citizens who pump oil that you buy to drive to the grocery. Play with this. Just thinking about one or two examples will get the point across.

BEYOND THE GHETTO: SAFE SPACE VS. ISOLATION

When you're just coming out, one of your most important pieces of healing is to end the isolation you felt growing up. Coming into a group of men where you can be yourself without editing, hedging, or lying about your identity feels wonderful. It's like stepping from a black and white movie into color, or from a street war into Disneyland. At first, it's hard to get enough. Often, being around other men-loving men feels so safe that it's tempting to hang out there as much as possible — to the point of letting go of anyone who isn't in on the secret. In a big city, where you have the luxury, your network can extend until it includes almost everyone in your life. You go to your Gay dentist, your Gay doctor, your Gay mechanic, eat at Gay restaurants, shop in Gay stores, and even take your Gay dog to a Gay groomer.

Probably none of us fully outgrows the need for positive Gay space. Not only does it help heal old wounds, it also provides an ongoing source of validation and support. At the same time, though, there's a danger in becoming too exclusively identified with any one group. After the initial period of healing, unless your connections support you in moving back toward full participation in society, your all-Gay support network starts to look more like a confining ghetto that perpetuates separation and keeps you in hiding.

Like it or not, men who love men exist in every part of society. Like it or not, that is also right where we belong — everywhere. Living in a ghetto — whether physically, or by choosing not to deal with anyone else — is only a single step from the closet. It just makes the closet bigger. It's got windows now, skylights maybe, and a **marvelous** view, but it's still a closet. It is safer for a while, and definitely a step toward healing. It is not, though, the final answer.

The first time I encountered this idea, I was furious. "What do you mean 'Ghetto'?! What's wrong with living totally separate? Why the hell would I want to help **them** anyway, all they ever did was hurt me? Screw em!" It took a while for me to calm down and look at things more objectively. When I did, I recognized the very vehemence of my reaction as a sign that I still had some wounding to deal with.

The closet/ghetto, however comfortable, ultimately keeps you in a state of half-citizenship. Total separation robs you of the opportunity to fight conditions in the larger society — like homophobia, negative stereotyping, and societal rejection of same-sex love — that hurt you in the first place. Think about it. If you don't vote because neither political party supports Gay marriage, you've given up your voice in the decision making process. If you skip the condo meeting because "they're just a bunch of hetero jerks," the hetero jerks will be the ones who make the rules you have to live with. Only by moving beyond separation — when you're ready — are you able to claim your full health and power.

To change the world, you have to be part of it. Yes, people did hurt us, but the hurt is a symptom of a greater pattern of disease. Homophobia is a disease that ultimately hurts everyone. Like racism, greed, poverty, and environmental misuse, it is a disease of humanity. Think of these issues as auto-immune problems affecting society. Just as HIV, lupus, and other conditions make some cells in a body attack others, societal diseases place groups of people at odds with each other to the detriment of the whole. To heal the problem, fight the diseases, not the people.

The world is changing quickly and dramatically. Issues that were inconceivable twenty years ago — Gay marriages, Gay parenting, openly Gay priests, soldiers, and Congressmen — are now front page news. The ghetto is rapidly becoming outdated as we integrate more openly and fully into the whole of society. As old models change, maybe it's time to consider defining ourselves in new ways. Should we still view ourselves as "Gay" or "Bi" first, with whatever else we are or do as secondary? Or shall we place our sexuality within the broader context of our full selves? Of course, how we love will always be integral to who we are, yet why can't we honor that part as we expand our horizons to include our total identities? Can we not act fully and openly everywhere in the world? It will take time, of course, but in the long run we have to claim our right to live in the world on our own terms.

Gay and beyond

Exercise

4. *It's natural to share yourself within many different contexts. No single group or individual could possibly meet all your diverse needs, interests, and ways of being. Review the list of affiliations you made in Exercises 1-3. Mark each group that is exclusively Gay with a big "G".*

In the other groups, how open are you about being Gay? How much of yourself are you able or willing to share in each setting?

Are there other groups that you'd like to join but haven't because of being Gay? If so, what are they?

This exercise is intended as food for thought, not as fodder for judgment. Each of us has to find his own balance of Gay and non-Gay interactions. At times the balance shifts one way, at others it shifts back. This is a very natural process. Just observe where you are.

SHARE YOUR GIFTS

Your gifts don't just belong to you alone. Whatever they are — beauty, talents, insights, material abundance, skills in any area — they gain in value when you share them with others. If you keep them hidden, or refuse to explore them fully, your gifts atrophy and go away. Think about a painter who won't show anyone his masterpieces, or a magnificent singer whose only stage is the shower. Any gift you have is a gift of Spirit. The only way it can enter the world is **through** you. When you share your gifts, you are the hands of Creator, nurturing and enriching all of Creation.

Almost every spiritual tradition speaks about the importance of dedicating part of yourself to the pursuit of higher goals. *"Do not hide your light under a bushel." "Share the visions given you by Great Spirit to help the People."* There is wisdom here that warrants attention. Life is short. Living only for yourself may feel good for a while, but ultimately leaves you unfulfilled. Opening beyond self by making whatever contribution or service you can gives your life meaning and depth.

True service is not the unhealthy, self-sacrificing martyrdom most of us were taught to believe. Indeed, it's not about giving yourself up at all, but about meeting your own needs and desires in ways that help others, too. Service is a call to be all you can, to reach your full potential, and express every bit of yourself with enthusiasm and vigor.

Healthy service actually feels wonderful. Each gift carries an inherent desire to express. Remember how badly you wanted to be sexual with another man before you came out, or how strong the desire gets if you go too long without? Your gift of sharing sexual intimacy demands expression. Your other gifts call with the same urgency. If you're an artist, you can be horny with the desire to paint or draw. If you're a dancer, every cell in your body cries out for the release of movement. If your gift is humor, compassion, organizational skill, the ability to cook a good meal, or to walk in heels, it lives in you always, craving expression. Do yourself a favor. Give in and share.

➤ Honor your gifts

5.a. *List ten of your talents, the ones you might put on a resume — good communication skills, great singer, caring and compassionate doctor, skilled auto mechanic, good teacher. Don't be modest, be honest.*

b. *List ten more. This time, list things that might not make the "official" list, smaller or off the wall talents you might have overlooked — make a great barley leek soup, score 200 at bowling, funny with kids, remember jokes, patient with older people, give a great blow job, whatever.*

c. *List five positive traits other people notice about you.*

Leave a little space after these lists in your journal. Later, when you think of other talents and gifts you haven't listed, return and record them here.

THE CALL OF THE WORLD

The world needs your gifts, now. It needs them not just a little, but desperately. I bet you can think of fifty problems that need attention without even trying hard — ranging in scope from AIDS, world hunger, and terrorism to the traffic congestion on your block or lack of water pressure in your apartment building. Indeed, we face a collective crisis of worldwide proportions. Even if there were no more than just numbers to consider — and there is **much** more — the fact that human population is expected to reach nearly 10 billion people by the mid-21st century will place an almost unimaginable pressure on institutions, governments, resources, and social interactions. Beyond doubt or denial, it is crisis time. Every person on the planet is called to join the search for solutions.

Are you breathing? Trying even to contemplate the enormity of the problems — much less **solve** them — is enough to put anyone into overwhelm. Indeed, that's already going on in most of society, as the sheer volume of frightening, disheartening information causes many of us to shut down in self-defense. Shutting down, though, only lets the problems go unaddressed and we dig our collective hole deeper and deeper.

It is possible to break out of overwhelm. In fact, it isn't even that hard. To start, recognize that you don't have to work alone. The fate of the entire world does not rest only on your two shoulders. Yes, you have a part to play, but your task is no bigger than you can handle. You have allies, each of whom does his or her part as well. The key is to think of yourself not just as an individual, but as part of the whole organism. The problems you face are problems of the collective. As you learn to align, your individual efforts become more powerful and effective because they draw on the strength of the whole. Change comes when we work together, one small step at a time, in the direction of healing.

You'll feel incredibly good about yourself when you learn to act effectively in the world. You've spent a good deal of time developing your skills. Go ahead and dare to use them!

The call of the world

Exercises

6. Use the following exercises to help you focus on the issues in the world that call you the most strongly.

a. *List five problems in the world that you think are important.*

b. *List five issues that concern you within the Gay community.*

c. *If you wrote down any "unresolved business" in Exercise 2 at the beginning of this chapter, review that list. Use it to direct you to where you might help others. For example, let's say you suffered rejection as a boy because your family couldn't deal with your being Gay. Maybe it's appropriate to reconnect with your family at this time. Maybe it's not. In either case, you might get great satisfaction from helping boys at a youth center deal with similar problems.*

d. *Do a little imagining. If you had all the money and time you ever needed, what contribution would you like to make to the world? Ask your heart. Ask your body. Ask your soul. Write a few sentences describing what contribution you'd like to make.*

e. *Narrow the scope. There's no way for you to address every one of these concerns at the same time. Look through the three lists you just made and put a star beside the single issue that calls the strongest. Of course they're all important. For now, just choose one.*

7. *Acknowledge where you already contribute your talents and energy toward making the world better. List the things you do that feel important, satisfying, helpful, meaningful, and service oriented.*

- I volunteer at the Community Center.
- I raised $300 in the AIDS Walk.
- I take Mrs. Porter to the store each Wednesday.
- I donate to the Nature Conservancy.

Don't be shy here, or underestimate your own contributions. Pat yourself on the back for each one. When you've finished your list, put a star beside each item.

ACTION

You already have all the power, strength, wisdom, and *chutzpah* you need to make powerful, rewarding contributions in the world. You've done your homework. You've established ways to heal old wounds and give yourself ongoing support. You've connected with the guidance of your Inner Council, empowered yourself as Shaman, Warrior, and Explorer. You are ready to act. Your final step is to bring all these parts of yourself into alignment with the goals you choose in the world. In preparation for that final step, take a moment to review the principles of empowered action.

First, be as **clear as you can personally**. Before you act, examine your motives. Where you come from almost always determines the results you get. Energetically, like attracts like. Actions that arise from anger tend to create anger and resistance in response. Actions that come from martyrdom, judgment, or blame tend to attract and reinforce those same negative qualities. Since the most effective action comes from a place of spiritual clarity, work inside yourself to release negativity and stay centered. When you draw on the energy of the spiritual Warrior, even very small actions can bring big, positive results.

Second, **focus on a very specific situations**. A popular bumper sticker sums this up as "Think Globally, Act Locally." You may want to end homophobia, save the rainforests, and create equal opportunity for every human being, but you can't do it all at once, nor can you do it all alone. Trying to do too much is the shortest way to burnout. Choose goals in line with your highest principles that are small, tangible, and realistic. Choose goals in which you can enlist other people. Each step you complete successfully is a step in right direction. Small steps add up to big changes.

Choose areas of focus that allow you to share the gifts you most enjoy sharing. Contributing to the world is a joy when you find the right forum. Like to sing? Teach music to children. Like to work with people? Coordinate volunteers for the Gay helpline. Like to cook? Prepare meals for a sick friend twice a week. Ideally, sharing in the world is an important forum for your own expression.

Third, **claim your feelings.** When faced with the immensity of imbalance on the planet, most of us tend to go numb. Otherwise, the enormity of the pain is too great to bear. By closing down, though, we sacrifice the ability to take action. When you learn to focus within a single sphere, your feelings are an important source of power. When you claim the rage, pain, and grief you feel and then transform their energy into appropriate action, your power is immense.

Finally, **call on Spirit.** Call on the power of your own dreams and the dreams of all humanity. Call on the strength and clarity of the archetypes within you. Call on the desire of Earth and humanity for healing. These powers are greater than any single individual. Your clarity and intention allow them to flow through you.

➤ Move into action

Exercise

8. It's time to access the energy directly. The following movement meditation recalls the procedures you learned for accessing the Warrior and the Explorer. Here it will help you focus on a single issue. By using your body to move beyond mind, you access wisdom and power that make your actions much more effective.

a. *To begin, set aside 10-20 minutes in which you won't be disturbed. Get your movement music ready. Take a few moments to breathe, stretch, and get calm.*

With your eyes closed, create your sacred space. Call your Inner Council and the Tribal Circle to stand around you. When you feel centered within their supportive energy, turn on your music and begin.

Allow your body to move gently for about a minute on its own. Notice where the breath flows easily. Notice how it feels to be connected with the Earth. Notice how it feels to breathe into each joint and into every other part of you.

b. *When you're ready, allow your Inner Council to guide you to the top of a tall mountain. Continue to move gently as you imagine seeing the entire world spread out below you. As you look down at it, all the challenges of humanity are laid out before you. These problems need solutions. Each one calls to you.*

Notice the problems that deal with the entire planet, things like hunger and disease. Notice the issues that deal more specifically with Gay people. Notice the challenges in your own personal situation. Don't try to act on any of these situations right now. Just watch them and notice how you feel.

c. *Ask your body to show you which of the issues calls the most strongly right now. "Show me where I can act most effectively now." As you repeat the question, all the other issues will fade into the background as your attention focuses on a single issue. What is it? For the rest of the exercise, focus on this single issue.*

Ask your body to show you the feelings you have about it — "Show me the feelings around this issue. Show me the feelings... " Let them come into your body. Whatever they are, feel them. Is there anger that this situation exists? Is there pain? Is there longing, hope, grief, or rage? Let the feelings fill you as you breathe and move. When you're as full as you can be, move to the next step.

d. *Using terms you're comfortable with, call Spirit to be with you inside the feelings. Imagine a strong white or blue light that flows through the top of your head right into the center. "Body, let Spirit come into this place. Let Spirit come into this place." Then move.*

Your body will show you a new Warrior dance. Feel the strength that comes from joining the power of Spirit with the depth of your feelings. Feel the movement that results. Dance for a few minutes, continuing to call Spirit into the place where your feelings are.

e. *Ask your body to show you the most appropriate way to use this energy. "How can I act to ease this problem?" As you repeat the request, your body will move differently. Let it give you sensations, images, faces, ideas, or other indications of specific actions you might take.*

Continue to move until you feel complete. Then let the movement come to a gentle conclusion. Thank your allies and release the energy. Record your insights in your journal.

TURN INTENTION INTO ACTION

What now? How do you begin opening to the world? With very small steps, that's how. Ask yourself, "What is the smallest first step I can take toward my goal of working in the world." To make that first step really effective, be sure it reflects where you are right now. Your desire to contribute to the world should align with your personal exploration. Bill, who's still just coming out, realized that his first steps are all personal ones. He needs to get clear in his personal life before he can be more open and "out there" in the world. Jack, who's been out for years and is now dealing with questions around his own aging, decided to work with men at a senior center. Sam saw that his best contribution would be to come out at work. Jim recognized that his frustration with the political process could transform if he volunteered for a voter education program.

Once you decide on a course of action, don't wait for the world to give you validation. Validate yourself. Give yourself permission to act. Then, do the best you can. Be flexible. You may need to adjust a particular course of action, or redirect it entirely, to get the response you desire. Don't let that throw you or make you feel defeated. The fact that you are acting at all is a major victory in itself.

Once you learn to take action in one area, you'll be drawn toward others. Maybe you'll help in your neighborhood. Maybe you'll be inspired to work within the Gay community. Certainly, hundreds of important issues could use your input. Be sure to balance your desire to act within the rest of your life, but don't limit yourself. Just like everyone else, you have a serious stake in the whole world. If you feel called to work with an environmental group or the local school board, do it! Whatever you do, be yourself. Working as an openly Gay man in any realm helps the cause. Just letting people see who you are — Gay, powerful, open, committed — is radically transformative. Just being yourself, you fight ignorance and promote understanding. You'll also feel great about yourself.

Action plan

Exercise

9.a. *Write down your first goal for contributing to the world.*

Break that goal down into the very smallest steps you can think of. Even if it seems overwhelming at first, you'll make it more accessible by breaking it down. How might you begin? Do you need more information? Are there individuals or groups you could connect with?

List five very small, tangible steps that will move you in the direction of your goal.

Make a commitment to complete the first step within the next week. Is that possible? If you need to adjust the timing, do so. Just be clear with yourself that you will take the step.

Do it and enjoy!

16 The Journey Continues

LOOK HOW FAR YOU'VE COME

Congratulations! You made it. You've come a long way since the beginning of this journey. Acknowledge the courage it took to dive into your depths and challenge the fears, wounding, and darkness that lived there. Acknowledge the strength it took to break old chains and overcome defenses you no longer need. Acknowledge the wisdom and power you now access. Honor yourself for a job very well done.

You've shifted and grown more than you even know. You're already aware of new attitudes and perspectives. A major part of your transformation, though, has taken place outside your conscious knowing. In your cells, you've replaced old limiting beliefs with new empowerment. In your heart, you've released fears, worries, and old hurts. In your relationship with Spirit, you've opened to new dimensions. Because they take time to manifest externally, these other changes may be a little hard to see at first. Expect to be surprised over the next few months as you unconsciously respond to situations and people in entirely new ways. You **will** notice changes. Every shift you've made inside will be mirrored in the world. You'll:

- **Stop** attracting situations and relationships that reflect old negativities. Negative people and situations will show up less and less often.

- **Stop** feeding the old blocks in yourself and others. Fear, homophobia, and limitation will have less power.

- **Start** resonating at a higher, healthier level of energy by not buying into things that used to bring you down. You'll attract people who acknowledge you as a valid, powerful human being.

- **Open** to receive help and support from within yourself, other people, and Spirit.

- **Free** up energy that used to be bound in struggle with yourself. You'll have more energy to do what you want — write songs, start a business, enjoy making love, dance.

- **Start** to have a greater, positive outlook and impact in the world. You become part of the solution, no longer part of the problem.

Do you appreciate how much you've done? Sometimes it's easy to forget. When you take a long hike, you can get so involved with the rhythm of the steps and the beauty of the scenery that you lose all sense of time and distance. Then, all of a sudden, the trees fall away and you stand on a rocky summit with the whole journey spread out below you. Hills and valleys are compressed by the distance. The river that threatened to swallow you earlier is reduced to a slender stream. The patches of desert where you felt alone and afraid look smaller, their harshness softened. Some of the challenge may seem diminished, the peaks less high, the valleys less dark, and you might forget just how far you've come.

Take advantage of this moment to survey the whole journey and claim it as your own. Lay the groundwork for your **next** steps while the insights, awareness, and enthusiasm are still fresh. Use your new tools to create the direction, support, and commitment you'll need in the next portion of your life.

Recapitulation

Exercise

1.   **Review your journal**

   One of the best ways to digest and integrate what you've learned is to review the whole process. Recapitulating, you remind yourself of how far you've come, where you've grown, and where you'd like to explore further. This process might take half an hour. It might take longer. Move as quickly as you like, but don't rush. Give yourself all the time you need to enjoy yourself.

   a.   **Goals**

   Return to your first list of goals for the journey ("Goals," page 30). How do they sound to you now? How many of your initial goals have you accomplished? How many of them have shifted as you proceeded?

   b.   **Attunement**

   Repeat the first movement meditation ("Attunement," page 65). How does your body feel in comparison to the first time you did this exercise? Are you more comfortable asking its guidance? Are you more accepting of your body now than you were then?

c. *Use your journal to review your entire journey from the first steps right to this point. As you read through your responses, don't try to remember each detail. Keep your focus on the bigger picture. Notice the high points and keep the following questions in mind:*

- *What parts were the most challenging?*
- *Where did you gain the greatest insights?*
- *What have you learned about yourself that will be useful from now on?*
- *Where did you change harmful attitudes?*
- *What gifts did you recover for the first time?*
- *Where did you receive unexpected support or create actual positive change in the world?*
- *What areas would you like to explore further?*

Highlight anything that seems especially pertinent or that you'd like to return to later.

2. **Movement meditation**

The following movement meditation helps you access through your body all the growth you've accomplished. Again, take the time to enjoy yourself.

a. *Start with the music you've used throughout your process. Pay attention to your breath. Let it help you get quiet inside. Be aware of your feet on the Earth and the way your breath flows through your whole body.*

Create your sacred space. When you're ready, call upon your Inner Council and the Tribe of Men who Love Men. Stand in the center of these circles. Feel their presence around you and bow deeply to thank them for their help.

b. *One at a time, ask the members of your Inner Council to move within your body. Begin with the Magic Boy. As you move, ask him to remind you*

- *where he's already active in your life,*

- *where to call on his help when you need it, and*

- *what gifts he shares with you.*

After a minute or so, release the Magic Boy and call on the other archetypes, one at a time — Sacred Androgyne, Lover, Shaman/Healer, Elder, Warrior, Explorer. Invite each to share your body and move for a minute or so.

c. *Invite the Self Who Knows to move in you as well. Feel how he embodies all the other archetypes as part of your own unique Self. Ask your body to move its wholeness. Watch and feel whatever comes through. Continue to move for as long as you like. If you have any questions you'd like to ask your Self, do so now. Watch the movement for his response.*

d.   *When you feel complete, thank your Inner Council for their help and support. Follow your breath back to normal awareness and release the energy you raised. Reach around and give yourself a big hug to appreciate all you've done.*

Record your insights and observations in your journal.

CREATE ONGOING SUPPORT

You stand at a new doorway. The same steps you take to complete this journey propel you across the threshold of another. What will that new exploration be? Where will you go? What will you accomplish? One thing is sure — whatever direction you choose, whatever goals you set, **you'll need support on your new path.** On this part of the journey, you've learned to receive support from a number of sources. As part of moving into the next, take a moment to review how you can reinforce and expand your network to ensure you have all the support you need.

Support yourself

At the beginning of your journey, you made commitments to support yourself at many levels. This is a good time to review those commitments and revise them if needed. How can you best support yourself in the following areas?

Body — What will you do for exercise? How often? Does your present program work or do you need to update it? How well are you giving yourself good nutrition and adequate rest?

Heart — How well are you supporting yourself emotionally? Are you being gentle on yourself? Are you actually using the tools you've learned? Are your relationships supportive? Could you commit to a weekly check-in to assess honestly where you are emotionally?

Creativity/Social/Play — All work and no play makes for one dull, unhappy boy. What do you do for recreation? What could you do to treat yourself? What would you like to explore creatively? Could you spend more time with friends? Could you set a date once a week to be with your Magic Boy?

Spiritual practice — How successful are you at staying centered and aligned? How are you doing with the practice you've chosen? Is there something that might work better? Is there a part of this journey — journaling, movement meditation, dance, writing meditation, or something else — you'd like to explore more fully?

Service — How well are you engaged with the world? Is there somewhere you'd like to help others? Could you write one letter a week in support of a worthy cause? Could you volunteer once a month to help a local AIDS service organization, assist at a shelter for the homeless, plant trees, or tutor a child in math?

Supporting yourself is a matter of balance. Find a mix of activities that meets your needs as well as possible. Stay flexible. You may need to adjust or fine tune your program from time to time as your needs shift.

Create a support group

As you support yourself more fully, you'll attract other people who support you as well. Pay attention to these people. Supportive friends make staying on the path easier. Friends who acknowledge the importance of spiritual issues and encourage you to reach for your goals are a great source of strength. Understanding companions will mirror your progress, help you maintain your perspective, and celebrate victories and milestones along the way.

How do you create a support group? Start where you are. Which of your friends already share similar interests? Who can you call on for support right now? Who might be interested in meeting from time to time to discuss spiritual issues? Create opportunities to share what really matters to you. You could create a group that meets regularly for a potluck and discussion. You might arrange periodic lunches, maybe once a month, to share what's going on with each other. Be creative and enjoy the camaraderie.

As you complete this part of your Gay empowerment journey, consider leading another group of men through the same process. Who might be interested in exploring exercises from this book? Can you call together a group of friends? Could you start a group by placing a notice in a local Gay publication? There are many people who'd benefit from the insight and empowerment you've gained. You'll also be surprised at how much new insight comes to you as you go through the process a second time with others. By creating an ongoing support group, not only will you help yourself stay focused, you'll also make a valuable contribution to the community at large.

Beyond your own friends, you might find support in a group or congregation that already exists. The number of organizations addressing Gay spiritual concerns is rising very quickly. Some have come about in response to the health crisis, while others focus in different areas. More and more churches welcome Gay people to worship in settings that range from alternative to traditional. There are also Gay groups affiliated with mainstream religious denominations — Gay Episcopals, Catholics, Lutherans, Jews, and so forth. Check sources like local Gay newspapers, community centers, and helplines to seek out groups in your area.

If you find a group that seems to meet your needs, give it a try. Remember, though, to **be true to yourself.** You're the only person who can determine your spiritual path. In your desire to be part of a group, do not subvert your own needs and knowing. If a group turns out **not** to meet your needs, **stop going.** Beware of fundamentalism of any stripe. Beware of any group that is too focused on dogma or that proclaims itself as the "only way." There are **many** paths to Spirit. If any group asks you to change who you are, if it is not 100% supportive of your being Gay, it is simply **not** your group.

In the same spirit, feel free to outgrow any group that may have suited you in the past. Beliefs and practices that once worked well may not meet your needs as you grow and change. Beliefs and practices evolve naturally. Let them. Don't worry about what used to work or what someone else says "should" work. Be concerned only with what works for you now.

The support of Tribe

Men who love men are on a spiritual journey together. As a Tribe, we're coming out together, healing together, demanding respect and validation from the rest of humanity together. At the level of energy, we are all connected. We share the energy of our beliefs. We share the energy of self-respect, self-validation, and love.

Your personal experiences are part of the shared Tribal journey. Because your process resonates within the Tribal whole, each step you take affects every other man-loving man. Remember the four-minute mile, the barrier once thought to be the absolute limit of human running ability? Once Roger Bannister broke that limit, it was broken over and over by others. Each day, you face your own four-minute miles — when you stand up against discrimination, help a sick friend, end an abusive relationship, break an addiction, or dance for the joy of being alive. Each step, small or large, infuses that much more health into our collective experience. Each step you take assists other men to take the same step, whether or not you know them personally, whether or not you ever exchange a single word, whether they live next door or across the world.

By the same token, because others are choosing to live with power, integrity, and satisfaction, you have support on your path as well. Even alone in your room, you can call on the strengths, insights, and guidance of the Tribe. Do the work and you help the Tribe. Do the work and the Tribe helps you.

Ongoing support

Exercise

3. **Self-support**

   Review the ways you already support yourself. Be sure to address your needs on every level — body, heart, mind, spirit, and service to others. Jot down any adjustments you'd like to make in your present program.

4. **Group support**

   If you feel the need, create an action plan for developing a support network. Where will you begin? What friends can you call on? What is the first step you can take toward getting a group together? Is there a group in your area that addresses your needs? Where can you find out? How can you connect?

5. **Tribal support: The Lodge of Dreams**

   The following visualization helps to strengthen subconscious Tribal connections. Use it before bed to connect with other men on a similar wavelength. You could also use it as a shared experiment within your spiritual support group. You'll be surprised at how many insights show up in your own dreams and the parallels that develop when you share them with others.

   Read through the visualization once or twice, until you feel comfortable taking yourself through it on your own. If the details shift slightly when you're in your own reality, let them. You'll get very comfortable with the process after one or two times. Enjoy!

   ### The Lodge of Dreams

   As you get ready to sleep, close your eyes and imagine the following scene:

   Go inside. Find yourself standing in front of a huge temple, a beautiful place with trees, vines, and tall spires. In front of you, a path leads toward a graceful gateway. Walk along the path. As you do, become aware of all that you've carried to this place — all the cares, burdens, worries, and concerns of the day. Feel them on your skin, in your clothing. It may feel as if you've had a very long and tiring journey. Now is the time to rest. Walk easily along the path toward the temple.

   At the gateway, two men step forward to greet you with smiles and embraces. "Be at home, Brother!" You feel their welcome, feel yourself relax as they escort you through the gates and into an inner atrium. Here, the light is dimmer, shadowy, and it takes your eyes a moment to adjust. Listen to the sounds of gently splashing water. Smell the fresh aroma of cleansing herbs. You make out a deep pool in front of you. Water enters the pool through two carved fonts and you notice that warm steam rises from its surface. Several other men are already in the pool, washing themselves or soaking quietly.

Let go of your dirty clothing and step into the warm pool. Feel the water wash your skin and hair. Feel any cares you brought with you wash away gently and easily. Rest in the pool until you feel entirely cleansed. When you're ready, step from the water and follow the others through a doorway on the far side of the pool.

As you enter, different men gently dry your body with soft towels and wrap you in a heavy, soft robe. Notice your surroundings. You are in a small chamber that opens into the main part of the temple. The light inside is very dim, and you see the still forms of brothers already asleep. The air is pleasantly aromatic and the sounds of gentle breathing are deeply comforting.

At the entry to the temple, an older man greets you quietly. You feel warm and relaxed by his manner and you sense that he knows you very well. This Elder is your guide. He asks what you'd like to address this night in your dreams. Is there some issue around which you seek clarity? Do you need guidance, healing, ease, relaxation, or insight? Tell the Elder what concerns you the very most. As you speak, he takes out a rolled up scroll, and you see your words appear on the white space.

Your guide leads you into the main room of the temple, where a place is already prepared for you. The top of the temple is open to the stars and the silvery light outlines the forms of the sleeping brothers around you. You feel their presence as you lie down, comfortable, safe, and secure. Follow your breath as you begin to drift off. Feel your thoughts start to weave with the dreams of the others. As you breathe and relax, you hear the Elder whisper that you'll remember everything of importance in the morning when you wake. It all feels right and good.

Whenever you wake up, jot down any impressions you have of your dreams. Using the techniques for interpretation outlined in Chapter 11, let your dreams guide you in light of the questions you asked. Don't be afraid to ask the same question several nights in a row until you feel clear about the response. If you let it, the Dream Lodge will become an important, supportive part of your inner reality.

REAFFIRM YOUR COMMITMENTS

Spirituality is a lot like gardening. You've already done the big enthusiastic Spring push — the backbreaking digging, turning over the soil, planning, planting, feeding, and mulching. You have a whole new set of tools — rake, shovel, hose, tiller — and a shed to put them in. You've set your course. Now, you have a choice. You can keep going — from now on it will probably take less work to stay on track — or you can sit back and rest on your laurels. You can let the tools rust in the shed, or you can use them to feed and water your tender new seedlings and keep the weeds from taking over.

The easiest way to stay on course is to create a plan to support yourself. That way you don't have to keep reinventing the path. You can just follow what you've set up and let the structure work for you. In the garden, your plan might involve deciding when to water, how often to weed, when to harvest or replant. Your empowerment plan involves choosing new goals and making commitments about how you'll pursue them. With either plan, you're free to be flexible, to adapt to unforeseen circumstances, or make changes as the need comes up.

➤ Set your course

Exercise

6. *Revised goals*

    Title a new page in your journal "REVISED GOALS."

    Under the title, write a set of goals that will guide you for the next three months. Take into account the goals you set up at the beginning of your journey and want to revise. Include the goals you set up for supporting yourself and for creating a support group. Include any new areas you'd like to explore.

    Remember to make your goals concrete and tangible. Be as specific as possible. Break big, long-term goals down into small, discrete pieces. Finally, make sure you're being realistic and choosing goals you can reasonably complete in three months. Start small. Set goals you can complete. Set yourself up for victory.

7. **Commitment**

    Make a formal commitment to yourself to pursue the goals you've chosen. After you complete them, you can renegotiate, revise your goals, try a new tack if you like, and begin another round.

    Copy the following statement into your journal, revising it into your own words if you like, and sign it:

"I, (your name) _____ *, commit that for the next three months, I will do my best to focus on the following goals (list your goals from above)* _____

_____

_____

_____

_____

I commit to value myself and to do all I can to support myself with a full, healthy, and fulfilling lifestyle. I commit to support myself by … (list your support commitments from above).

I commit to honor and treasure myself and my capacity to love myself and other men. I commit to be patient with myself and to treat myself as the special, important individual that I am. I commit to encourage myself, to catch negative thoughts and judgments and reframe them into positive affirmations of my wholeness and worth.

I commit to accept all the help that comes to me. I am willing to open to the possibility of being all I can."

Date _____ *Signature* _____

SPREAD YOUR WINGS

You are not in this alone. Your willingness to grow and your intention to live in alignment opens you to support from unexpected quarters. Spirit will help you in many ways. Guidance will come from within yourself and from other people. Situations that used to seem vague will become clearer. You'll face challenges, both old and new, with more strength and alignment. Insights will come when you least expect.

Accept the help. Allow the miracles. Accept the fact that you are more than your body, more than your thoughts, feelings, and emotions. Welcome assistance from inner guides and outer angels — hunky, horny, man-loving angels. Open to new possibilities beyond your wildest dreams. The way that you love is part of your spiritual path. Let it lead you to the fullness of your own self. Let it help you join the Tribe in creating a new reality.

We're creating this new reality already. Ten years ago, I had a vision of a Gay healer's council, a circle of men who'd come together to share touch, love, healing, and wisdom. At the time, I imagined that the council existed somewhere on the level of dream or archetype. I wrote it down with a feeling of longing. "Wouldn't it be nice!"

Already, I've seen that council in the flesh many times. I've sat with forty Gay men atop a mountain, sharing counsel and healing. I've sat year after year with a hundred others in a great, heart-filled family circle. A group meets in Tennessee, another on an island in the Puget Sound, another in New York, others in California, Hawaii, England, France, Australia. More are forming every day. The vision we share is powerful. We are creating safety, health, support, and fulfillment for ourselves. We are empowering ourselves to take our rightful place in the world.

You're on this path. You were born in this Tribe, born to be great. Dare to hold your Vision with your whole being. Dare to be healthy, to live, dream, create, and enjoy being all you are. Above all, dare to be yourself.

Findhorn Press has been publishing books filled with spirit, inspiration and hope for almost thirty years. If you would like to learn more about us please visit our website

http://findhornpress.com

or send for our free catalog at the addresses below –

In the USA or Canada:

Findhorn Press
PO Box 13939
Tallahassee, FL 32317

toll-free 1-877-390-4425
e-mail info@findhornpress.com

In the UK and the rest of the world:

Findhorn Press
The Park
Findhorn, Forres IV36 3TY
Scotland, UK

freephone 0800-389 9395
e-mail books@findhorn.org

You may also wish to visit the website of the Findhorn Foundation in Scotland, an educational spiritual organization. Among all their many workshops and conferences, they also offer Gay Spirit and Self Empowerment workshops.

http://www.findhorn.org

APPENDIX
BIBLIOGRAPHY AND FURTHER READING

Abbott, Franklin. *Boyhood, Growing Up Male: A Multicultural Anthology.* Freedom, CA: Crossing Press, 1993.

_____. *Men and Intimacy: Personal Accounts Exploring the Dilemmas of Modern Male Sexuality.* Freedom, CA: Crossing Press, 1990.

_____. *New Men, New Minds: Breaking Male Tradition; How Today's Men are Changing the Traditional Roles of Masculinity.* Freedom CA, Crossing Press, 1987.

Balka, Christie and Andy Rose. *Twice Blessed: On Being Lesbian or Gay and Jewish.* Boston: Beacon, 1989.

Barzan, Robert. *Sex and Spirit: Exploring Gay Men's Spirituality.* San Francisco: White Crane Press, 1995.

Bass, Ellen and Kate Kaufman. *Free Your Mind: The Book for Gay, Lesbian, and Bisexual Youth — and Their Allies.* New York: HarperPerennial, 1996.

Berger, Raymond M. *Gay and Gray: The Older Homosexual Man.* Binghamton, NY: Harrington Park Press, 1996.

Bernstein, Robert. *Straight Parents, Gay Children: Keeping Families Together.* New York: Thunder Mouth Press, 1995.

Berzon, Betty. *The Intimacy Dance: A Guide to Long-Term Success in Gay and Lesbian Relationships.* New York: Dutton, 1996.

_____. *Positively Gay: New Approaches to Gay and Lesbian Life.* Berkeley, CA: Celestial Arts, 1992.

_____. *Setting Them Straight: You Can Do Something about Bigotry and Homophobia in your Life.* New York: Plume, 1996.

Borhek, Mary V. *Coming Out to Parents: A Two-Way Survival Guide for Lesbians and Gay Men and Their Parents.* Cleveland, OH, Pilgrim Press, 1993.

Boswell, John. *Christianity , Social Tolerance, and Homosexuality.* Chicago: University of Chicago Press, 1980.

Bouldrey, Brian, ed. *Wrestling with the Angel: Faith and Religion in the Lives of Gay Men.* New York: Riverhead Books, 1995.

Boyd, Malcolm. *Take Off the Masks.* Rev. ed. San Francisco: HarperSanFrancisco, 1993.

_____. *Are You Running with Me Jesus?* Rev. ed. Boston: Beacon Press, 1990.

_____. *Gay Priest: An Inner Journey.* New York: St. Martin's Press, 1986.

_____. *Go Gentle into that Good Night.* Columbus, MS: Genesis Press, 1998.

_____. *Look Back in Joy: A Celebration of Gay Lovers.* Rev. ed. Boston: Alyson Publications, 1990.

Boykin, Keith. *One More River to Cross: Black and Gay in America.* New York: Anchor Books, 1996.

Brelin, Christa, ed. *Strength in Numbers: A Lesbian, Gay, and Bisexual Resource.* Detroit: Visible Ink Press, 1996.

Brimner, Larry Dane. *Being Different: Lambda Youth Speak Out.* New York: Franklin Watts, 1995.

Broughton, James. *Coming Unbuttoned: A Memoir.* San Francisco: CityLights Books, 1993.
_____. *Making Light of It.* San Francisco: City Lights Books, 1992.
_____. *The Androgyne Journal.* Seattle: Broken Moon Press, 1991.
_____. *Special Deliveries: New and Selected Poems.* Seattle: Broken Moon Press, 1990.
Bull, Chris and John Gallagher. *Perfect Enemies: The Religious Right, the Gay Movement, and the Politics of the 1990's.* New York: Crown, 1996.
Cameron, Julia. *The Artist's Way: A Spiritual Path to Higher Creativity.* New York: Jeremy P. Tarcher/Putnam, 1992.
Campbell, Joseph with Bill Moyers. *The Power of Myth.* New York: Doubleday, 1988.
Carpenter, Edward. *Intermediate Types Among Primitive Folks: A Study in Social Evolution.* London: George Allen & Company, 1914.
_____. *Selected Writings,* vols 1-3. London: GMP Publishers, 1984.
Cashorali, Peter. *Fairy Tales: Traditional Stories Retold for Gay Men.* San Francisco: HarperSanFrancisco, 1995.
Chermoyeff, Catherine, Jonathan David, and Nan Richardson. *Drag Diaries.* San Francisco: Umbra Editions/Chronicle Books, 1995.
Clark, Don. *As We Are.* Boston: Alyson Publications, 1988.
_____. *Loving Someone Gay.* Berkeley, CA: Celestial Arts, 1987.
Clark, J. Michael. *Beyond our Ghettos: Gay Theology in Ecological Perspective.* Cleveland, OH: Pilgrim Press, 1993.
Connor, Randy P. *Blossom of Bone: Reclaiming the Connections between Homoeroticism and the Sacred.* New York: HarperCollins, 1993.
Dawson, Jeff. *Gay and Lesbian Online.* Berkeley, CA: Peachpit Press, 1996.
Dean, Amy. *Proud to Be: Daily Meditations for Lesbians and Gay Men.* New York: Bantam Books, 1994.
Driggs, John H. and Stephen E. Finn. *Intimacy Between Men: How to Find and Keep Gay Love Relationships.* New York: Dutton, 1990.
Due, Lennea. *Joining the Tribe: Growing Up Gay and Lesbian in the 90's.* New York: Anchor Books, 1995.
Eichberg, Rob. *Coming Out: An Act of Love.* New York: Plume/Penguin, 1990.
Fairchild, Betty and Nancy Hayward. *Now that You Know: What Every Parent Should Know about Homosexuality.* New York: Harvest/HVJ, 1989.
Fahy, Una. *How to Make the World a Better Place for Gays and Lesbians.* New York, Warner, 1995.
Feinberg, Leslie. *Transgender Warriors: Making History from Joan of Arc to RuPaul.* Boston: Beacon Press, 1996.
Ford, Michael Thomas. *The World Out There: Becoming Part of the Gay and Lesbian Community.* New York: New Press, 1996.
Glaser, Chris. *Coming out to God: Prayer for Lesbians and Gay Men, their Families and Friends.* Louisville, KYL Westminster John Knox Press, 1991.
_____. *Uncommon Calling: A Gay Christian's Struggle to Serve the Church.* Louisville, KY: Westminster John Knox Press, 1988.
_____. *The Word is Out: The Bible Reclaimed for Lesbians and Gay Men.* San Francisco: HarperSanFrancisco, 1994.

Goldberg, Natalie. *Wild Mind: Living the Writer's Life.* New York: Bantam New Age, 1990.

_____. *Writing Down the Bones.* Boston: Shambala, 1986.

Gomes, Peter J. *The Good Book: Reading the Bible with Mind and Heart.* New York: William Morrow, 1996.

Grahn, Judy. *Another Mother Tongue: Gay Words, Gay Worlds.* Boston: Beacon Press, 1984.

Griffin, Carolyn Welch, Marian J. Wirth and Arthur G. Wirth. *Beyond Acceptance: Parents of Lesbians and Gays Talk about their Experiences.* New York: St. Martin's, 1996.

Halifax, Joan. *Shaman: The Wounded Healer.* New York: Crossroads, 1982.

Harner, Michael. *The Way of the Shaman: A Guide to Power and Healing.* San Francisco: Harper & Row, 1980.

Harrison, Gavin. *In the Lap of the Buddha.* Boston: Shambala, 1994.

Hartman, Keith. *Congregations in Conflict: The Battle over Homosexuality.* New Brunswick, NJ: Rutgers Univ. Press, 1996.

Harvey, Andrew, ed. *The Essential Gay Mystics.* San Francisco, Harper San Francisco, 1997.

_____. *Hidden Journey: A Spiritual Awakening.* New York: Arkana\Penguin, 1991.

Hay, Harry. *Radically Gay.* ed. by Will Roscoe. Boston: Beacon Press,1996.

Helminiak, Daniel A. *What the Bible Really Says about Homosexuality.* San Francisco: Alamo Square Press, 1994.

Herdt, Gilbert and Andrew Boxer. *Children of Horizons: How Gay and Lesbian Teens are Leading a New Way Out of the Closet.* Boston: Beacon Press, 1993.

Hopcke, Robert. *Jung, Jungians & Homosexuality.* Boston: Shambala, 1989.

Hopcke, Robert, Karin Lofthus Carrington, and Scott Wirth. *Same-Sex Love and the Path to Wholeness.* Boston: Shambala, 1993.

Isay, Richard. *Becoming Gay: The Journey to Self-Acceptance.* New York: Pantheon Books, 1996.

_____. *Being Homosexual: Gay Men and their Development.* New York: Farar, Strauss, and Giroux, 1989.

Isensee, Rik. *Love Between Men: Enhancing Intimacy and Keeping your Relationships Alive.* Boston: Alyson, 1990.

_____. *Reclaiming your Life: the Gay Man's Guide to Love, Self-Acceptance, and Trust.* Los Angeles: Alyson, 1997.

Jastrab, Joseph with Ron Schaumburg. *Sacred Manhood Sacred Earth: A Vision Quest into the Wilderness of Men's Heart.* New York: HarperPerennial, 1994.

Katz, Jonathan. *Gay American History: Lesbians and Gay Men in the USA.* New York: Crowell, 1976.

Kaufman, Gershen and Lev Raphael. *Coming Out of Shame: Transforming Gay and Lesbian Lives.* New York: Doubleday, 1996.

Kettlebach, Guy. *Dancing Around the Volcano: Freeing our Erotic Lives: Decoding the Enigma of Gay Men and Sex.* New York, Crown, 1996.

Kominars, Sheppard B. and Kathryn Kominars. *Accepting Ourselves and Others: A Journey into Recovery from Addictive and Compulsive Behaviors for Gays, Lesbians, and Bisexuals.* Center City, MN: Hazelden, 1996.

Leyland, Winston ed. *Queer Dharma: Voices of Gay Buddhists.* San Francisco: Gay Sunshine Press, 1998.

Mains, Geoff. *Urban Aboriginals: A Celebration of Leathersexuality.* San Francisco: Gay Sunshine Press, 1984.

Matousek, Mark. *Sex, Death, Enlightenment.* New York: Riverhead Books, 1996.

Merla, Patrick, ed. *Boys Like Us: Gay Writers Tell their Coming Out Stories.* New York: Avon Books, 1996.

Mickens, Ed. *The 100 Best Companies for Gay Men and Lesbians.* New York: Pocket Books, 1994.

Miller, Neil. *Out of the Past: Gay and Lesbian History from 1869 to the Present.* New York: Vintage Books, 1995.

Milton, Adrian. *Lavender Light: Daily Meditations for Gay Men in Recovery.* New York: Perigee/Berkeley, 1995.

Monette, Paul. *Becoming a Man: Half a Life Story.* New York: Harcourt Brace Jovanovich, 1992.

Moore, Robert and Douglas Gillette. *King Warrior Magician Lover: Rediscovering the Archetypes of the Mature Masculine.* San Francisco: HarperSanFrancisco, 1990.

Moore, Thomas. *Care of the Soul: A Guide for Cultivating Depth and Sacredness in Everyday Life.* New York: HarperCollins, 1992.

Muchmore, Wes and William Hanson. *Coming Out Right: A Handbook for the Gay Male.* Boston: Alyson, 1991.

Neisen, Joseph H., Ph. D. *Reclaiming Pride: Daily Reflections on Gay and Lesbian Life.* Deerfield Beach, FL: Health Communications, Inc., 1994.

Odets, Walter. *In the Shadow of the Epidemic: Being HIV-Negative in the Age of AIDS.* Durham, NC: Duke University Press, 1995.

O'Neill, Craig and Kathleen Ritter. *Coming Out Within: Stages of Spiritual Awakening for Lesbians and Gay Men (The Journey from Loss to Transformation).* New York: HarperCollins, 1992.

Osborn, Torie. *Coming Home to America: A Road Map for Gay and Lesbian Empowerment.* New York: St. Martin's, 1996.

OUT Magazine, editors. *The Gay and Lesbian Address Book.* New York: Perigee/Berkeley, 1995.

Perry, Troy. *Don't Be Afraid Anymore: The Story of Reverend Troy Perry and the Metropolitan Community Church.* New York: St. Martins, 1990.

_____. *The Lord is My Shepherd and He Knows I'm Gay.* Los Angeles: Universal Fellowship Press, 1972.

Pollock, Rachel and Cheryl Schwartz. *The Journey Out: A Guide for and about Lesbian, Gay, and Bisexual Teens.* New York: Puffin, 1995.

Preston, John ed. *Friends and Lovers: Gay Men Write about the Families They Create.* New York: Plume, 1995.

Ram Dass and Mirabai Bush. *Compassion in Action: Setting Out on the Path of Service.* New York: Bell Tower/Crown, 1992.

Ram Dass and Paul Goorman. *How Can I Help?* New York: Alfred A. Knopf, 1988.

Ramer, Andrew. *Angel Answers: A Joyful Guide to Creating Heaven on Earth.* New York: Pocket Books, 1995.

_____. *Revelations for a New Millennium.* San Francisco: HarperSanFrancisco, 1997.

_____. *Two Flutes Playing*. San Francisco: Alamo Square Press, 1997.

Raphael, Lev. *Journeys and Arrivals: On Being Gay and Jewish*. Boston: Faber and Faber, 1996.

Rasi, Richard A. and Lourdes Rodriguez-Nugues. *Out in the Workplace: The Pleasures and Perils of Coming Out on the Job*. Los Angeles: Alyson, 1995.

Roberts, Elizabeth and Elias Amidon. *Earth Prayers from around the World: 365 Prayers, Poems, and Invocations for Honoring the Earth*. San Francisco: HarperSanFrancisco, 1991.

Roscoe, Will. *Changing Ones: Third and Fourth Genders in Native North America*. New York: St. Martins Press, 1998.

_____. *Living the Spirit: A Gay American Indian Anthology*. New York: St. Martin's Press, 1988.

_____. *Queer Spirits: A Gay Men's Myth Book*. Boston: Beacon Press, 1995.

_____. *The Zuni Man-Woman*. Albuquerque: University of New Mexico Press, 1991.

Sadownick, Douglas. *Sex Between Men: An Intimate History of the Sex Lives of Gay Men Postwar to Present*. San Francisco: HarperSanFrancisco, 1996.

Saks, Adrien and Wayne Curtis, eds. *Revelations: Gay Men's Coming Out Stories*. Boston: Alyson, 1994.

Schneebaum, Tobias. *Where the Spirits Dwell: An Odyssey in the Jungle of New Guinea*. New York: Grove Press, 1988.

Schneider, David. *Street Zen: The Life and Work of Issen Dorsey*. Boston: Shambala, 1993.

Schwartzberg, Steven. *A Crisis of Meaning: How Gay Men are Making Sense of AIDS*. New York: Oxford University Press, 1996.

Sears, James T. *Growing Up Gay in the South: Race, Gender, and Journeys of the Spirit*. New York: Harrington Park Press, 1991.

Sherrill, Jan Michael and Craig A. Hardesty. *The Gay, Lesbian, and Bisexual Students Guide to Colleges, Universities, and Grad Schools*. New York: New York University Press, 1994.

Signorile, Michelangelo. *Outing Yourself: How to Come Out as Lesbian or Gay to your Family, Friends, and Coworkers*. New York: Random House, 1995.

Somé, Malidoma Patrice. *Of Water and the Spirit: Ritual, Magic, and Initiation in the Life of an African Shaman*. New York: Putnam, 1994.

Stern, Gary J. *A Few Tricks Along the Way: Daily Reflections for Gay Men, Queer Boys, Magnificent Queens, and the People who Love Them*. Freedom, CA: Crossing Press, 1994.

Stevens, Anthony. *Archetypes: A Natural History of the Self*. New York: Quill/William Morrow, 1983,

Sutcliffe, Lynn. *There Must be Fifty Ways to Tell your Mother*. New York: Cassell, 1995.

Thompson, Mark. *Gay Body: A Journey Through Shadow to Self*. New York: St. Martin's Press, 1997.

_____, ed. *Gay Soul: Finding the Heart of Gay Spirit and Nature with 16 Writers, Healers, Teachers, and Visionaries*. New York: HarperCollins, 1994.

_____, ed. *Gay Spirit: Myth and Meaning*. New York: St. Martin's Press, 1987.

_____, ed. *Leatherfolk: Radical Sex, People, Politics, and Practice*. Boston: Alyson Publications, 1991.

Tilleraas, Perry. *The Color of Light: Meditations for All of Us Living with AIDS*. San Francisco: Harper/Hazelden, 1988.

Timmons, Stuart. *The Trouble with Harry Hay*. Boston: Alyson, 1990.

Walker, Mitch. *Men Loving Men: A Gay Sex Guide and Consciousness Book*. Rev. ed. San Francisco: Gay Sunshine Press, 1994.

_____. *Visionary Love: A Spirit Book of Gay Mythology*. Berkeley, CA: Treeroots Press, 1980.

White, Mel. *Stranger at the Gate: To be Gay and Christian in America*. New York: Simon and Schuster, 1994.

Williams, Walter. *The Spirit and the Flesh: Sexual Diversity in American Indian Culture*. Boston: Beacon Press, 1986.

Wilson, Nancy. *Our Tribe: Queer Folks, Jesus, and the Bible*. San Francisco: HarperSanFrancisco, 1995.

Woods, James A. with Jay H. Lucas. *The Corporate Closet: The Professional Lives of Gay Men in America*. New York: The Free Press, 1994.

Newsletters and Journals

RFD: A Country Journal for Gay Men Everywhere. P.O. Box 68, Liberty, TN 37095.

White Crane Journal. P.O.Box 1018, Conifer, CO 80433-1018.

Touching Body and Spirit. The TBS Network, P.O. Box 957, Huntington, NY 11743.

Visionary. Newsletter of Gay Spirit Visions. P.O. Box 339, Decatur, GA 30031-0339. *http://gayspirit.home.mindspring.com*

Video

Messages from the Sixth World. video made by Brian Helder and John Williams, featuring Andrew Ramer, Franklin Abbott, John Stowe and the other men of Gay Spirit Visions, 1992. available from Rubicon Pictures, 242 Howard St., Atlanta, GA 30317 ph: (404) 378-0841 or FAX: (404) 373-0167.